Rome De

Book three of the “Guardian of Empire” series

By: William Kelso

Visit the author's YouTube site

William Kelso is also the author of:

The Shield of Rome

The Fortune of Carthage

Devotio: The House of Mus

The Veteran of Rome series (9)

Soldier of the Republic series (11)

Guardian of Empire (3)

Published in 2025 by KelsoBooks Ltd. First Edition

A CIP catalogue record for this title is available from the British Library.

Dear Reader,

I hope that you will enjoy this book. 'Rome Defiant' is the third instalment of the 'Guardian of Empire' series. A fourth book will be published later in 2025.

As an independently published author, I do not command huge marketing resources so, if you are so inclined, please do leave me a review or a rating.

For those visually inclined have a look at my short historical themed YouTube videos at

The Story So Far...

This book series tells the story of three brothers. Corbulo, Veda and Munatius. The brothers are the descendants of the characters from my **Veteran of Rome** and **Soldier of the Republic** book series. Their ancestral home is the farming estate on the isle of Vectis just off the south coast of Britain. It is the year 261 AD, and the brothers have not seen or heard from each other in seventeen years. Since they were split up at an early age their lives and fates have developed separately. But the three of them share a secret that will always bind them together. A terrible secret that over time has come to affect each brother in different ways.

In the troubled East, in Roman Syria, Corbulo, the eldest brother is rising through the ranks of the imperial Roman army. A natural born leader who fights for Rome and who is keenly aware of the deeds of his illustrious ancestors. In Britain, Veda, the middle brother has given up on his aimless life pursuing pleasure and has found new purpose working for a Roman banking house, doing the dirty and dangerous jobs that no one else wants to do. While growing up in captivity in free Germany, presumed dead by his family, Munatius /Ignatz, the youngest brother has become the outlaw leader of a Frankish war-band, determined to lead a life dedicated to war. His ambition - to become known as the greatest and most famous band of mercenaries for hire east of the Rhine.

Book III of the Guardian of Empire picks up the story...

Chapter One - The Final Triumph of Anarchy

Spring 261 AD. The Imperial palace, Mediolanum, Northern Italy

Striding down the corridor towards the grand double doors beyond which lay the great imperial state hall, the two Roman officers did not speak. The sound of their hobnailed boots rasped purposefully across the stone floor. Their faces were set. Calm and composed like seasoned soldiers accustomed to stress, hardship and conflict. Long spatha swords were hanging from their belts. While their worn coats of mail body armour gleamed in the dim torch light and their shoulders were covered by short red dyed woollen cloaks fixed with a brooch across the right shoulder. Their cloaks emblazoned with the proud insignia of emperor Gallienus's newly created cavalry army.

Ahead, coming from the direction of the great state hall, Corbulo could hear shouting and angry, raised voices. As if a furious row was taking place, but he could not see what was going on. Soon, he thought, he was going to find out whether emperor Gallienus was the man he had hoped he would be or whether he had led his men on a long, foolish, mistaken mission by leaving one shit emperor only to join another. The long-awaited moment of truth was finally here.

Approaching the closed double doors at the end of the corridor and the three praetorian bodyguards who were guarding the entrance, Corbulo and his companion came to a halt as the duty officer stepped forward to block their path. The man's hand raised.

"Sorry Sir," the officer said. "But no one enters the hall until the emperor calls for you and he is busy right now."

“We will wait,” Probus, Corbulo’s companion replied.

“Very well,” the duty officer said remaining where he was, blocking access to the doors.

“You are all a bunch of fucking leeches!” an enraged voice suddenly roared from behind the closed doors. “You and the Senate suck and suck and suck some more. Like a greedy baby at a mother’s teat. Like it was your goddamn given right to demand anything from me. That is all you do! You demand and you whine. Well, I am fed up with it. Everyone is fed up with you! You and the ungrateful populace of the city of Rome suck the very lifeblood out of this empire and then when you are done you leave me and the army to handle the mess that you have left behind. I am the fucking emperor, and I said my decision was final! What part of that do you not understand?”

Standing out in the corridor behind the closed doors the five Roman officers and soldiers remained silent as the shouting and swearing from within the great hall continued. The praetorians looking sheepish. No one speaking. No one moving. Looking up at the ceiling as he waited to enter the hall Corbulo pretended to admire the painted hunting scenes. At nearly thirty-one he was a handsome man. Eldest of three brothers he was tall, lean and cleanshaven. His black hair was cut short with long straight sideburns while his neck was adorned by a green tattoo of a wolf’s head and on his finger, he was wearing Gamo’s gold ring.

“What’s that you say!” the angry voice yelled from within the hall beyond the closed doors. “You think that just because my family were born into the Senatorial class that I am going to automatically look after your interests! That’s just fucking cheeky. Of course, I am my father’s son, but Valerian failed. He lost the war in the East and allowed himself to be captured by those scumbag Sasanians. He made mistakes but I will not be like him. I may be of Valerian's blood but now that I am in sole charge of the empire things are going to change. I have my own ideas on how to rule and they include a reduced role for you and the Senatorial class. The Senate is the past. The city of Rome is the past. The equestrian officers and the frontier provinces are the future. It is they who are going to save Rome and I don't give a shit that you are not happy about it!"

Waiting outside in the corridor Corbulo idly turned to examine the battle scars that were stitched across his left hand before glancing at his companion whose eyes were patiently resting upon the doors. In his late twenties Probus was of medium height but built like a brick with short closely cropped hair and bulging arm and leg muscles hardened by much physical workouts. The man was young to be the commander of the equites Mauri. The elite Moorish cavalry who provided security to emperor Gallienus. But that just spoke of his skill and courage as a soldier Corbulo thought. Probus was a rising star in the army.

He had first met him just a few months back when he and his vexillation from the Rhine; a battlegroup comprising of the infantry from 1st Cohort of the Thirtieth Legion and the two attached companies of Frankish auxiliary cavalry from his own 1st Cohort of Salian Franks; had landed at Byzantium in Europe having successfully absconded from the army of the usurpers Macrianus and Balista. Their aim - having decided which emperor they were going to fight for; to join the forces that were still loyal to the rightful and legitimate emperor - Gallienus.

Probus had been there waiting on the quayside at Byzantium to meet his sister Claudia who had escaped with him. The commander of the equites Mauri had been grateful to him for helping Claudia escape the clutches of the usurpers and the two of them had quickly become friends.

“You dare to lecture me!” the angry voice roared from withing the state hall. “You dare to call me idle! A womaniser! I know that I am married but I am the goddamn emperor! It is none of your business or anyone else's for that matter where I put my cock! She is a woman. Pipara was given to me by king Attalus of the Marcomanni when we concluded our treaty. She is his daughter, but my hostage and I have every damn right to do with her as I please and right now the princess pleases me. Which is more than I can say about you lot! We are done here. Your petition is denied. Get out and fuck off back to Rome!”

A moment later sensing movement in the hall and anticipating what was about to happen the duty officer hurriedly gestured for Corbulo and Probus to step aside. And just as they had done so the doors to the great state hall were flung open and a party of senators, clad in their fine white togas, came marching out. Their sandals stomping across the stone floor. The city fathers were looking grave and flustered. None of them glancing at the waiting soldiers as they quickly strode off down the corridor without speaking a word.

“What’s next?” an annoyed voice cried out from within the hall.

“In you go Sir,” the duty officer said hurriedly turning to Probus.

Entering the great imperial state hall, side by side, Corbulo and Probus approached the throne upon which Gallienus was seated. The emperor was in his early forties and sporting a narrow and neatly clipped, curly beard that ran under the chin from ear to ear. His face had the look of a stubborn, determined man and he was wearing his coat of mail body armour over which he was clad in a splendid cloak coloured in imperial purple. His fingers, bedecked with expensive rings, were tapping impatiently upon the arm rest of his throne and to Corbulo's surprise Gallienus was wearing eye make-up and an earring.

Gathered around the emperor his entourage of advisers and soldiers looked on in silence. Some of the officers were stony faced. Others grave. Some of the imperial slaves looked pale and nervous as if they were worried that they would be blamed for the disastrous audience with the senators while the praetorians stationed around the hall just looked bored as if they had seen it all before. But as he and Probus approached the emperor and bowed before him Corbulo was aware of many eyes studying him. Hard, cruel and merciless eyes. As if he were fresh meat to the slaughter. An easy inexperienced picking. The courtiers like wolves waiting for him to make just one small mistake before they would devour him. The imperial court pregnant with hostile tension.

"Ah it's you, Probus," Gallienus called out sounding relieved as he stopped tapping his fingers against the wooden arm rest. "I hope you are here with some good news for me."

"Honest news Sir," Probus replied flashing a smile.

"Good. Give it to me straight and simple. Another reason why I thought it fit to promote you to be my commander of the Mauretanian guard," Gallienus replied. The emperor's positive reaction to the new audience swiftly improving the mood inside the hall as the courtiers followed Gallienus's lead. "Did you see those senators on your way in?" Gallienus snorted. "The good lords of Rome thought they could petition me to restore their old rights - the same rights which I only took away from them a few months ago. The sheer arrogance! Thinking they could tell me what to do. We are just one step away from the final triumph of anarchy my dear Probus and all they can think about is themselves and their careers. The whole world is going to shit in case you have not noticed."

"You and the army will hold the empire together Sir," Probus replied in a breezy, confident voice as he and Corbulo stood before the emperor. "I have no doubts."

"Maybe," Gallienus said looking away with a sudden resigned look. "But wherever I look I see anarchy and catastrophe. The barbarian tribes press us all along the frontier. The West is lost as is the East and in the city of Rome the populace expects the rest of us to subsidise them when they do fuck all to help themselves. And the Senate just wish to enrich themselves. How did it all come to this eh," Gallienus said turning to Probus with an amused smile. "And the people expect me to take care of all this shit without raising taxes."

Then Corbulo was suddenly conscious that he was being observed by a pair of shrewd, keen eyes.

"And who are you?" Gallienus barked.

"Sir," Probus replied as Corbulo coolly and silently gazed back at the emperor. "This man here is called Corbulo. Prefect of the 1st Cohort of Salian Franks. Recently returned from service in the East. He is the officer who managed to extract his command from the clutches of the usurpers Macrianus and Balista. He brought back nearly a thousand experienced soldiers to serve you Sir, and he now wants to join your new cavalry army. We are here to ask you to confirm him as the prefect of the new cavalry unit that is being created - the all-German cavalry ala, the equites foederati Germanica. I believe general Aureolus recently submitted a report regards the expansion of the new cavalry army..."

“Ah yes, I remember now. Aureolus did. So, this is the job interview,” Gallienus replied lifting his head as he carefully sized Corbulo up. His fingers starting to tap the wooden arm rest on his throne. “So, you are the officer who escaped from Syria and who brought me nearly a thousand valuable soldiers. That was a brave decision. But why? Why take such a risk when you could have simply served Macrianus and Balista? Don't my rivals pay their soldiers like I do?”

As the court fell silent and all eyes turned towards him, waiting expectantly for him to speak, Corbulo kept his focus upon Gallienus. It was the first time he had ever seen the emperor in person even though for years he had seen the man’s image depicted on imperial coins.

“I did not like Macrianus or Balista,” Corbulo replied. “They were traitors to your father. They wanted him to fail at Edessa. They used that defeat to further their own interests. They betrayed Rome and they murdered my friend. And yes, it is true that the colour of their money is the same as yours but there is no honour in fighting for those men. Only shame. You are the true legitimate emperor and my men, and I will fight for you, and you alone Sir.”

"I see," Gallienus replied glancing quickly at his courtiers, "now why do I get the impression that it is I who is being interviewed here," the emperor's remarks eliciting a smattering of polite laughter.

Then turning to study Corbulo from his throne, Gallienus appeared to mull upon Corbulo's answer. The great hall falling silent. The emperor's crafty, calculating eyes resting upon him and suddenly Corbulo was aware that behind the foul-mouthed imperial facade lay a sharp, clever, highly sophisticated and educated mind. Gallienus was no fool. And in that same instant

Corbulo understood that Gallienus was the man he had been hoping to find. An emperor he could do business with. A man he would now gladly fight for.

“Your men are Salian Franks and Batavians, Germans recruited mainly from the lower Rhine delta are they not?” Gallienus said at last, his expression showing that he was unimpressed by Corbulo's answer. “Foederati, treaty bound allies. So why not fight for that prick Postumus who has stolen the western provinces from me. He is of German origin like your men. Your soldiers must surely have family still living in the lost provinces. So, would they not prefer to fight for that usurper Postumus than for me? It would make sense would it not? Postumus would be delighted if you went over to him. He would pay well too.”

“The home base of the infantry of the 1st Cohort of the Thirtieth Legion is at Colonia on the Rhine Sir," Corbulo replied. “You are right when you say that most of my men are of German origin and were recruited from that province. It is also true that my men are now cut off from their families and our parent unit in the West,” Corbulo continued, “as am I from my own family. So, for each one of us there is a personal cost, but we shall pay it. My men and I took an oath to serve you and your father Valerian, and we are bound by that oath. We are loyal to the one true emperor. Loyal to our military oath. We are soldiers. Not hired mercenaries who are willing to sell ourselves to the highest bidder. We shall fight for you Sir.”

"The changed political situation in the West is the main reason why we are forming this new all German speaking cavalry ala, the equites foederati Germanica," Probus interrupted addressing the emperor who ignored him.

“So, you fight for honour and your oath,” Gallienus said. “Well, that is not good enough. Not good enough for me. I am sure that there are many in the armies of these usurpers who are decent honourable men but that would not stop them from cutting off my head if they got the chance. Why should I trust you? For all I know you could have been sent here by my enemies to assassinate me or betray me when the critical moment comes. Maybe you are a spy. If you want to join my new cavalry army you will have to do better than try to seduce me with talk of honour."

Coolly Corbulo stood his ground.

"I was born on the isle of Vectis Sir in the province of Britannia, but I grew up along the Rhine," he replied. "My family have a long history of service to Rome. I can recall each of my ancestors and their deeds back to the time of Hannibal. For it is the custom among the Celtic inhabitants of those distant islands to remember the names of their forefathers and their deeds. To recite their names directly before going into battle. So, when I say that I fight for honour, I mean I fight for their honour. For my forefathers. To make them proud. It is they who guide me and they would not want me to aid these usurpers. It would not be right."

Reaching up Gallienus rubbed his beard with his hand. His expression pained and thoughtful.

"Still not good enough," the emperor exclaimed raising a finger in the air. "You must have known you would get an audience with me. You could have prepared that little speech in advance. I am the emperor," Gallienus continued, his expression hardening as he glared at Corbulo. "And my job is about the most dangerous job in the entire imperium. Do you know how many people are out to kill me, young man? Do you know how many have already tried?"

"And yet you are still here Sir," Corbulo replied refusing to yield. "I want this position. I want to be the prefect of the equites foederati Germanica. I have been trained for this. The army is my life, and I am ready. I will serve you well. You will not regret your decision to promote me. I ask you to take a gamble on me Sir."

"Come on!" Gallienus thundered making one of his slaves jump and whimper in fright. His eyes blazing. "You can do better than that! I have not survived longer than any of my predecessors in the last thirty years by being a fool. If you want this job, then show me who you are. Show me who you really are or else get the fuck out of my court."

"Sir...," Probus tried to intervene but in response Gallienus held up a solitary finger silencing him, his eyes resting upon Corbulo.

"I was the last Roman to have seen your father!" Corbulo called out, his words cutting through the hostile hall. "I saw Valerian in Sassanian captivity. In the heart of the enemy capital of Ctesiphon. The reason why I was there was because I and two companions risked our lives to try and rescue him, but we failed. So, if that is not good enough for you Sir then respectfully - screw you. I was mistaken to think you were worthy of my service."

On his throne Gallienus's expression seemed to change and for a long moment he did not speak.

"Out! Out! Out!" the emperor yelled at last turning to his courtiers and officials. "Everyone out except for the praetorian guard. Out! Out! Now!"

As the courtiers and imperial advisers hurriedly left the hall, their footsteps receding, Corbulo and Probus remained standing. The two friends quickly exchanging a silent look. Then Corbulo lowered his gaze to the floor. He'd blown his chance. This was not looking good. The hall empty, no one spoke. The great imperial state hall silent like a terrified mouse in the presence of danger. The departure of the court officials leaving only the imperial bodyguards standing positioned around the hall like stone statues. And the brooding emperor sitting upon his throne.

"You saw my father after he was captured at Edessa?" Gallienus said at last in a changed voice. "Speak."

"I did Sir," Corbulo said respectfully raising his head to look at Gallienus. "After the emperor, your father was captured by the Sassanians at Edessa a rescue mission was attempted. I led that mission. A small group of us travelled to Ctesiphon to try and rescue Valerian. It was not my idea to do so originally. It was Antoninus, Claudia's husband, Probus's brother-in-law, who first suggested it. He was governor of Emesa and most loyal to your father... but he is dead now. Balista murdered him. But it was Antoninus who convinced me to make the attempt."

"I know who Antoninus was," Gallienus said. "Continue."

"So, we managed to cross the desert and slip into Ctesiphon," Corbulo went on. "I managed to do some reconnaissance once inside the city. The Sassanians they were..." for a moment Corbulo paused as he struggled to find the right words. "The Sassanians Sir, they had placed your father in a cage and put him on public display for all to see. They were humiliating and mocking him."

"In a cage," Gallienus blurted out, his eyes fixed upon Corbulo. "They put my father in a cage like some wild animal?"

"Yes Sir," Corbulo nodded. "I walked past him myself. I was as close to him as you are now. He was alive and seemed to be in good health. Later," Corbulo continued lowering his gaze, "we planned to free him and smuggle him back to Roman territory, but we were betrayed and discovered before we could act, and we barely made it out alive. I am sorry Sir. We failed. The mission was unsuccessful. But I would try again if you ordered it."

As Corbulo stopped speaking the great hall seemed to grow cold. No one speaking. No one moving. Then at last Gallienus stirred and rose to his feet.

"Did you know about this?" Gallienus said glancing at Probus. "Did you know that an attempt was made to rescue my father? And if so, why the fuck was I not told about this sooner?"

"Sir," Probus said in a strained sounding voice. "I was aware of the attempt, but I thought it better if the details of the rescue mission came from Corbulo himself. No one was trying to withhold this news from you. It was just a matter of finding the right time to tell you. That is all."

"The right time..." Gallienus shot back giving Probus a displeased look. "Now you speak like a woman, Probus. What happened to giving it to me straight and simple."

Then not bothering to wait for an answer Gallienus turned his attention back to Corbulo and something seemed to have changed in the emperor's attitude.

"So, there you are at last," Gallienus said, his eyes gleaming with a sudden strange fervour. "There is the real you on display for all to see. Anger cannot be dishonest. I see you now Corbulo, prefect of the first cohort of Salian Franks. That was a brave thing to do. To try and rescue my father. But you said you were betrayed? Who betrayed you and why? Who did not want my father returned to us? Speak and speak well."

“The second wife to King Odaenathus of Palmyra,” Corbulo replied. “Her name is Zenobia. She betrayed us to the Sassanians Sir. I have no proof, but it was her. I met her in Palmyra before the start of our mission. She did not want to see Valerian freed. I do not know why.”

“Queen Zenobia of Palmyra!” Gallienus exclaimed looking suddenly troubled. “That woman has some nerve preventing me from getting my father back. She must harbour ambitions of her own. Great ambitions," Gallienus added in a thoughtful voice, "for her to take such a risk.”

“It is outrageous Sir,” Probus agreed. “You should send a messenger to her husband King Odaenathus at once demanding that he hand Zenobia over to us immediately. Then bring her here to Mediolanum so that she can explain her behaviour to you in person. Her betrayal is an insult. It is an open challenge to your authority. It cannot be allowed to stand.”

“I hear you Probus,” Gallienus said quickly raising his hand, “but we cannot be hasty here. We must think this through carefully. Our situation is precarious, and our resources are limited. The usurpers Macrianus and Balista control much of the East and if they manage to seize Egypt, they can cut off the supply of grain to Italy. The Alemanni invaders may have been driven back for now and the Marcomanni are riven by civil war but their neighbours to the east, the Quadi are growing restless and once again threatening the Danube frontier. On top of that, that arsehole, the governor of Upper Pannonia, Regalian, has also just risen in rebellion against me at Carnuntum. Egypt too is ripe for rebellion against me."

For a moment Gallienus paused, looking a little overwhelmed. "So, you see dear Probus," he continued. "I do not have the resources to fight all of them and that usurping Batavian bastard

Postumus in the West while at the same time also guarding the frontiers against renewed attacks by the Germanic tribes. I mean there is only one me and one cavalry army. I can only be in one place at one time. You forget that we are just one step away from seeing the final triumph of anarchy. If I fall," Gallienus exclaimed beating his chest with his fist, "then so does the whole empire. So, we must be cautious and smart. And right now, I cannot afford to offend King Odaenathus with a request that he hand over his wife to me. For we are going to need the good King to help us crush Macrianus and Balista."

"So, we do nothing?" Probus exclaimed.

"I did not say that!" Gallienus shot back. "I am taking all possible measures to restore the empire to its former greatness. To reunite Rome under one rule. I mean that is my sole fucking purpose right. The relentless quest to save the empire. And let's be honest about it. That is the only reason why the people and the army support me. Because they believe that I am the only one holding the whole thing together. The only one standing between anarchy and civilisation. But don't worry dear Probus. I shall succeed. I must succeed. Everything depends on my success. It is however going to take time for my plans to mature so you need to be patient, Probus."

"Very well Sir."

"And as for you," Gallienus went on turning his eyes towards Corbulo. "They say that a man who does not gamble now and then is afraid of life. And I am forced to gamble all the time whether I like to or not. So, I am going to take a chance on you. As of now you are promoted to prefect of the equites foederati Germanica. I hear your Frankish warriors are first class fighters. They had better be because there is a shed load of shit coming down the road. Welcome to my cavalry army, prefect!"

Chapter Two - We are the Ones to Turn the Tide

It was getting late and the noisy city tavern in the centre of Mediolanum was packed with people. The large single room with its straw covered floor and the L shaped bar at one end was heaving. The clientele chatting, shouting, singing and laughing as groups of men and women were sitting around small wooden tables. The mood of the drinkers was boisterous. The atmosphere jovial and here and there team colours were visible adorning people's clothing. While the inevitable bored looking prostitute was leaning against the ladder that led to the loft above the pub, examining her painted fingernails and the tavern owner was feverishly working behind his bar replacing a barrel of wine. The smell of stale, unwashed bodies and woodsmoke filled the room but no one seemed to mind. Sitting in a corner around their small table in the dim flickering light coming from an open fire, Probus grinned as he raised his cup of wine in a toast to his two companions.

"To you Corbulo!" Probus exclaimed as he was swiftly joined by his sister Claudia, "on your promotion to the commander of the newest unit to join the cavalry army - the equites foederati Germanica. This is a good day. A great day!"

Touching their wooden cups together Corbulo nodded and smiled modestly as the three of them drunk their toast.

"Well done, Corbulo," Claudia said turning to him with a pleased smile, her blond hair illuminated in the firelight as to his surprise she reached out and placed her hand over his. The young attractive woman was in her mid-twenties and clad in her white woollen winter cloak. "The empire is stronger as of today. The emperor is a lucky man to have you in his army," Claudia continued with a mischievous look. "Now I am certain that we are going to win this civil war."

Carefully withdrawing his hand from under hers Corbulo looked thoughtful as he once again raised his cup of wine in another toast. “To those who we left behind,” he said glancing at his two companions. “To Antoninus.”

At the mention of her dead husband, the smile faded from Claudia’s face, and she quickly nodded and drank, lowering her eyes as if the mention of his name had brought back bad memories.

“The new cavalry army that is forming here in Mediolanum,” Probus said raising a finger, “is going to form the spearhead of Gallienus’s attempts to reunite the empire. After what the Alemanni did during their recent invasion of Italy Gallienus decided that he needed a large body of trained horsemen who could move fast towards any point of danger along the frontier and there are so many such local crises. He is not wrong when he says that the final triumph of anarchy is close. The empire is splintered and under threat like never before. But we my friend are going to be the empire’s fire brigade. The imperial elite. First into danger. First into battle. We are going to be the ones to turn the tide.”

“Sounds like fun,” Corbulo replied.

“Oh yes,” Probus replied unable to check his enthusiasm. “Not counting your Germans Corbulo, the cavalry army right now numbers twelve thousand men. Most of the cavalry units are not new and have existed for some time of course but no one has ever concentrated them together in one army. Not like this, not under one unified command. The equites Dalmatae are the most numerous, five thousand of them. Then there are the equites Promotii and Scutarii. The old legionary cavalry. Then there are my own equites Mauri. I have eighteen hundred Moors, and they are the best horsemen in the world. Wait till you see them ride. They are the descendants of Hannibal's Numidian light cavalry who were once the terror of the legions. Fierce tough little fuckers afraid of nothing. And now making up a fifth group we have your Germans. Your Salian Franks. There was supposed to be a sixth regiment," Probus said eagerly licking his lips, "the equites Sagittarii, eastern horse archers. But Valerian took all of them to the East and they were either destroyed at Edessa or are now serving the usurpers Macrianus and Balista."

"So, it seems that I and my men will be keeping illustrious company," Corbulo said looking pleased. "My men will enjoy that, no doubt. But you are wrong about your Moors. Wait till you see my Salian Franks. My Germans are the best horsemen in the world. They live for war. They are born to it. They crave it."

"We should have a contest," Probus said smiling as he took up the challenge. "To see who is best. Moor or German. But seriously. How many men do you think you will be able to muster?"

"Hard to say right now," Corbulo said idly glancing across the packed tavern towards the bored looking prostitute. "My unit is still forming. The call has gone out for German speaking volunteers serving in other army units to come and join us, but I do not know if any will come or be assigned to my command. I am also awaiting my horses without which we will not be a proper cavalry ala." For a moment Corbulo paused as he inspected the whore. "I brought nearly a thousand men back from Syria," he continued at last, "but four fifth of them were infantry who had never ridden a horse before. I have my two cavalry companies of Salian Franks of course, veterans to a man, but they are severely understrength and with the situation in the West being what it is I do not expect to receive any reinforcements from the Rhine. It is going to take some time to reorganise, re-equip and train my men."

"I don't think we are going to have much time," Probus replied his expression growing serious. "You heard the emperor. Our enemies are stacking up against us. Regalian the governor of Upper Pannonia has just rebelled, and he has been joined by the Fourteenth Legion at Carnuntum. And if that were not bad enough. Intelligence suggests that the Danube frontier is in danger of being overrun by the Quadi and their Vandal allies and the intelligence from the East is especially bad. Gallienus expects that Macrianus and Balista will soon cross into Europe and march on Italy. The loyalty of the Danube legions is suspect too. Gallienus thinks Macrianus is going to try and force the issue of who is emperor. So, it is likely that we are either going to be sent into battle against Regalian, the Quadi or against the Macriani usurpers or all of them and it will happen soon. So, my guess is that you have just a couple of months to get your men into shape. That's if there is no other crisis before that which requires our immediate presence and attention."

"And Aureolus?" Corbulo said giving Probus a wary look. "Our commanding officer. He is a good general?"

"Aureolus," Probus said leaning back in his seat with a sober look as if the question had caught him off-guard. "He is a bully, and he is an ambitious man. He is disliked by many at court because he despises civilians and because he was once a lowly goat herder from Dacia, but he is the best cavalry general that I have ever served under. A soldier's soldier as his supporters like to call him. I would not call him a friend, but Gallienus was wise to appoint him to the command of the new cavalry army. Aureolus knows how to win battles."

“Speak plainly with Corbulo and do not hide the truth from him," Claudia interrupted remonstrating with her brother. "Just say it. You hate Aureolus's guts. He stands in your way Probus! He is a rival."

"Maybe it is true," Probus said giving Corbulo a cryptic smile.

"Aureolus may be a good soldier but that is about his only talent,” Claudia continued frowning at her brother, “and do not be so sure it was wise of Gallienus to give him such power. Power corrupts brother. And loyalty wears thin like ice on a hot day. What is to stop Aureolus from at some point trying to overthrow Gallienus and install himself as emperor? What then for us?”

Glancing at his sister Probus just shrugged. “Such are the times we live in,” he replied. “Gallienus knows the risks but what else can he do. Aureolus is good at his job. He is needed. Now more than ever. The emperor must take risks, that is his job. He has no choice.”

“And what about Gallienus,” Corbulo said, carefully eyeing Probus, “today was the first time that I have ever met the emperor. What struck me was that he did not seem very close to Valerian - his father. I was expecting him to order me back to the East to try and mount another rescue mission to free Valerian, but he said nothing. He did not seem interested in the idea.”

Quickly Probus turned to look around the tavern, but no one seemed to be listening in to their conversation. Exchanging a brief wary look with his sister he at last turned back to Corbulo.

“What you say is true,” Probus said lowering his voice. “Few know this. But Gallienus was already estranged from his father before Valerian even left for his campaign in the East. The two of them did not see eye to eye on many things. It had got to the point where Gallienus had started to number his own victories separate to those of his father. The two were officially co-emperors but they had different ideas on how to rule. In public they were a unified front but in private they were arguing all the time. So maybe it was a blessing when they decided that Valerian would rule in the East and Gallienus would do so in the West. Valerian was a traditionalist who gave the Senate much power. He respected his fellow senators for after all he was one of them. But Gallienus is not like his father. He by contrast is a reformer. A moderniser who wants to promote talent before birthright. Thus, under his rule the equestrian class is now in the ascendency and the political careers of the Senatorial class have been restricted. It's because Gallienus fears the Senate," Probus continued, his eyes gleaming. "Gallienus thinks that if there is another major rebellion against him, its leaders will come from the Senate. He trusts the lower social orders more than his own class. Which is why he is so popular among the common people and the army. He understands that to survive we must start to do things differently. Because the world has changed. Because it is growing darker. And we should be grateful to Gallienus for that because men like you and I," Probus added pointing at Corbulo, "would never get promoted otherwise."

"So, he is a reformer," Corbulo said turning to idly inspect his cup of wine. "I am glad to hear it. I was hoping he would turn out to be such a man."

"Why?" Claudia said sharply, gazing at Corbulo with a questioning look. "Why do you care what kind of man Gallienus is?"

"Because I want something from him," Corbulo said coolly replying to her with a little cryptic smile. "Because one day the emperor is going to do something for me. Something very important."

"I support Gallienus because the emperor is going to be good for me and my family," Probus replied lowering his gaze, choosing his words carefully. "But Gallienus has had a hard time of late. Last year he lost his father and both his eldest sons and heirs. His eldest boy Valerian II was murdered by the usurper Ingenuus at Sirmium on the Danube and his second son Saloninus was murdered by Postumus at Colonia. Both were killed within just a few months of each other. Gallienus is assailed on all sides by usurpers and barbarians and an ungrateful Senate," Probus continued. "The West and East are lost. Plague stalks the land. The imperial coffers are bare, and inflation is rampant. Everywhere you look there is a crisis and anarchy. And yet he still stands and does his duty to the empire. That deserves our respect. Gallienus is the light that is keeping the world from being plunged into darkness."

"I agree brother that Gallienus will be good for us," Claudia said, her eyes gleaming with sudden fanaticism. "Valerian may have been old school but at least Valerian was not wrong about the Christians," she said, her lips curling in disgust. "He did the right thing to continue to persecute the Christians. The Christian cult with their belief in just one God represents a mortal threat to the empire. The Christians are already dividing the populace at a time when we should be united. They deserve to be punished for that. They deserve nothing but death. We should continue to hunt them down and burn them in the arena!"

"Ah the Christians," Probus said wearily as Corbulo shifted uncomfortably in his seat. "I suppose you are right sister, although it is a tedious issue. One best left until that moment when you have nothing more to talk about."

“Does Gallienus take a different view towards the Christians than his father did?” Corbulo asked.

“We don’t know,” Claudia said sharply, turning her large zealous eyes towards Corbulo. “He has made no public announcements yet regards the Christians, but the rumour is that he is soft on the cult and will tolerate them. Apparently, he does not share his father’s conviction that they should be hunted and persecuted. Gallienus is weak in that way,” Claudia added her voice turning bitter. “He is too nice. Too sophisticated. Too blinded by his tolerance. He should rule with a much harsher and firmer hand. He should root out these Christians and destroy their cult. They are a menace that cannot be tolerated. A threat to the very foundations of our empire which cannot be allowed to fester.”

Lowering his gaze Corbulo suddenly appeared sombre and he made no effort to offer a reply and for a moment an awkward silence descended upon the little table. Then suddenly Claudia’s hand was once again resting on top of his own. Her fingers pressing into his flesh. Her expression softening as if she had noticed the sudden change in his mood.

“Are you worried about them,” she asked sounding concerned, “about your family back on the isle of Vectis? You are thinking about them now, aren’t you? You look worried Corbulo.”

Raising his gaze to look up at her for a moment Corbulo studied Claudia as if she were a stranger. Then he turned away.

“What’s this?” Probus interrupted glancing from Corbulo to his sister and back again with a puzzled look. “What is this about your family?”

"You should tell my brother. He should know," Claudia said studying Corbulo with a knowing look. "Maybe he can help. It is time he knew."

Ignoring Claudia Corbulo turned to Probus with a resigned look.

"My loyalty to emperor Gallienus is not without a personal cost," he said carefully clearing his throat. "When I abandoned the usurpers and brought my men back to the West I put my family on the isle of Vectis in Britannia in grave danger. Before this Balista had threatened them if I were to prove disloyal and he is a powerful man with a long reach. Balista is also a vindictive man, and I have no doubt that he will have tried to carry out his threat by now. So, you see; by remaining loyal to Gallienus I have put my family in mortal danger."

Sitting on his stool Probus stared at Corbulo. Then he swore.

"I sent my aunt Helena a letter as soon as I was able to," Corbulo continued. "Warning her of what was coming but with the imperial postal system as it is who knows how long it will take before the letter arrives or indeed if it will ever arrive. I have had no news from Vectis in over a year."

"So, you do not know what has happened to your family?" Probus muttered.

"I have no idea what has become of them or the fate of the ancestral farm," Corbulo replied. "They could all be dead if Balista has managed to carry out his threat. I just don't know. And if the worst has happened then that would be on me. I will have killed them all. Loyalty is not without cost."

"Indeed," Probus murmured. "But the western provinces have rebelled and broken away under Postumus," he went on. "Maybe the political change has limited Balista's reach. He is after all in the East and your family are far away in the West. You should hold onto that hope," Probus added, nodding with growing confidence. "No news is not necessarily bad news."

"Indeed. Hope," Corbulo replied looking grateful.

For a while the three of them did not speak as they drank their wine.

"Before you leave for war Corbulo," Claudia said at last, changing the subject, her fingers tightening their grip on his hand, "why do you not come out with me. I could show you how to hunt wild boar in the forest. It would be fun. Take your mind of things. Just the two of us."

Turning towards Claudia Corbulo hesitated as he took in her mischievous inviting smile, sensing that the woman wanted something else from him, something deeper and more meaningful. But she had still completely missed it he thought.

"I don't think I am going to have the time for hunting," he replied in a measured voice withdrawing his hand from her grasp. "I am sorry. There is a lot to do to prepare my command but thank you for the offer, Claudia. Another time perhaps, when we have got to know each other better."

"When we have got to know each other better!" Claudia exclaimed looking startled and confused by his rejection. "I think I know you well enough by now Corbulo. Excuse me," Claudia added as she hurriedly rose from her seat and headed towards the public toilets.

For a moment Corbulo watched her go before he felt Probus tugging at the sleeve of his cloak.

“What’s this?” Probus said shooting Corbulo a little amused smile. “You are turning down the opportunity to get to know my sister. To have sex with her. She likes you Corbulo. She likes you very much. I can see. So why turn her down?”

“It would not work,” Corbulo replied with a shrug. “I don’t have time for a wife. I am a soldier. The army is my life.”

“Oh, come on,” Probus exclaimed. “You are also a man. What do you do when you need a woman?”

For a moment Corbulo hesitated. “When I need a woman, I go to see a prostitute,” he said at last looking up at Probus. “That’s how it has always been for me. I pay women for sex. It's just easier and more convenient that way. There are no complications. No strings. No commitments. Just a simple transaction. But a woman like Claudia she wants…she needs more than just an affair. I have got to know her well these past few months that we travelled together. She wants a husband. A new Antoninus. She wants marriage, children, a home. None of which I can give her so it would not work between us, and I do not want to raise her hopes. That would be cruel, and she has already suffered enough.”

Swearing softly Probus stared at Corbulo. Then he looked away and sombrely lowered his gaze.

“Fair enough,” he murmured. “But if you change your mind Corbulo I will whole heartedly support you and give my blessing to your union with my sister. Having you as my brother-in-law would be a prudent move for both of us.”

For a moment the two of them remained silent. Then just as the commander of the equites Mauri was about to speak again Corbulo suddenly spotted Linus pushing towards him through the crowded tavern. The nineteen-year-old youth with his long blond hair tied back in a ponytail looked worried and as he noticed Linus's expression Corbulo felt a sudden sense of dread. Something appeared to be wrong. He could tell instantly.

"What is it Linus?" Corbulo said sharply rising to his feet in alarm.

"Sir," Linus gasped, his face contorted with concern. The youth close to tears. "I am so sorry to disturb you Sir but its concerning Badurad. They said that I could find you here. I came as quickly as I could."

"What!" Corbulo growled his expression darkening. "What's the matter with Badurad? What has he done?"

"He's been arrested again Sir," Linus blurted out. "The city watch caught him brawling in a whorehouse. They arrested him. He is being charged with public disorder offences and criminal damage. He told me to find you at once. You must come with me Sir. Right now. It's urgent. He's in trouble!"

"What!" Corbulo exclaimed in disbelief. "Fighting! Badurad has been brawling again! I can't believe this. After I specifically told him not to get into trouble. Wait till I get my hands on that useless, wretched boy!"

"I am so sorry Sir," Linus whined.

"You will have to excuse me while I tend to this emergency," Corbulo said hastily turning to Probus. "Badurad is my cousin. He is family. I must sort this out. I must go."

Chapter Three - Loyalty

Following Linus down the dark deserted street Corbulo's growing fury was concealed by the night. His boots rasping across the cobblestones. His hands clenched into fists. His eyes hard as flint. Badurad was about to get an earful and a proper beating. His young cousin appeared to have lapsed into his old bad habits. Despite all his promises to the contrary he had not changed. He was still a rebellious youth who enjoyed getting into trouble with authority. Leading the way Linus had set a blistering pace. The young man and Badurad's best friend not daring to look back at Corbulo as if he sensed his growing outrage. It had been the venerable Hostes, Badurad's soldier father back in the Colonia on the Rhine, who had originally sent his nineteen-year-old son to join Corbulo's vexillation, who had at that time been seconded to the Syrian frontier. Hostes in his letter had tasked him Corbulo, with making a man and a soldier out of his son, Corbulo recalled and with Badurad had come Linus, his spineless childhood friend. The two youth's completely inseparable. That had been a year ago and since then much had happened. When he had first joined Corbulo's unit in the East, Badurad had proved to be a rebellious young man. Difficult to handle. Insubordinate. Constantly getting into brawls and trouble from which he'd had to be rescued. But eventually the boy had started to mature and listen to him. Promising to stay out of trouble. To become the man Hostes had wanted him to become. Or so he had thought until tonight, Corbulo thought savagely.

"Where are we going?" Corbulo said, frowning as he quickly drew level with Linus. "You said that Badurad was arrested by the city watch. Are they not holding him at their police post? If so, we're going the wrong way! The guard station is in that direction."

“They didn’t take him to the station Sir,” Linus said hurriedly, not daring to look at the older man. “When he was arrested Badurad told the watch who you are and that he is your cousin. He convinced them to put him under house arrest. The city watch took him to your house. They are keeping him there until you arrive. Badurad thinks that you will be able to get him released and the charges dropped. Because you are an important man Sir.”

“Oh great!” Corbulo said swearing out loud. “So, I am supposed to look the other way because he is family. No fucking way! Badurad is going to get the punishment that he deserves. Brawling! What again! I thought he had grown up, but it seems that I was wrong about him. He is still a boy.”

“That’s what I told him you would say. I am so sorry Sir,” Linus gasped as the two of them rounded a corner and hurried down the street towards the civilian house where Corbulo had been billeted.

Glaring at the darkened building Corbulo could see no soldiers on guard outside. His home appeared quiet and deserted like the rest of the street. Taking over the lead as Linus respectfully slowed his pace Corbulo marched up to the front door, inserted his key in the lock and barged into his house before abruptly coming to a confused halt. The front room was cloaked in darkness. No lights were on, and he could see nothing. What was this? Where were the city watch. Where was his cousin? Then suddenly from the darkness close by he heard a female giggle and a moment later several oil lamps burst into light, illuminating the room.

“Ha! Got you old man!” Badurad cried out with a broad delighted grin as he came bounding towards the startled Corbulo and gave him a bear hug. “Happy birthday uncle. You thought we had forgotten hadn't you! Well, you are wrong. Welcome to your surprise birthday party!"

Staring at his young cousin Corbulo remained rooted to the ground. Caught completely off-guard. Then his gaze shifted to the four young attractive women sitting together on the couch gazing up at him with amused smiles, already holding cups of wine in their hands as if they had been waiting for him. The women were clearly in on the prank. Then swiftly Corbulo turned to look round at Linus who was standing behind him. The youth was grinning from ear to ear.

"So, you were not arrested for brawling in a whorehouse?" Corbulo growled at last turning his attention back to Badurad.

"Nah uncle," Badurad smiled, looking amused. "That was just an excuse to get you to come back. I sent Linus to fetch you, and we thought it would be fun if you thought that I had been arrested. Just like the old days in Samosata, eh. Ha! You should see your face right now. That's just priceless."

"I see," Corbulo said relaxing, his hands unclenching. "Shame because I was just about to give you a thorough beating."

"Did he buy your act?" Badurad said turning to Linus.

"Oh, he did," Linus cried out in delight as he stood in the doorway. "He never suspected anything. He was furious with you Badurad. No offence meant Sir. We just thought we would play a practical joke on you."

"It's your birthday, uncle," Badurad continued taking over and opening his arms wide in a smooth, disarming gesture, displaying his youthful charm. "We thought we would throw you a surprise party. Come on. Let's have a good time. The night is still young. We have been planning this for a week."

“Is that why there are four women sitting on my couch,” Corbulo said turning towards the four ladies.

“Four very expensive prostitutes, uncle,” Badurad beamed. “Two for you and two for me and Linus will just have to sit and watch and take notes because he does not like women. What do you say, uncle? It’s your birthday and I have paid for everything with my own money. This is on me.”

“It’s true Sir,” Linus exclaimed. “Badurad paid for it himself. And when does that ever happen!”

For a moment Corbulo said nothing. His gaze sweeping over the occupants of the room. Then at last he turned and giving Linus a little slap across his cheek he closed the front door behind him.

“Maybe there is hope for you yet,” Corbulo said turning back to Badurad with a grave look as two of the women silently rose to their feet and came up to him, slipping their arms around his waist. “But you still got the date wrong, cousin. My birthday is tomorrow.”

***

It was still dark, the hour before dawn as Corbulo sat at the table in the back room of his two-room house. Already fully clothed in his uniform his sheathed spatha sword was lying on the table in front of him. The four prostitutes had already left and Badurad and Linus were still asleep in the front room and for the moment he was alone. The house was quiet and the city beyond was peaceful while the room was dimly lit by a solitary handheld oil lamp shaped like a human foot. The fragile light flickering and casting shadows across the wall.

On the portable army stove nearby the small copper pot filled with polentum, porridge was coming to a boil and as he watched his breakfast Corbulo looked resigned. Today was his birthday. He was thirty-one. At last, turning his eyes towards Gamo's gold ring that still sat upon his finger he sighed. As eldest son he had inherited the ring after Gamo his stepfather had died when he'd been just fourteen. But it was not a valuable gift to be cherished. Nor did it bring fond memories of Gamo. Instead, he'd worn it for the past seventeen years to remind himself of the grave, dishonourable thing he had once done. For one day he would have to atone for his actions before the assembly of his illustrious forefathers. One day he would have to tell Hostes, Gamo's brother, what he had done.

Gamo had been his stepfather. His mother's second husband. A Batavian from lower Germania who had served as a centurion in the garrison at the Roman city of Colonia on the lower Rhine. Gamo had abused him and his younger brothers, Veda and Munatius. Gamo had been dreadful. A violent, sadistic bully. The abuse continuing for years until he could no longer take it Corbulo thought lowering his eyes as he remembered. So, one day when he had been fourteen and Veda had been twelve and Munatius just eight, the three of them had conspired to murder their stepfather. Munatius had lured Gamo into the ambush where he Corbulo had been the first to stab Gamo with a knife while Veda had followed up delivering the final killer blow. The three brothers swearing to each other afterwards to keep their murderous secret just between themselves. And they'd done just that, remaining loyal to each other, for no one had ever found out what they'd done.

Reaching out with his other hand Corbulo fidgeted with the ring as the memories of that day came flooding back. Shortly after the murder, Hostes, Gamo's brother, a good man unlike his brother, completely unaware of what they had done, had taken over the responsibility for raising the three brothers. Hostes had become a father figure to him Corbulo thought, a man he deeply respected. Hostes too had early on decided to separate him from his brothers. Sending Veda and Munatius back to live with their aunt Helena and sister Cata on the ancestral farm on the isle of Vectis in the province of Britannia while he Corbulo was to be prepared and trained for a career and leadership position within the Roman army. But something had gone wrong and on their journey to Britain Veda and Munatius had been attacked by Frankish raiders and eight-year-old Munatius had been taken captive by the Germanic tribesmen and was presumed to have perished.

Staring at Gamo's gold band on his finger Corbulo took a deep breath. It had been seventeen years now since he had last seen Veda his brother and his aunt Helena and his sister Cata. His family were becoming strangers, and he was finding it increasingly difficult to remember what they looked like. They would all be older now if they were still alive. If Balista had not already managed to carry through on his threat to have them eliminated. Would his letter to his aunt warning her of the danger arrive in time? He doubted it. Before the break-up of the empire, once a year he had written to his aunt and sometimes he had received a letter in reply. The correspondence taking months to arrive. Each letter a treasure to be kept. But now with Postumus declared emperor in the West it was likely that no more letters would be able to get through. The imperial post system was broken. The world was descending into anarchy and ruin.

"You are up early, uncle," Badurad said as he came shuffling into the backroom, looking hungover, hungrily eyeing the bubbling breakfast in its pot.

“We have a full day ahead of us,” Corbulo replied reaching out to stir the boiling porridge. “So, get yourself ready and wake Linus. I want to be at the barracks by dawn. There is a lot of work to do. I must get the men ready, and time is short. War is coming. Probus thinks we may be sent against the usurper Regalian or the Quadi or the Macriani usurpers when they finally cross over into Europe. And I still don't have any damn horses.”

“Oh yeah, happy birthday, old man,” Badurad replied as he pulled up a stool and without asking started to help himself to the porridge, pouring it into his bowl. “You enjoy yourself last night?” the youth added.

“I enjoyed the fact that you paid for it all,” Corbulo said as he too started to help himself to the breakfast.

But Badurad did not seem in the mood for idle talk. Eating his porridge, he remained silent. His expression suddenly brooding.

“You know there is something that I have been meaning to speak to you about uncle,” Badurad began. “Something important. Maybe you can help me understand.”

“Go on,” Corbulo said between mouthfuls.

“Hostes is my father. Gamo was yours,” Badurad said frowning as he turned towards Corbulo. “Hostes raised you pretty much after Gamo died even though you were not his son. Hostes trained you to be a soldier, uncle. He got you your first position as an officer with the Thirtieth. He used his influence to give you a good start. You and I, we owe everything to Hostes. He made you. He made me. So here is my problem. Our families are in Colonia and in Britannia. In the West where we grew up. So, I keep asking myself this - why the fuck are we fighting for

Gallienus? Why should we be loyal to him? Should we not be fighting to defend our homes and our families. They need us. Hostes needs us. I know he does. It doesn't make sense. We should be fighting for Postumus, uncle. He is the emperor in the West. He should be our man. Not Gallienus."

Abruptly Corbulo stopped eating. His expression souring. Then he turned towards Badurad studying him coolly.

"Do I really need to explain this to you," Corbulo said at last sounding disappointed. "We are fighting for Gallienus because all of us, those of us in the West, swore a sacred oath of allegiance to the emperors Valerian and his son Gallienus. We are soldiers and we will do our duty. To the emperor. To Rome. And when we accepted the emperor's silver, we made a contract with Gallienus and so far, the emperor has kept his promise to us. Postumus however is a usurper, he is illegitimate, and he will meet the same fate as all usurpers and you Badurad will not bring this subject up again, understood."

"I want to go to home," Badurad said defiantly and angrily placing his spoon on the table. "I miss home. I miss my family. Hostes. Holda. Jutta. Do you not want to see your brother Veda again? Your aunt Helena, your sister? We are fighting for the wrong side uncle. We should return home - to the Rhine. To Germania. To Britain. The mountain passes are open again. From here we could be home within a week. We are needed at home, and I am not the only one who thinks like this. There are others - under your command - who feel the same way as I do, uncle. They too want to go home. They too think we are fighting on the wrong side. Screw Gallienus! This is all wrong!"

"Enough!" Corbulo barked slamming his fist down on the table. "I said that this conversation is over!"

“No fuck you,” Badurad retorted rising to his feet and pointing an accusing finger at Corbulo. “You got it wrong this time. We are needed at home. Not here! Eat your breakfast old man but I am going to sleep at the barracks from now on. Don’t try to change my mind!”

And with that Badurad turned on his heels and was gone, angrily slamming the door behind him as he left the house.

Staring at the door Corbulo did not move. Then he took a deep breath and turned his attention back to his porridge.

“Badurad is upset Sir,” Linus said gingerly as he suddenly appeared in the doorway to the back room. “He misses home that is all. We have been gone for over a year now. It’s a long time.”

“If he speaks to me like that again,” Corbulo growled without looking up, “then I shall have him flogged in front of the troops.”

“He’s just upset,” Linus repeated as he sat down on the stool vacated by his friend. “But he doesn’t mean what he said. You know Badurad. His anger does not last. He will get over it. By tomorrow he will have forgotten all about it all and something else will be occupying his mind. I will speak to him Sir.”

“Let’s hope so,” Corbulo said finishing his food and quickly reaching for his spatha to attach it to his military belt. “Good. Thank you, Linus,” he added rising to his feet and giving the youth an appreciative glance. “Please put some sense into that boy’s head.”

Chapter Four - The Equites Foederati Germanica

“Attention!” the guard officer cried in a loud voice as Corbulo entered his command post. The group of Roman officers who were already inside the tent waiting for him, sprang stiffly to attention. Their arms pressed tightly against the sides of their bodies. The military salutes coming in rapid succession as Corbulo acknowledged his principal subordinates with a curt nod. Crastus, the big, brash centurion with an air of aggression about him. A tough soldier in his forties who despite his age could take you out for a great night of drinking and wild tavern brawling. Harald tall, calm and serious. Fifteen years older than Corbulo, Harald, with his short spiky hair, was an officer of the old school. A strict disciplinarian who was not afraid to rebuke his superiors if he thought they were doing something wrong. Both he and Crastus were battle-hardened veterans who had been part of the original vexillation from the Thirtieth that had been sent to shore up the East from their homebase along the Rhine frontier.

It was dawn and across the barracks just outside the city walls of Mediolanum the camp was a hive of activity.

“Alright gather round, I have important news,” Corbulo called out in German summoning his subordinates to him. “Yesterday I had an audience with the emperor who confirmed my position as prefect ala and with that confirmation the equites foederati Germanica have now been officially added to the army lists. We are in business, gentlemen! We are now part of Gallienus’s cavalry army and under the direct command of general Aureolus. Some of you are going to have to learn how to ride a horse!”

And as the news was announced the small group of Roman officers began to stamp their boots on the ground in approval.

"So as of today," Corbulo went on, "we are no longer a vexillation from the Thirtieth legion detached for duty in the East. We are now an independent ala, the equites foederati Germanica and all our existing units will be amalgamated. The old unit names and insignia will be dropped and new ones adopted. A complete reorganisation, gentlemen. Your 1st infantry Cohort Crastus," Corbulo said turning to the big man, "will be retrained to become horsemen. Aureolus's staff have assured me that we shall be provided with the necessary horses and equipment as soon as possible."

"So we are to become cavalry," Crastus replied. "I have no objections to that Sir, but my men are not used to riding horses. We were trained to fight on foot and in a shield wall. The men have little experience of riding into battle or fighting in that manner. It will take me some time to get them ready."

"Which is why I am breaking up the 2nd and 3rd cavalry companies of Salian Franks," Corbulo replied, "and distributing our surviving riders among the newly forming companies. Our Franks are the best and most experienced horsemen we have got and as such they are now going to act as instructors to the rest of the unit. I want them to share their riding experience and skill with the rest of us. So, the Salian Franks will oversee training and teaching your men how to ride and fight Crastus and I want you Harald, "Corbulo said turning to the tall officer with his short spiky hair, "to oversee that training regime. I need you to get us ready to fight on horseback. Which means I want you and Crastus to work together."

"Very well Sir," Harald replied in German, looking resigned, "how much time do I have?"

"A couple of months if we are lucky."

“If we are now to fight as cavalry Sir,” Crastus said, “then does that mean the pay of my men will increase accordingly to their new status? Cavalry get paid more than infantry. My men are going to ask Sir.”

“No. There will be no increase in the soldier’s pay,” Corbulo replied shaking his head. “I was told very firmly by the imperial fiscus that there can be no extra funds allocated to us. None. Money is in short supply right and the situation is not expected to improve any time soon now that the West and East have broken away. It is just the way things are right now,” Corbulo added, “but once we are on campaign the men should be able to supplement their income from the spoils of our defeated enemies. And if we are sent across the imperial frontiers there should be plenty of opportunities for unconditional looting.”

For a moment Corbulo paused to look around at his subordinates but no one spoke up in protest.

Crastus was probably his most courageous officer Corbulo thought. A one-man battering ram with the strength and appetite of an ox who liked to lead from the front. A man who was very popular and respected among his soldiers. A veteran fighter who you would want at your side in the thick of a shield wall and close contact with the enemy. Harald by contrast was more reserved and serious. An excellent organiser and planner with an iron sense of duty and discipline and a natural disdain for his more boisterous and unruly colleague. The rivalry between the two officers, both of whom were vying to be promoted to become Corbulo’s deputy, was well known among the soldiers, to the extent that rival marching songs had been written about it. But Harald was also a close friend Corbulo thought. For Harald had like himself, been trained by Hostes, the old and wise warrior from the Rhine who had adopted Corbulo when he was still a boy and to whom he owed his whole advancement and military career. That shared bond between Corbulo and Harald had helped to secure their friendship and trust over the years.

"Now in addition to our old vexillation, the men from the 1st infantry cohort of the Thirtieth and our Salian Frankish cavalry," Corbulo continued, "I have also been informed that we will be receiving reinforcements from the 2nd Batavian auxiliary cohort. Well to be more precise we will be receiving all the survivors from that unit. Until recently they were posted to defend the Danube frontier. They are a mixed cohort, part infantry, part cavalry. It appears though that they have had a hard time up there on the Danube and I am told that they have suffered substantial casualties, so we have been instructed to amalgamate them into the equites foederati Germanica. The two units are to become one."

"The 2nd Batavian auxiliary cohort!" Crastus growled rubbing his hands together with a happy grin. "Our brothers in arms from the Rhine are going to join us! This is good news Sir."

"I know their commander," Harald added, "a good soldier by the name of Oskar. He served with Hostes before Sir. I agree that this is good news, and we can sure do with the reinforcements."

"Well with the changed political situation in the West," Corbulo went on in a measured manner, "like us, the 2nd Batavians have now been cut off from their homeland and families. Like us they cannot go home. So, the imperial administration has decided to assign them to me. To concentrate all the surviving Batavian and Salian Frankish units into one all German speaking command. The 2nd is therefore being pulled from the frontier and sent to us, to bring us up to strength. For logistical, political and command reasons they want all the German speaking soldiers from the lower Rhine concentrated in one unit. I am expecting them to arrive within days and when they do, we shall have to integrate them into our own companies."

Inside the tent no one spoke. The officers watching Corbulo expectantly as they sensed that more important news was still to come.

"So, all in all," Corbulo went on summing up, "with the six hundred survivors from the old 1st infantry Cohort of the Thirtieth Legion and the hundred and sixty-five Salian Franks plus the survivors from the 2nd Batavians we should be able to form eight new cavalry companies of a hundred and twenty riders apiece. Our total strength will be about nine hundred and sixty men. I am going to form these eight companies into two battlegroups of four companies each. Four squadrons of thirty men to a company each squadron led by a decurion. You Crastus will be in command of the first cavalry cohort and you Harald will oversee the second cavalry cohort. You will both report directly to me. I am going to need daily reports on the progress that you are making for time is short. Select your subordinate officers and submit their names to me for approval as soon as you can. I also want you each to take half the men from the 2nd Batavians once they arrive and spread them around your companies in equal measure. We need to build a single cohesive and effective force. So, see to it that each of your companies is assigned some experienced horsemen. I know that it will take time and won't be easy, but there it is. That's your task. See that it is done. Alright. You have your orders."

"Yes Sir," Crastus and Harald called out before quickly glancing at each other. Their rivalry briefly showing.

"Good," Corbulo said looking pleased.

"So, as we are now the equites foederati Germanica," Harald said soberly," we are going to need a new battle-standard Sir.

The men need to have pride in their unit and that starts with our battle-standard. It must reflect who we are, and we are clearly no longer just a vexillation from the Thirtieth."

"Indeed," Corbulo said nodding in agreement, his enthusiasm showing. "This is a new start for us as an independent unit. A great day! A historic day! So, we must seize this opportunity with both hands. For it is not every day that you get a chance to create a new unit from scratch but here we are, gentlemen. Here we are. Ready and able to create our own traditions. To start something that may go on to last for hundreds of years. But at the same time as we look to the future, we must not forget who we are or where we came from. So, I propose that we keep the symbols and battle-honours from our old banners in honour of our history, heritage and our past service. We will keep the wolf's head depicted on our shields, but we will add a new motto to our standards. One that we shall become known by. *Gallienus's Finest. Loyal and Faithful - First into Battle*."

But as Corbulo finished speaking he was met by a wall of silence.

"I see what you are trying to do but it's a bit long Sir," Harald said at last looking dubious.

"It's a shit motto Sir," Crastus burst out laughing unable to contain himself. "What happens when Gallienus is no longer emperor. Then we are stuck with an outdated motto. Whoever wears the purple next is not going to be very impressed are they especially if Gallienus is done away by a rival general who then becomes our commander. Gallienus's Finest - indeed. Ha!"

"I am aware of that," Corbulo replied coolly glancing at Crastus and then at the others, "but what you are not aware of is the fact that the very existence of the equites foederati Germanica is tenuous at best. We have enemies at the imperial court. The emperor has agreed to include our unit on the army lists but there are voices at the imperial court close to him who do not wish for us to exist at all. Voices who whisper that we cannot be trusted that the money could be better spent elsewhere. And these voices are especially persuasive now that the West has broken away and our homeland and families serve another emperor. Gallienus worries about this. So, this motto - I know it flatters Gallienus," Corbulo added looking grave, "but for us to survive we must make a name for ourselves. We must prove our worth to the emperor."

"Did we not already prove ourselves," Crastus growled, his smile fading away, "when we risked all to desert the cause of usurpers in the East. I mean for fucks sake; we broke away to join Gallienus. If that bastard Balista had caught up with us our heads would be rotting on spikes by now."

"It is not enough," Corbulo said shaking his head. "Like I said we have enemies at court and few friends. No one knows who we are right now. We have powerful enemies who dislike our existence and who would like to see us undone. Who would like to see us disbanded - and I cannot allow that to happen. I am a soldier. The army is my life. Soldiering is what I do. So, if the equites foederati Germanica are to survive gentlemen, and I intend for us to survive, then we must make a name for ourselves on the battlefield. Something no imperial bureaucrat can just erase with his stylus. And it all starts with the choosing of a new motto for that is how the world is going to get to know us. That is what will end up being written on our tomb stones. This motto is about who we are!"

For a moment the Roman officers remained silent, mulling on what had been said.

"Then shorten it to just *Gallienus's Finest*," Harald exclaimed.

"Fuck that," Crastus growled shooting Harald a contemptuous look. "How about *Loyal and Faithful* instead."

As the tent fell silent all eyes turned to Corbulo as the officers waited for his reaction and for a while he kept them waiting.

"*The Emperor's Finest, First into Battle,"* Corbulo said at last turning to look at his officers as he made up his mind. "There! That should stand the test of time. That will be our motto, gentlemen."

"It's going to piss off the other cavalry regiments," Harald said raising his eyebrows. "There will be many who will wish to dispute the fact that we are claiming to be the emperors finest. For what I am hearing Sir is that Gallienus's cavalry army is to be no ordinary army. The emperor is bringing the elite of the Roman army together under one command. We are going to be fighting alongside some very prestigious and accomplished regiments. All of whom who are senior to us, all of whom who are much older and more established than us."

"Good," Corbulo responded. "The intention is to piss them off. To get their attention. No doubt we shall be looked down upon as being just another border defence detachment from the lower Rhine, but it is my intention to make a name for ourselves as the finest fighting force in the world. So, screw our enemies, screw the imperial bureaucrats and screw anyone who stands in our way. Are you with me, gentlemen! Are you with me on this journey!"

"Sir. Sir," Crastus and Harald said hurriedly as the officers inside the tent started to stamp their boots on the ground in approval.

"And what about me," a fed-up sounding voice suddenly called out as the stamping died away. "You have not told me what I am supposed to be doing? With respect Sir but I have been bored out of my fucking mind ever since we got here. You know me. There are two things that I can't stand and one of them is being bored. Not employing me is a waste of precious military resources. So, I do hope that you have got something interesting for me to do Sir."

Turning to Atlas, Corbulo hesitated as he carefully sized up the young officer who was in his mid-twenties. The soldier was still wearing his keffiyeh scarf around his neck as if he had just emerged from the Syrian desert. Atlas was the sole speculatore, intelligence officer, attached to the old vexillation from the Thirtieth. Like himself, Crastus and Harald, Atlas had been there from the start - when the original contingent of soldiers had set out for the East from their base camp on the lower Rhine some years before. An oddball. A loner. The offspring of a German barbarian and a Greek woman, Atlas had a talent for learning languages. He'd also proved to be a bit of a weirdo. Difficult to handle. Insubordinate and often rude. Disappearing off on his own for weeks on end without any explanation or contact. Popping up only when he needed something or had something important to report. For most of the time Corbulo had no idea what Atlas was up to. His work was carried out in the shadows. But that he was a first-class intelligence officer was not in doubt. He'd tolerated the man's behaviour because Atlas got results.

"It's actually quite nice seeing you looking so frustrated and bored, Atlas," Corbulo replied his comment eliciting grim satisfied looks from the faces of the other officers gathered inside the tent. Each one of whom had had their own history of personal run-ins with Atlas and who had been the victim of his practical jokes. "But as it happens, I do have a task for you. Something that I think you will enjoy," Corbulo continued. "It is not right that you should remain our sole speculatore. If we were to lose you, we would have no replacement. So, I want you to select someone from the ranks you think is suitable and I want you to start training them in the art of intelligence gathering. I want you to teach them what you do and what you know," Corbulo said patiently, "so that we will end up having two of you. Two intelligence officers are better than one and the work you do is important. So, select your apprentice and start work."

For a moment Atlas did not reply as he stared back at Corbulo, appearing to be thinking it over. Then he screwed up his face as if he were in pain. "I will think about it and let you know Sir," he said moodily before slouching out of the tent without saying another word.

***

It was afternoon and Corbulo was standing inside his command post with Harald discussing the new cavalry training regime plan when the watch commander came hurrying up to him.

"Sir," the officer said hurriedly, glancing towards the tent entrance, "there is a man waiting outside who claims to have been assigned to your staff Sir. He's a civilian. He gave me this as his form of identification," the officer continued handing Corbulo a tightly rolled scroll.

Accepting the scroll Corbulo frowned as he spotted the wax seal of the fiscus, the imperial state treasury. For a moment Corbulo stared at the seal before, looking baffled, he turned his head in the direction of the tent entrance. But his view of the man waiting outside was obstructed by the canvas.

"The fiscus!" Corbulo muttered as he broke the seal and unrolled the parchment letter. "What do they want?"

Quickly reading through the correspondence Corbulo's frown deepened. Then abruptly he handed the letter to Harald and without speaking he turned and strode towards the tent entrance, accompanied by the watch commander. Emerging from his command post Corbulo stopped as he caught sight of a figure standing waiting outside. The man was in his forties. Sporting a narrow, neatly clipped curly beard that ran from ear to ear under his chin as if he were imitating emperor Gallienus's style. A brown leather satchel was slung across his shoulder. His demeanour was calm and patient like a man who knew what he was about. His appearance screaming precision and efficiency. His smart Greek style tunic and cloak showing off that he was indeed a civilian.

"Prefect!" the man called out swiftly raising a hand before Corbulo had a chance to speak, "let me introduce myself. My name is Tobias, second secretary to the department of military administration within the imperial fiscus. I have been assigned to your staff. Everything that you need to know is contained within my letter of appointment that I just handed to your soldier. Now I would be happy to answer any of your questions but maybe afterwards you would be so kind as to show me to where I shall be billeted. My slave needs to know where he should take all my belongings to you see."

Still frowning Corbulo stared at the bureaucrat.

"I was not informed that you would be joining us," Corbulo replied curtly. "A civilian! This is unusual and a bit of a surprise. When I met with the emperor's staff just yesterday, they did not mention you. Why are you here?"

"Ah then you didn't read my letter properly," Tobias exclaimed gently looking away and standing his ground with an air of calm, confident authority. "The emperor and the imperial bureaucracy do not need to explain everything to you prefect," the man continued. "Suffice to say that my role on your staff will be to ensure that all public funds that are transferred to your command are properly accounted for. I am an accountant by profession, and I assure you I am very good at what I do. I am the guardian of the rules, our fiscal rules that is. My job will be to record all your unit's expenses and income. To audit your finances. To uncover any corruption and misappropriation and report it to the fiscus. Money is what allows us to wage war prefect. Not soldiers. The public have a right to know and demand that their taxes, which after all pay for your troops, are properly accounted for. Would you not agree?"

"I see," Corbulo replied stony-faced. "You are an accountant. So, I am to allow a civilian onto my staff. Your letter states that you are to report not to me but directly to general Aureolus and the fiscus. So, I have no authority over you?"

"Correct," the accountant said smiling. "Your instructions prefect are to allow me to attend all your war councils and to provide me with unlimited access to your accounts and answer any questions that I may have. Full access! I and I alone am the guardian of the fiscal rules as set by the imperial fiscus and the emperor. I am to physically supervise your unit's gold and silver reserves and any potential new income from the battlefield. The fiscus - prefect - is determined to ensure that scarce public funds are spent in the most optimal and efficient manner. For this is how we shall eventually win the war."

"I see," Corbulo repeated. For a moment he hesitated. Then he turned to look away, his mind working. "Very well then, so be it," Corbulo continued sounding resigned. "Welcome to the equites foederati Germanica. You will find us an honest unit. My officers and men are of German stock from the lower Rhine. So, we are used to speaking in German at our war councils. Do you speak German?"

"No, prefect, I do not," Tobias replied.

"We shall accommodate you then in Latin," Corbulo said turning to the accountant. "And one more thing. A man of your accomplished and educated position will need an assistant to show him what is what. So, I am assigning one of my men to you. He will show you how things work within the camp. His name is Badurad. He will act as a liaison between you and me."

"I do not need an assistant, prefect," Tobias scoffed. "I am perfectly capable of getting around by myself."

"Maybe. But your letter makes no specific mention of this," Corbulo said sharply, "so I am assigned you an assistant. I am the commander of this unit. That is my right, and you will agree not to interfere in any military decisions that I make. You shall confine yourself strictly to your specific fiscal tasks. If that is clear, then you and I shall get on splendidly."

"On that I can agree," Tobias replied, dipping his head in acknowledgement.

"Good," Corbulo said curtly. "Wait here."

Then he turned to his watch commander. "Go find Badurad and tell him to report here at once," he said swiftly switching to German. "Inform my cousin that he is to assist this arrogant prick."

And with that Corbulo re-entered his command post leaving a suddenly lost looking Tobias waiting outside. Quickly coming up to commanding officer Harald however was suddenly looking troubled. The officer handing Tobias's letter of introduction back to him.

"You heard that conversation?" Corbulo said angrily, flicking his head in the direction of the tent entrance.

"I did," Harald murmured in disapproval. "A civilian attending our war councils. Well. Well. When does that ever happen? That stuff about auditing our finances is just a cover to justify his presence here I reckon. You mentioned earlier Sir that we have enemies at court. Could they have sent him here? The man must be a spy. Sent here to spy on us. If you ask me Sir, either our enemies or the emperor has dispatched this man to keep an eye on us. To check up on us. To gage our loyalty and to report back if he discovers a plot to rebel. That must be it and if I am right and this has been done on the emperor's orders that means Gallienus does not fully trust us."

"Maybe," Corbulo replied lowering his gaze with a thoughtful look. "I don't know. But if it is Gallienus who has sent him then we cannot blame the emperor for that. So many army commanders have already rebelled. Gallienus must be feeling a little paranoid."

"Well, we did not rebel," Harald grumbled. "We did not mutiny. We risked everything to get away from Macrianus and Balista and to rejoin Gallienus. I hate to admit it, but Crastus was right when he spoke about that earlier. Do you want me to arrange a little accident for our new accountant friend? A military camp full of rough soldiers can be a dangerous place after all."

"No, no," Corbulo replied quickly shaking his head and reaching out to place a hand on Harald's shoulder. "Nothing like that. I am assigning Badurad to be his liaison officer. If Tobias is here to spy on us, then I shall get Badurad to spy on him in turn. Two can play this game. I will handle Tobias."

“You are placing a lot of trust in young Badurad,” Harald said with a frown.

“He’s my cousin,” Corbulo replied in a sudden weary voice. “He needs a task to keep him focussed, busy and out of trouble.”

Chapter Five - The New Officer

With his principal officers and bodyguards gathered around him Corbulo stood just outside his command post watching the column of soldiers from the 2nd Batavian auxiliary cohort coming in through the gates of his camp. Clad in his tight coat of mail body armour and wearing a plumed helmet upon his head, a short red cloak covering his shoulders, he cut a dapper, handsome figure. While his standard bearer, a splendid wolf's head draped over his helmet, was standing beside him proudly holding up the new war banner of the equites foederati Germanica. It's traditional metallic discs and crescent moons and animal symbols gleaming in the clear sunlight. While the image of the Batavian warrior god Hercules Magusanus was depicted below them together with the unit's new motto inscribed on a bronze placard together with four battle honours, Rhine frontier, Samosata, the Cilician Gates and Tarsus neatly displayed beneath.

It was morning and thronging both sides of the large sandy parade ground, forming a narrow corridor, the men from the equites foederati Germanica, fully clad for war, were keenly watching the arrival of their new comrades. The whole unit having turned out to witness the event. The soldier's dark shields adorned with a white wolf's head emblem. No one speaking as the promised reinforcements came marching into the camp carrying their weapons, shields and marching packs. The newcomer's helmets adorned with two simple feathers. The atmosphere full of expectation and excitement. The crunch of hundreds of hobnailed boots ringing out. The creak and rattle of horse-drawn wagons and the braying of mules loaded down with baggage and equipment filling the parade ground.

Shifting his gaze Corbulo glanced at Tobias who was watching the new arrivals. The impeccably turned-out accountant conspicuous in his civilian attire among the mass of burly body-armour clad soldiers. Then Corbulo's eyes shifted to Badurad who was standing at Tobias's side looking awkward and ill at ease as if the youth really did not want to be there. For a moment Corbulo eyed the pair. Badurad had kept his word and after their quarrel he had taken to sleeping at the barracks. His cousin resolutely avoiding him whenever he could. Sulking. Refusing to talk. The quarrel between them very much still ongoing.

"Their numbers appear to be correct Sir. I count just over two hundred men. Just like what we were promised," Crastus said as Corbulo turned his attention back to the marching column who were heading straight towards him. "But I don't see any cavalry among them. Were the 2nd Batavians not supposed to be a mixed unit Sir?"

"Yes, they were," Corbulo replied. "They must have lost or surrendered the last of their horses. No matter. We will get them new mounts."

Saying nothing more Corbulo's eyes had come to rest upon a tall lanky man in his thirties who was leading the party of reinforcements from the 2nd. The officer was at least a head taller than all his companions and resting across his shoulders he was carrying a massive, spiked club. The man's long legs taking huge strides as he approached. His long blond hair tied up in a traditional Swabian knot to the side of his head. While his cheeks and chin were unshaven.

"Gods look at the state of them," Crastus exclaimed his earlier enthusiasm seeping away as he eyed the officers and men from the 2nd Batavians. "Look! They are carrying unauthorised weapons and clothing too. And have they forgotten to bath and shave. They look filthy. I can smell them from here Sir and where the fuck is their war banner? Surely, they have not lost it!"

"Well, I remember Crastus that I could smell you and your men too after the retreat from Samosata," Corbulo replied.

"Don't be so hard on them Crastus," Atlas interrupted as he stood directly behind Corbulo, his eyes fixed upon the newcomers. "These men have been up on the frontier. They have had a hard time. Show some respect. They are our brothers from the lower Rhine after all."

"My brothers, not yours, you stink like a Greek," Crastus retorted.

"I am as German as you are," Atlas sniffed refusing to be silenced. "Your problem Crastus is that you do not respect anything."

"There is always chaos on the frontier," Crastus growled without turning around to look at his colleague. "And of course I know they are our blood brothers but if they have lost their war banner that would be disgraceful. Remember Atlas, I must get them ready to fight again. Not all of us can live the idle life like you do! Some of us must do proper work."

"I do not spend my time in idle boredom," Atlas countered.

"Have you selected your apprentice yet?" Corbulo said quickly refusing to take his eyes from the approaching column. "Your colleague in intelligence work. How is that going?"

"No. Not yet, I am still thinking about it," Atlas replied sourly.

"Where is Oskar, the prefect of the 2nd, their commander?" Harald suddenly blurted out, frowning in confusion. "He should be leading his men, but I cannot see him anywhere. Where the fuck is he?"

Watching the newcomers marching towards him Corbulo did not reply as the tall officer with the Swabian knot and carrying the spiked club finally brought the column of soldiers to a halt directly in front of the unit's battle-standards, his deep booming voice ringing out across the parade ground. The men behind him coming to an abrupt crashing halt. The sound of the officer's voice immediately followed by a few seconds of utter silence. As if the parade ground was holding its breath. The men keen to get a glimpse of what was going to happen next. Then the tall officer turned towards Corbulo and rapped out a smart salute before with an extravagant and gallant gesture he bowed his head and respectfully got down on one knee.

"Prefect," the officer cried out in German, speaking with a thick Frankish accent, his eyes lowered to the ground. "I am prince Gummar of the eastern Franks. Second son of Jonar and brother to king Adalheim. Outcast. Faithful ally of Rome and emperor Gallienus. I and my men from the 2nd Batavian cohort are at your service Sir!"

"Rise prince Gummar," Corbulo said in German beckoning for him to get back to his feet, conscious of hundreds of eyes resting upon him. "There is no need to kneel before me. This is the Roman army. Not some foreign court. A salute will do. On behalf of my officers and men I welcome you and your soldiers as brothers to the equites foederati Germanica. The only all German speaking ala within the new imperial cavalry army."

"Thank you, Sir," the tall man cried out quickly rising back to his feet with a broad pleased smile that revealed a couple of missing teeth. "It is good to once again hear the accents of the lower Rhine. To meet men from our homeland. It has been a long time since we were there."

"The same for us," Corbulo replied. "But forgive me I was expecting to see your prefect Oskar here. He is your commanding officer is he not. I hear that he served with Hostes before."

"Ah yes Sir," prince Gummar replied the grin fading from his face. "Unfortunately, Oskar is dead. Our prefect was slain along the Danube. I as the senior surviving officer assumed command of the cohort after he was killed. We had a hard time up on the frontier," Gummar continued his voice tightening as he quickly turned to survey his troops arranged behind him. "At one point we were surrounded by the enemy in our camp, but we managed to fight our way out. We got away. But it came at a cost. I lost half my command in the fighting against the barbarians along the river."

"Is that how you came to lose your cohort's battle-standard too?" Crastus called out with a contemptuous look. "I don't see your banner. Or perhaps you sold it along the way."

Coolly Gummar turned to stare at the big centurion. "Yes, it is true we lost our banner to the enemy," Gummar replied. "They overwhelmed us. You should know that Oskar our prefect tried to take the standard back and that is how he got himself killed. Oskar died like a warrior ought to. He was a brave man. He will no doubt be sitting in the feast halls of the gods and laughing at us right now."

"But the banner remains lost and that's a disgrace in my eyes," Crastus retorted refusing to let it go. "The very first thing you do is bring disgrace into our camp. In the old days your whole cohort would be disbanded for that. You do not lose your battle-standard, ever!"

“Enough Crastus,” Corbulo interrupted silencing his subordinate with a look. Then to prince Gummar.

“The loss of your battle-standard is unfortunate, but we shall give you a chance to redeem what was lost. You shall have a new banner, that of the equites foederati Germanica,” Corbulo called out gesturing at the new battle standard proudly displayed nearly. “Now I am aware of the long and illustrious history of the 2nd Batavian auxiliary cohort in the service of Rome,” he continued. “But as of today, the 2nd Batavian auxiliary cohort will officially cease to exist, and your men will become part of our new unit. And to honour your officers and soldiers we shall add your battle honours to our own and we shall all wear the feathers of the Batavians in our helmets. So, the memory of what the 2nd Batavians did shall continue in a new form, for a new day, carried by men who are now your friends.”

“That is most kind and honourable of you Sir,” prince Gummar exclaimed once again inclining his head to Corbulo in a respectful manner. “My men and I are pleased by this.”

“You should know too,” Corbulo went on, enjoying himself now as an amused gleam appeared in his eye, “that I too have a personal connection to the 2nd Batavians. For it is the same unit that one of my ancestors once served in long ago. His name was Marcus, and he was with the 2nd when it took part in the battle of Mons Graupius in Caledonia over one hundred and eighty years ago. So, you could say that your arrival here with the remnants of the 2nd to serve under my command is fate. That mighty Magusanus himself wishes it to be so.”

“Then I know that I and my men shall be in good hands Sir and that we are going to fight in illustrious company,” prince Gummar said grinning. “For Magusanus is always right.”

"Illustrious," Corbulo heard Harald mutter as the veteran officer raised his eyebrows.

"You said that you are an outcast?" Corbulo inquired.

"Yes, so I am Sir," Gummar replied stirring. "Outcast! Forbidden from ever setting foot in my homeland again on pain of death. I am the younger brother of Adalheim, a king of the Franks who live east of the Rhine in the lands beyond Roman control. My brother is a cruel man and my father was weak," Gummar added breezily. "Now my father is dead and my brother rules. My brother banished me. But that was a long time ago."

"So, you are king Adalheim's brother," Corbulo said raising his eyebrows. "Tell me prince Gummar, why were you banished? How come you ended up fighting for Rome and not for your brother?"

"Simple," Gummar exclaimed. "My elder brother saw me as a rival, a threat to his position and tried to kill me. So, I crossed the Rhine and offered my services to the Roman governor and swore an oath to Rome instead."

"I see," Corbulo responded, "and tell me, if your brother the king would ever offer you an amnesty, what would you do? If you could return home?"

"You are testing me now Sir," prince Gummar said smiling. "But you are not the first. You want to know what I would do if my brother was standing right before me. Well, I would put a knife in his neck. The bastard tried to murder me. That is not something a man easily forgets."

"And your men," Corbulo continued gesturing at the troops of the 2nd, "they are Batavians and Salian Franks. Like us they have family in the West along the lower Rhine. So why do they not leave to fight for the usurper Postumus? He is after all one of us. He is a Batavian."

"The 2nd Batavian cohort remains loyal Sir," Gummar replied with a shrug. "We made a contract with Gallienus and the emperor keeps his promise to pay us. But may I add that as the cohort's history appears to be coming to an end today, I would like to let it be known that they were loyal to the very end. None have left the 2nd without permission. My men are still here and are willing to serve emperor Gallienus because I will not let them serve the usurper Postumus. I won't them return home and that is how it is going to remain. The 2nd will follow me Sir. They trust me. They know me and now we shall fight together under your command."

Eyeing Gummar Corbulo remained silent. "Good," Corbulo called out at last. "Good. Now dismiss the men for the final time prince Gummar and tonight you and I shall toast the achievements of the 2nd. Harald," Corbulo continued quickly. "See to it that the new men are assigned to their company and unit sleeping quarters and get the kitchen to serve them some hot food. The men are to have the rest of the day off so that they can recover from their journey. But tomorrow at dawn we shall have our first joint parade. The first where the whole ala will be together. I shall be addressing the whole ala."

"Very good Sir," Harald replied clicking his heels together.

"Prince Gummar," Corbulo said as he turned back to the officer who towered over him. "You will follow me for a full debrief. Now if you please."

Entering his command post followed by his senior officer's bar Harald Corbulo strode up to his desk before turning to look back at his men. The officers gathering around him watching him closely as they waited for him to speak. Crastus still looking contemptuous. Atlas looking thoughtful. Tobias looking lost having not understood a word of the conversation outside. Badurad standing dutifully to one side like a statue as if he really did not want to be here. And then finally there was Gummar. The tall man's head nearly touching the top of the tent canvas. The Frankish prince appearing intrigued by something.

"I know that these are difficult times for all of us," Corbulo began, looking grave as he eyed Gummar before shifting his attention to the others. "All of us here are anxious about our families in the West. But we are soldiers, we swore an oath of allegiance. We made a contract with Gallienus and the emperor has kept his promise so we shall keep ours. So, we cannot go home. Not now that Postumus has seized power. Not until the usurper in the West has been defeated. Nor can we break an oath that was freely and solemnly given. So, I heard what you said outside just now prince Gummar, but will the changed political situation be a problem for you and your men? I need to know now if it will be."

"Well, it is hardly good news is it Sir," Gummar replied before booming with laughter that caused some of the Romans to glance at each other. "No Sir," the tall man added shaking his head. "The 2nd are loyal. They will do what I tell them to do as long as Gallienus continues to pay them. They are loyal to Gallienus and to me. I have given the emperor my personal assurance. You are right. We are soldiers and we swore an oath. We made a contract. We cannot break it now. That would be a terrible thing to do."

"A greater disgrace than losing your battle-standard?" Crastus interrupted giving Gummar a scornful look.

"Wait. You were granted an audience with emperor Gallienus!" Corbulo exclaimed looking startled. "You spoke to the emperor directly?"

"Yes," Gummar replied ignoring Crastus as he eyed Corbulo, his grin slowly fading. "I am a prince of the Franks. I may be an outcast, but I am still of royal blood. My rank allows me access to the emperor. He and I happen to be friends of long standing. The emperor is good like that. He knows how to motivate men. Gallienus hopes that one day I will return home, overthrow my brother and turn the eastern Franks into allies of Rome. That too is my ambition. But to succeed I need to become more famous than I am now. I need to accrue fame and a reputation as a great warrior for only with such a worthy name will I make my countrymen follow me and crown me as their king. And now that we are on this subject," Gummar continued, his eyes gleaming. "I am going to be your new deputy Sir. I am to be the second in command of the equites foederati Germanica. That's what the emperor promised me."

"What?!" Corbulo exclaimed as the other Roman officers turned to stare at Gummar in shock that swiftly turned to outrage.

"That's right," Gummar replied looking unperturbed. "I am to be your new deputy and second in command Sir."

"This in an outrage!" Crastus burst out unable to contain himself, blushing fiercely as he rounded on the tall man. "I have been with this unit from the very start. From when we first set out for the East from Colonia on the Rhine years ago. If anyone is to be promoted to deputy commander, then it should be me or at a stretch Harald. But certainly not a newcomer like you! A man who managed to lose his battle-standard. Who the fuck do you think you are?"

"Well, it is not your decision to make," Gummar said with a shrug, glancing across at Crastus. "The decision has been made by the emperor. I am to be the new deputy commander of the equites foederati Germanica. So that is that. The decision has already been made. And if you do not believe me Sir," Gummar added turning to Corbulo, "then please go to the imperial palace. They shall confirm my appointment. It's true."

"What is this?" Crastus hissed rounding on Gummar. "You think you can just show up here and be appointed deputy commander? Is this a joke? Until a few minutes ago no one had ever seen or heard of you before!"

"I understand your disappointment centurion," Gummar replied, his calm voice appearing to infuriate Crastus even more, "but I cannot help you. The matter has already been decided at the highest level. And as your superior officer you will address me as Sir from now on."

"You arrogant swine!" Crastus burst out, looking enraged.

"Swearing is not going to help you little man," Gummar retorted turning to square up to Crastus and as he did Corbulo was suddenly conscious of something about Gummar that had remained hidden until now. The Frankish prince appeared swift to bear a grudge. The man was easily provoked. "You really don't want to make an enemy out of me," Gummar continued his eyes narrowing. "I enjoy the emperor's favour. And one day with his help I am going to return home and overthrow that murderous brother of mine and become a king of the eastern Franks. So just remember who you are talking to."

"You are threatening me now?" Crastus hissed responding by taking a menacing step towards Gummar.

"Goddamn right I am," Gummar replied standing his ground. "I am your superior officer, and you will address me as Sir from now on."

"Enough Crastus," Corbulo called out silencing the big officer as Crastus was about to speak again. Then turning to Gummar Corbulo frowned. "This is highly irregular," he said. "I am the commanding officer of this ala, and I would expect to be able to appoint my own officers. I don't need a deputy. Why did the emperor appoint you without informing or consulting me?"

"I don't know why Gallienus did not inform you Sir," Gummar responded coolly, "but like I said he and I are friends."

"This is a fucking outrage!" Crastus growled, his fists clenched. His anger palpable. "This will not stand. It cannot stand."

"Well, I too have spoken with the emperor," Corbulo said looking thoroughly annoyed. "And Gallienus's instructions were quite clear. I am to turn the equites foederati Germanica into an effective and cohesive fighting force and that is what I intend to do. So, if you prince Gummar are going to start trouble within the ranks or between my officers then you will answer to me. I will not tolerate dissent among the ranks and emperor's friend or not you still serve under military discipline. Have I made myself clear."

"You have Sir," prince Gummar said.

Still looking thoroughly annoyed Corbulo paused as the tent around him fell silent, the tension rife as everyone waited for his decision. Gummar was going to be trouble Corbulo thought. There was no way Crastus or Harald were going to let this go but what choice did he have. If the man was indeed the emperor's friend, he was essentially un-sackable.

"Fine," Corbulo said at last glaring at the faces around the tent. "I shall send a man to the imperial palace to confirm your account Gummar. You shall be acting deputy and second in command on a temporary basis until I am satisfied that you are speaking the truth. That will be all!" Corbulo cried out swiftly raising his voice as the officers around him broke into furious protest. Their discontent clear. Their anger overflowing.

"Silence!" Corbulo bellowed. "Tomorrow at dawn I shall address the whole ala on the parade ground. You have your orders. See that they are carried out!"

Chapter Six - The Song of the Ancestors

Alone, sitting at his desk inside his command post, an oil lamp placed on the wooden surface beside him providing the solitary light, Corbulo was finishing the speech he was going to deliver later that day. His fingers moving swiftly as he scratched away at the soft wood. At last, laying down his stylus, pen he leaned back in his chair staring at the neatly scribbled speech, silently rehearsing the address he was to make to his soldiers.

It was still dark outside, and the dawn was still a couple of hours away. The camp around him was quiet. While immediately outside his tent he could hear the quiet murmur of his bodyguards talking to each. At last, closing the wooden tablet Corbulo reached up and rubbed his chin before looking down at Gamo's ring attached to his finger. The gold gleaming evilly back at him in the reddish glow of the oil lamp. For a moment Corbulo did not move as he stared at the band. Then softly he began to sing to himself. The old song he'd known since he had been a boy. The words coming swiftly and with ease.

"Flavius the carpenter was the first. A foundling with a mark. An enemy of Hannibal. A friend of Rome. He gave us our first home."

"His youngest son Julian went off to fight in Spain. To be a brave soldier. To become a friend of the great Scipio. And at Zama he achieved his aim and did accept the surrender of the Carthaginian and hence gave us our name."

For a while Corbulo's quiet voice filled the tent with his soft and tender melody.

"Corbulo was next. A veteran of the legions. First to come to Britannia. First to gain possession of our fair farm on Vectis. A hard man with many loves and a fondness for drink. A man with a taste for violence, to force all to bend, a character who drove his poor wife to her unhappy end. But who redeemed himself by his death and who gave us new breath."

"His son Marcus learned the ways of the Batavi. He went to Hyperborea and came back. Then to Rome where he became a senator. The only one of us who ever made it that high, he gave us the sky."

"Fergus son of Marcus followed. He became a soldier in the Twentieth rising from the bottom to the very top. He saw fair Mesopotamia and Germania and made our family wealthy with Dacian gold. He gave us five beautiful daughters one of whom grew to be very old."

"Briana eldest daughter of Fergus our guiding star was blessed with wisdom and a mind for business. She outlived all until she was ninety-five and protected our farm from ruin. She kept alive the memory of all those gone before. She was able to mend, and it is from her that you and I my dear boy descend."

Finishing his song Corbulo suddenly felt better and more upbeat as if the memory of his ancestors had given him new energy and purpose. His tiredness fading away. It had been his mother Tadia who had taught the song to him - as a way in which he would be able to remember and keep alive the deeds of his illustrious ancestors. But now the song needed another stanza he thought. Someone was going to have to write the next chapter, and it could not be him for the next stanza was going to be about him. But who then Corbulo thought. He had no wife, no children. Who would write the next chapter of his family's saga?

“Sir,” a voice called out softly but insistent from the entrance to his tent, the suddenness catching Corbulo off-guard. “Sorry to disturb you Sir, but its urgent.”

Rising from his chair Corbulo hurried across to the tent entrance as one of his watch commanders came up to him. The officer looking grave.

“Well, what is it?”

“I came right away Sir,” the watch commander said in an apologetic voice as he quickly rapped out a salute. “I must report some unpleasant news. I was on my rounds earlier. Checking up on the sentries around the camp Sir,” the officer continued hurriedly clearing his throat. “To see if none of the men were asleep on duty. And when I reached the sentry on guard at the stables, I found him bound and gagged Sir. The soldier claimed he was attacked just a few hours ago. His attackers overpowered him.”

“Attacked!” Corbulo blurted out, frowning. “By whom?”

“Our own men Sir,” the watch commander replied uneasily. “The sentry says he saw nine men before they blindfolded him. Soldiers. Our men Sir. And now nine horses are missing from the stables Sir.

“You certain of this!”

“Yes Sir. I checked the barracks before I came here. I am afraid that I must report that we have nine deserters Sir. Nine of our men are missing.”

“Deserters!” Corbulo growled, his expression abruptly darkening. “Fuck! How did they get out of the camp. Were the gates not closed and guarded? Did no one else report seeing these men?"

"The main entrance gates were indeed closed and guarded Sir," the watch commander replied shifting uneasily on his feet, "but no one on guard duty last night remembers seeing anything unusual. The camp was quiet but there is a narrow gap in the camp's perimeter that was damaged in a storm some time back and which has not yet been repaired. It is large enough for a man and a horse to slip through if they move in single file. They probably got out that way. I have already posted a guard to the spot to prevent future unauthorised leave."

"Oh great," Corbulo said looking away in dismay. "That's just fucking great! Just before I am to address the whole ala, we get nine deserters. That sets a great example that does. Any ideas as to where these men could have gone? Have you alerted the city watch? Have you interrogated their friends? I want those deserters found!"

"Not yet Sir," the watch commander replied blushing. "I am still getting round to that. But there is something else," the man continued, lowering his gaze, his unease making Corbulo frown. "It is why I came to your first. One of the deserters Sir. He is your cousin Badurad. He and that friend of his Linus, they are missing and cannot be found anywhere. I checked twice and, I am sure. Both men appear to have left the camp without permission. So, as Badurad is your cousin I thought you should be informed before I alert the city watch Sir. These deserters may have a few hours head start on us, and they have horses but if the watch catch them now, they will be all hanged for desertion."

“Badurad is one of the deserters!” Corbulo exclaimed his eyes widening in shock. Then abruptly he turned to look away, his face ashen.

“Thank you,” Corbulo said at last turning to his subordinate, regaining his composure. “You did well to come to me first. Now alert the city watch to what has happened and start to interrogate the friends of these missing men. I want to know why these soldiers deserted and I want them caught. And when you do, they shall be punished according to the regulations. No exceptions! Report back to me with your findings as soon as possible.”

Chapter Seven - The Omens Are Not Good

The tension inside the tent could be cut with a knife. The seriousness of the situation reflected upon the faces of the men. It was just after dawn and the small group of Roman officers were silent and waiting like a volcano that was about to blow. Their bodies taut with straining, explosive tension. The atmosphere inside the command post crackling with pent up frustrations and the whiff of violence. Corbulo's bodyguards were standing rigidly to attention beside the tent entrance like armed statues, barely daring to breath. While Crastus faced off against prince Gummar. The big fighter's arms pressed tightly against his body. His hands clenched into fists. His officers backing him up. The tall Frankish prince and deputy commander gazing back at Crastus with calm, confident contempt. The intense dislike and rivalry between the two officers palpable. While Atlas simply looked frustrated and Tobias the accountant, the only civilian present, was carefully toying with a ring on his finger. The watch commander who had first reported the desertions was standing to one side, silent, embarrassed, his gaze fixed upon the ground. Only Harald was missing from the emergency council.

Standing by the entrance to his command post Corbulo took a deep unhappy breath as he gazed out across the large sandy parade ground where the nine hundred and sixty officers and men of his command were standing rigidly to attention waiting patiently for him to address them. The Roman troops formed up in their cohort, company and squadron formations. Their officers positioned in front and directly behind the ranks. The soldiers war banners proudly held aloft. The Draco banners of the 1st and 2nd cohorts snaking in the gentle breeze from wooden poles. The soldier's shields were emblazoned with white wolf's heads painted onto the wood. While two Batavian feathers poked up from each side of their helmets. The equites looking quite magnificent in their full kit. The parade ground silent and expectant.

Looking displeased Corbulo at last turned back to the waiting officers inside the tent. As if his problems could get any worse, Harald had that morning been taken ill and confined to the military hospital. The army doctor moving him into the isolation tent and forbidding any visitors. The doctor fearing that Harald had caught the plague and had just days to live.

“We have a serious problem. Nine of our men deserted last night,” Corbulo said. “Nine of our men broke their military oath and their contract. I am told they overpowered the night watchman at the stables and stole nine horses. I have instructed the city watch to start looking for them. But it is unlikely that they will be found. They will probably have been planning this for some time and by now they will be far away. So, we will let the city watch handle the search. For we have a bigger problem, gentlemen. If nine of our men are willing to risk deserting knowing the punishment that would follow if they were caught, then how many more are willing to do so?”

“I agree. This is a most a serious and unpleasant development,” Tobias said in Latin before anyone else could reply - the accountant turning to subject Corbulo to an angry, reproachful look. “If this is how you run your ala, prefect then I am not hopeful about the future. Not only have we lost nine men and nine valuable horses, saddles and other military equipment but I understand that provisions were also stolen from the storeroom. And on top of that I need to report that the young man, the liaison officer you assigned to me, is one of the missing men and that before he left this same young man stole my own private purse and the silver coins that were inside. It's not a very auspicious start to the equites foederati Germanica is it,” Tobias snapped. “You Batavians were supposed to have a reputation for honesty and loyalty, but it seems that I am instead surrounded by thieves and oath breakers. You know," Tobias went on pointing an accusing finger at Corbulo, "that I will have to report this all to the fiscus and to general Aureolus. The financial and reputational loss is considerable. This cannot just be swept under the table."

"Our liaison officer stole your private purse," Atlas said with a mocking smile as he turned to Tobias. "That's such a shame."

"Regards the nine deserters Sir," Crastus said sharply, turning to Corbulo, "did they by any chance include any men from the 2nd Batavians who arrived with prince fuck-face here? Because I remember him very clearly bragging that the men of the 2nd would not desert because he would not let them leave."

"What did you just call me?" Gummar cried out losing his cool and taking a threatening step towards Crastus. "This is your last warning. You will address me as Sir, or you will be flogged in front of the men for disobedience. I am your superior officer! You will do as you are told."

"Two of the deserters belonged to the 2nd Batavians Sir," the watch commander said hurriedly turning to address Corbulo. "Five others were members of the old 1st infantry Cohort of the Thirtieth. The final two were assigned to the old 3rd company of Salian Franks."

"Ha!" Crastus hissed. "Thought so. He lied!"

"One more word from you..." Gummar retorted raising a threatening finger.

"Enough both of you!" Corbulo said turning to Crastus and then to Gummar with a stern warning look. "So, some of the deserters were from your old unit and some were from yours and some belonged to the company that I used to command. So, both of you have lost men. But I am in command. I am responsible for everything that goes on in this ala. So, if blame is to be assigned for this fuck up then it lies with me and me alone. Got that. Continue with your report," Corbulo added quickly turning to his watch commander.

"Sir," the watch commander said hurriedly. "Well, I have completed interrogating the friends of the deserters. No one seems to know anything. They all claim to be surprised by what happened. No one saw it coming and no one knows why they would do such a thing or where they would have gone. That none want to say anything is to be expected Sir," the watch commander added. "None of these men want to get into trouble but I suspect that some of the men know more about these desertions than they are willing to share. So, if you want the friends of these deserters to talk then I will need to flog them."

"No, that won't be necessary," Corbulo said shaking his head. "That will just make matters worse."

Abruptly Crastus lunged. His head lowered like a bull as he charged at Gummar, the big man catching the tall Frankish prince in a low tackle that sent both officers crashing and tumbling backwards onto the ground. The Roman command post erupting in yells of outrage. On the floor the two senior officers were frantically kicking and punching at each other in a frenzy of blows, the two men giving it their all as they rolled over the ground, snarling and screaming obscenities. The sudden brawl catching everyone off-guard.

Rushing into the fight Corbulo had managed to get hold of Gummar's arm as he tried to break up the brawl but just as he did so, Crastus's fist, aiming a blow at Gummar, struck him in the face instead. The powerful punch sending Corbulo staggering backwards in shock and pain, his hand clasping his bloody nose. But his intervention appeared to have done just enough for suddenly Crastus hesitated, aware of what he had just done.

“Strike the prefect again - big man,” Atlas said coolly as he appeared directly behind Crastus, a blade suddenly gleaming in his hand, “and I will cut your throat. And you know I will do it.”

“Sorry Sir,” Crastus stammered, his chest heaving from exertion, his breath coming in gasps as he staggered backwards onto his feet staring at Corbulo. “I did not mean to punch you. It was an accident.”

“What the fuck! Fuck!” Corbulo roared looking livid as he inserted himself between his two brawling officers. Blood streaming from his nose. “What is this? You are the two most senior officers in this ala, and you decide to start a brawl in the middle of a council like common soldiers! Like boys! The whole ala is standing out there right now waiting for me to address them,” Corbulo yelled furiously pointing in the direction of the parade ground, “and instead I am here inside this tent because my officers are messing things up. You are making us look like idiots! You are both a fucking disgrace!”

“Well, he started it Sir,” Gummar hissed spitting some blood onto the ground, as he glared at Crastus with a murderous look. “I demand punishment. He struck a superior officer. Twice! That is an offence under military regulations.”

“Both of you - shut the fuck up and listen!” Corbulo yelled as he turned to glare at Gummar and then back at Crastus as he stood in between them. “If I catch you two brawling again, I shall have both of you publicly flogged in front of the men and then dismissed from the army. Both of you! And I don’t care who started it. I don’t care if you are friends with the emperor. This is my command. You Crastus will not strike your superior officer again and you," Corbulo said turning to Gummar, "will not provoke him. Instead, you will learn to work together, and you will set an example to the men."

"That's hardly fair Sir," Gummar hissed. "He attacked…"

"Silence!" Corbulo bellowed. "There will be no brawling! This will not happen again. Understood! That is an order."

For a long moment the tent remained silent, angry, murderous looks being exchanged between the officers.

"Yes Sir," Crastus said at last lowering his gaze.

"Yes Sir," Gummar said looking away.

"Good," Corbulo said glaring at his subordinates as he reached up to wipe some of the blood from his nose. "Back to business! Now I know why our men deserted. They have gone to join Postumus in the West. That is what this is all about. They have gone to fight for the usurper. Which presents us with a problem. For we do not know how many more feel the same way as these deserters. And if the ala were to gain a reputation for unreliability, then the emperor will become suspicious of us. All our careers will be in jeopardy, maybe our lives too. We cannot allow this to happen. So how can we stop more men from deserting?"

Inside the tent however no one appeared willing to offer an answer.

"Maybe the men deserted because of money Sir," Atlas said at last in a quiet, soft voice. "Maybe Postumus simply pays his soldiers more."

"There can be no increase in the men's pay," Tobias said rounding on Atlas in alarm. "Don't make this the problem of the fiscus. Military budgets are non-negotiable and have been set by the central committee. There can be no change. I thought I made that clear already."

"Yes, so you said," Atlas said gazing at Tobias with a thoughtful look. "But I am sure you bureaucrats in the fiscus, and the imperial administration know exactly how to play the system. How to rig the books. How to conceal unauthorised expenditure or hide a bribe from prying eyes. I have often wondered why the imperial administrators always look so happy."

"Are you saying that I am corrupt?" Tobias called out raising his eyebrows as he confronted Atlas. "Be careful. That is a very serious accusation that you just made. So, make it again and I hope that you have got evidence for this accusation for else I will sue you for slandering an imperial administrator. I am an honest accountant. I do not steal from the emperor!"

"Maybe you don't have the balls to steal from the emperor," Atlas retorted. "But I know a guilty man when I see one," Atlas continued abruptly switching to German. "Let me tell you something you little shit. I have eaten sheep's eyes with the Bedouin amid the desert. I have watched a man be boiled alive. I have known the skill in which Indian women make love, but I have never actually come across an accountant who has been honest."

"What's that you are saying?" Tobias said glaring at Atlas. "Speak in Latin. What did he just say?" the accountant called out looking around the tent for support but not finding it. No one prepared to translate Atlas's words. "Well screw the lot of you," Tobias said in a bad-tempered voice. "I may be a civilian but mess with me at your peril. Just remember who I report to."

"Alright that is enough," Corbulo said shooting Atlas a quick warning look as he held his hand up to his bloodied nose. "Tobias has a job to do just like the rest of us. We will let him get on with it. And I am still waiting on you Atlas to report to me about the training of your apprentice and how that is going."

"I will Sir," Atlas replied.

"Well, if the fiscus were to provide my men with better quality coins," Crastus said glaring at the accountant, "then maybe they would be happier. The silver content in our coins has become ridiculously low as to be practically worthless. Inflation is out of control and prices are rising all the time. The fiscus is responsible and it's a fucking disgrace if you ask me."

"You are not very bright are you," Tobias responded rounding on the big man. "The fiscus is not responsible for the silver content of our coins. That is the responsibility of the state mint. Not my department. Not my problem. If you have an issue with the quality of our coins, then I suggest you take it up with the mint and stop slandering the fiscus which remains a most excellent organisation."

"Weasel words, civilian," Crastus retorted jutting his chin at Tobias. "Most excellent, my arse."

"Listen," Corbulo said seizing back the narrative as he turned to glare at his officers, his nose still dripping blood, "our men deserted because they believe we are fighting for the wrong emperor. Postumus rules in the West now and that is where our homeland and families are. The pull of home is strong. We all feel it. My cousin and his fellow deserters left us because they wanted to go home. They think that they should be fighting for Postumus."

“So, what are you going to do to stop it from happening again?” Gummar said sniffing unhappily as he turned to Corbulo with the slight air of a challenge. “What is the solution Sir?"

“I am going to address the men and give them a reason to stay and fight,” Corbulo said coolly turning to eye his deputy. Then to the rest of his officers. “Our soldiers are worried about the safety of their families in the West. We all know about the Frankish raids across the Rhine. I get it. But for now, we are just going to have to trust that Postumus will do his best to protect the Rhine frontier, to defend our people and homeland. The man may be a usurper, but he is still a Roman and he will still do what he can to defend the frontier. He certainly won’t remain in power for very long if he neglects the border defences. For the only reason people tolerate an emperor, a strong man, these days is because they need an emperor to protect them. And if he can’t do that then what use is he. And I am going to remind the men that we have all signed a sacred contract to serve Gallienus,” Corbulo continued eyeing his officers one by one. “I am going to remind them of the eternal shame and dishonour that comes from breaking an oath. And then finally I am going to give them the argument which is going to make them want to stay and fight. Which is that with Gallienus they are going to get far more opportunities to get filthy rich from looting the enemy's possessions than if they fought for Postumus. For gentlemen - with Gallienus,” Corbulo called out, “we are going to see far more action than we would possibly see if we sat out this war in a camp along the Rhine. I am going to win over our men with the promise to make them rich.”

As the gathering broke up and the officers headed out of the tent Corbulo quietly caught hold of Crastus’s shoulder signalling for him to remain behind. Then when the two of them were alone Corbulo spoke.

"Listen," he said eyeing the big man with a grave but patient look. "I don't like the situation with prince Gummar either but there is nothing I can do. The man has the ear of the emperor. I can't just get rid of him. So here is what you are going to do. I want you to obey his orders. He is your superior officer. He has the right to expect you to obey him and for this command to work properly I cannot afford for another incident as like what just occurred. But if there is something you really don't like or agree with then you are to come to me with it and I will make a ruling. Understood? Do this for me. Can I count on you big man?"

Studying Corbulo, Crastus hesitated. Then at last he nodded his acceptance. "I should have put a bit more power into that punch," Crastus replied. "Alright Corbulo, for old times sake."

***

It was evening and the military camp was settling down to its routine, the parade ground empty, the men back inside their barracks as Corbulo, attended by just one of his bodyguards, headed for the hospital. But as he approached the isolation tent the army doctor came hurrying up, trying to block his path. The man looking concerned.

"I can't let you enter Sir," the doctor stammered. "I am sorry Sir, but we have not yet established whether he has the plague. And if it is the plague, it will be contagious. Please Sir, think of the risk to the men!"

"I need to see him," Corbulo replied calmly pushing on towards the tent. "I have witnessed plague before in the East. I will take the necessary precautions, doctor. You have my word."

"Sir," the doctor protested but Corbulo silenced him with a raised hand. Then leaving his bodyguard outside by the entrance, alone, he pushed aside the tent flap and entered the isolation ward.

Harald was lying on a camp bed, looking weak and pale with a medical screen placed around him but as he noticed Corbulo the old veteran gave him a little weary smile. Halting a couple of yards from the bed Corbulo studied his friend.

“It’s not plague Sir,” Harald called out in a weak voice. “The doctor is an idiot. He has never seen plague before. The other one we had in the East was far better. All I did I think was eat something bad and now I just feel like shit. I need to rest. I will be back on my feet soon.”

“Good,” Corbulo said with a nod. “Good. What I need you to do right now is to recover and regain your strength. I have asked prince Gummar to take over the training of our men and supervise their conversion from infantry into cavalry. There is a lot of work to be done.”

"Keeping the men busy keeps them out of trouble," Harald said.

Nodding again Corbulo paused, and it was clear he had something on his mind.

“Talking about trouble. I heard there was a fight between Crastus and Gummar in the command post,” Harald said in a weak voice. “Explains that bloody nose of yours I suppose. How did you handle that then?”

“Badly,” Corbulo said sourly turning to look around the tent. “The command of the ala is a proper mess right now. Crastus and Gummar cannot stand each other but I cannot get rid of prince Gummar. He enjoys the emperor's favour. Atlas is dragging his heels over training up his apprentice and takes too much delight in provoking Tobias and the accountant is not our friend. I think he is spying on us. And you are ill. When you have recovered, I am going to need your help in keeping Crastus and Gummar apart from each other," Corbulo added in a weary voice. "They would have tried to kill each other if I had not been there to stop it. Those two cannot be left alone together, that is for sure. Not even for a brief period."

"Fine. I will do my best to keep them apart Sir," Harald murmured. "You will find a way to sort it all out."

"So, from one crisis to the next," Corbulo continued. "For there is more. There is another problem. Nine men deserted yesterday including Badurad and Linus. I think they have gone to fight for Postumus."

"I was expecting something like that," Harald muttered. "It is inevitable. The omens are not good then. This civil war continues to divide us."

"So, it does," Corbulo said sombrely. "I suppose that I shall not be seeing Badurad again now. He has made his choice and chosen his side. It's just a shame that we had to leave on such bad terms. And it is a shame too that I failed Hostes. He entrusted me with turning Badurad into a man - into a soldier - and I failed in my task. I have let him down."

"You did your best Sir," Harald said weakly from his bed. "Badurad made his choice and now he will have to live with the consequences. Like a man. He will just have to learn the hard way."

"He was not a bad kid," Corbulo said looking resigned.

"No just a bit hot-headed and impulsive," Harald replied. "Remember that time at Samosata along the Euphrates when Badurad and Linus single handedly charged the Sasanian lines.

They nearly destroyed us that day. And who came to your rescue Sir?"

"You did," Corbulo said. "But I am not here to talk about that. Or about our command. I am here because I want your advice on something."

"My advice?" Harald said looking surprised. "Oh, this sounds like it is serious."

"Yes, it is," Corbulo said looking away and hesitating as if he were suddenly unsure of himself. "You and I Harald, he continued at last, "we were both raised under the watchful gaze of Hercules Magusanus and as you know along the Rhine the Batavians and the Salian Franks worship Magusanus like a father. A true warrior god of the people of the northern light. So, I ask you now," Corbulo said lowering his voice and turning to look down at Harald, "what happens when a man turns his back on a god, he has believed in all his life?"

"You are renouncing Magusanus!" Harald replied frowning. "I don't know. I suppose the god will not be pleased. But you are a man, and you have a free will. Why? What has Magusanus done to you, to upset you so much that you are considering renouncing him?"

Chapter Eight - Corbulo Chooses his Path

Alone in the heart of Mediolanum, Corbulo paused at the street corner and cautiously turned to look around, taking in his surroundings. It was noon and in the narrow, busy and smelly streets the crowds of civilians were hurrying on by - intent on their own affairs. The populace going about their business. An ox drawn wagon laden with goods was trundling on down the road towards him. The driver sitting high up on the vehicle, staring straight ahead. Across the road from Corbulo a group of excited youths were loitering. The teenagers egging each other on as they eyed the entrance to a whorehouse, Meanwhile the shop owners and the street stalls were doing a brisk trade, competing for customers. The market district was alive with the traders loud and humorous sales pitches and from out of sight, a dog was barking franticly as if in warning. While the scent of woodsmoke and the pong coming from an open sewer blanketed the city in an insufferable stench that seemed to bother no one.

Wearing a civilian cloak drawn over his army tunic, Corbulo warily eyed the crowds, his weapons concealed underneath his clothes. But no one appeared to be paying him any attention. At last satisfied that he had not been followed into the city from the army base Corbulo turned to look in the direction in which he had to go. The alley was straight and narrow and deserted. Hesitating, still undecided, for a moment he remained where he was. Once again picturing Hypatia standing in her underground aqueduct in Syria. Protecting her people from the Sasanian raiders. Her leadership that day, a year ago now, had impressed him. He could not deny it. Somehow, he could not get her out of his head. Remembering her curiously powerful conviction and the woman's resolute strength, Corbulo sighed.

If he did this he thought, there could be no going back. If he were to get caught it would likely mean disgrace and execution.

Slipping into the alley he left the congested main street behind. His army boots crunching quickly across the dirty paving stones. For a while he followed the alley before darting into another passageway which was barely a yard wide, glancing over his shoulder now and then to see whether he was being followed but he could see no one.

At last, entering another alley, squashed in between the rows of terraced stone buildings, Corbulo approached a green door set in the wall. Pausing he once again glanced over his shoulder to check he was not being followed, before hurriedly opening the door and slipping into the building.

Inside the small, confined storeroom the air was cool and slightly musty. The space was filled with stacks of freshly cut wood and hanging neatly on the walls were the iron tools of a carpenter. While from her basket a cat eyed him, watching him with her green and wary eyes as he moved towards the back room of the building. Pausing in the doorway Corbulo took a deep breath as he spotted the occupants of the house. A man and a woman and a girl no older than ten were sitting huddled around a small table eating soup and bread. While the large room was divided into two by a curtain which had been drawn across the middle of the space. And as the occupants of the house noticed him, they froze. Then the three of them stiffly rose to their feet in complete silence.

"I am ready," Corbulo said turning to address the man. "I am ready to do this. But it must be now. You said I could do this anytime that I wished."

"I see," the man replied quietly, "you were followed?"

“No, I don’t think so. I was cautious.”

“Good,” the man said. For a moment he hesitated. Then hurriedly he turned to his wife and gestured to her. The woman responded by pushing aside the curtain and vanishing from view. While the girl just stood staring at Corbulo with large fearful eyes and the cat appeared and came over to see what was going on.

“You say you are ready,” the man replied forcing a smile. “I am pleased for you Sir. But you know what is required. There is no turning back once you commit yourself. There can be no falseness in your heart. This is serious. You know the price that you must pay and the danger…”

“Yes,” Corbulo interrupted. “I understand the danger of what I am about to do but I am ready to face it. I have chosen my path. My heart is set, father.”

“Good,” the man said as a moment later the woman reappeared from behind the curtain and quickly nodded to her husband that all was ready.

“May I say Sir,” the man said still hesitating, carefully clearing his throat as he studied Corbulo, “in our gatherings you were always the most reluctant to speak. I got the impression that you were not always convinced by my teachings. So, what made you now decide to become one of us?”

“I am a soldier. I lead men into battle,” Corbulo said with a shrug. “Your god is more powerful than the others. So, I have decided I shall honour him. A soldier needs a powerful god on their side.”

“There can only be one true god,” the man said gently, “the others are just false idols.”

"So, you say," Corbulo replied sharply, "but others of your faith have said that it is possible to believe in your god and in the old gods at the same time. That there is nothing wrong in honouring all. If your god is truly the only one then that shall become clear to me in time, father."

Appearing unhappy the man did not immediately respond. Then with a resigned look he nodded.

"Follow me and obey my instructions," the man said quietly as he turned and pushed aside the curtain that divided the room in two. Following him Corbulo quickly took in the household church. The simple altar hastily placed beside the hearth. The little clay statues. The painted iconographs and finally the precious silver cross that had been hurriedly hung up on the wall. Moving past him the woman said nothing as she carefully placed a large bowl of water upon the altar. The girl appearing moments later in the part of the room dedicated to the household church. The cat following and miaowing as it demanded to know what was going on.

"Blessed you are Sir," the woman said softly as she turned to give Corbulo a brave smile. "This is a most joyous day."

Saying nothing Corbulo turned to stare at the bowl of water that stood upon the altar as the man carefully dipped his hands into it. Then loosening his fibula, he took off his cloak and carefully laid it on the ground before turning to the man who was watching him.

"Please sit, Sir," the man said gesturing for Corbulo to sit down as the woman brought him a chair. And as he did so the woman and the girl took a step back, both gazing at him as if they were about to witness a miracle.

Sitting in the chair with his back to the altar, clad solely in his army tunic, Corbulo took a deep breath as he stared straight ahead at the curtain while standing beside him the priest began to speak the ritual words in a soft but precise voice. The man's tone growing in strength and conviction. Then it was time and as the priest gently grasped hold of Corbulo's head with both hands and carefully immersed him backwards into the bowl of cold water, his soft voice rang out.

"I now baptize you in the name of the Father, of the Son and of the Holy Spirit."

"May God wash me clean and cleanse me of my sins," Corbulo murmured in response as he stared up at the roof, "for I repent and ask God for forgiveness. May I remain always true to the Christian path on which I now embark."

***

Making his way through the crowds as he headed back towards the army camp just outside the city walls, Corbulo felt like a man reborn. A man from who a load had been lifted. His stride confident. His heart soaring. His eyes alert as inside the palm of his clenched hand he felt the shape of the small fish amulet that Hypatia had once given him and which he'd kept hidden from prying eyes all this time. Even from his closest colleagues. The symbol of the Christians was giving him renewed strength. He was a Christian now he thought. A Nazarene. He had finally done it. From now on he would fight for the Christian god. For He was the most powerful of all the gods Corbulo thought. The Christian god was the future. The way forward.

The idea of becoming a Christian had been growing on him ever since Hypatia had given him the amulet nearly a year ago while he and Badurad and Linus had been on their way to the desert city of Palmyra. But Christians were outlawed too. Hunted by mobs. Betrayed for money. Lynched without trial. Detested by the majority pagan population. Persecuted by official imperial decree and so he would have to keep his conversion a secret. He could tell no one. Not even his closest friends. For if he was found out it would be the end of him.

But as he strode on through the bustling street Corbulo was unaware of the figure concealed among the crowds who had been trailing him ever since he'd set out from the barracks that morning. Their face concealed by a hood.

Chapter Nine - To War!

Early summer 261 AD

General Aureolus, the forty-year-old commander of the imperial cavalry army was an imposing figure. He dominated the room. A tall man with a shock of thick black hair styled in the shape of a cock and the colour of a crow. His hideous face was disfigured by old wounds and the lingering evidence of a nasty childhood disease. But the man oozed sheer courage and aggression. His expression set in a permanent angry scowl as if he were only happiest when about to kill something. He looked like a general ought to Corbulo thought as he took his place among the other senior officers who were gathered around the large campaign table. His colleagues were waiting for their commander to address them. It was only the third time he'd met the general Corbulo thought but Aureolus appeared to be living up to his reputation as a tough and experienced soldier. A bully according to some. But at least his commander would not tolerate any fools and for that Corbulo was grateful. For it was a sentiment which he shared. Fools got good soldiers killed for no reason.

Resting upon the large wooden table at the centre of the conference room inside the imperial palace was a magnificent miniature mock-up of the entire Danube frontier from the black sea to the foothills of the Alps. The miniature laced and dotted with roads, towns, harbours and the locations of every Roman army fort, base and supply depot. The military and naval units were denoted by coloured and numbered figurines of men, horses and ships. The room inside the imperial palace was stuffy and hot. While the excitement among the officers was growing.

“So, gentlemen our time of idleness appears to be coming to an end. We are going back to war and about fucking time too!” Aureolus boomed, unable to hide the glee in his voice, his eyes sweeping across the room. “This morning intelligence reached us that the usurpers Macrianus Major and his snivelling son by the same name have crossed over from Asia into Europe and are now camped in Thrace with their army. Soon they intend to advance northwards towards Mediolanum and contest the imperial throne. They intend to defeat us. The battle that we have all been waiting for since the summer of last year is finally upon us. The usurpers think they can destroy us, but they do not know me or you. They have no idea of the shit storm they are about to encounter when they meet my army,” Aureolus called out. “We are going to thrash these usurpers and drive them into hell! We are going to break their spines. We are going to stamp our boots on their faces. We are going to end their rebellion against the true emperor, Gallienus, once and forever!”

And as general Aureolus paused the room erupted with the rhythmic stamping of hobnailed army boots on the stone floor as the senior Roman officers made their approval clear.

“So as of an hour ago,” Aureolus cried out, gesturing for silence. “Emperor Gallienus has ordered me to destroy these usurpers. I am to prepare our cavalry army and the attached infantry units for battle. Soon we shall march south to confront the usurpers. To destroy them. We are going to war!”

“How many men have the usurpers brought with them Sir?” the prefect of the equites Dalmatae called out.

“Intelligence suggests around thirty-thousand soldiers,” Aureolus barked. “And unfortunately, they are set to be joined by vexillations from the Danube legions who have decided to join the usurpers. There is talk that the Danube legions have been bribed. But it cannot be helped. All the rebels will be crushed and will die at our hands. The imperial cavalry army is ready to show them what is what."

At the mention of the Danube legions a few of the officers exchanged looks with each other, the mood growing more subdued.

"Ah fuck those conniving little weasel bastards," Aureolus cried out as he sensed the changed mood. "None are going to be able to stand against us. For the first time in history gentlemen, Rome has gathered the finest cavalry from the empire. All in one place under one command. We are going to go through these rebels like a spear through a fat goose!"

"Well said!" Probus called out as he stood beside Corbulo in the crowd of senior officers. "Lead us to victory Sir!"

Turning to gaze at Probus, Aureolus hesitated for a moment, his permanent scowl deepening as if he were trying to gage whether Probus was being sincere or taking the piss.

"We march on the last day of the month," Aureolus cried out, shifting his focus back to assembled officers. "From Mediolanum we will take the old road to the fortress of Singidunum on the Danube and then follow the via Militaris southwards through Illyria and into Thrace. See that your men are ready and that they carry enough provisions to last them for a three-month campaign. But not you!" Aureolus barked, his voice cutting like a steel blade as he quickly pointed a finger at Probus, picking him out. "No, you Probus will have another task to complete before I allow you to wet your sword on rebel blood. As we all know the Quadi King Hildimer and his bastard allies the Vandals, German tribal scumbags from the darkness beyond the Danube, have recently taken the opportunity afforded to them by the disaster and chaos unleashed by that shit head usurper Regalian and the dismal performance of the Fourteenth, to cross the river and raid the province of Upper Pannonia. This barbarian invasion must be stopped," Aureolus boomed, glaring at Probus.

"Gallienus wants these raids to end," Aureolus continued. "But the barbarians think we are weak. They no longer fear us. They think they can cross the Danube whenever they fucking please, so I want you Probus to remind them that Rome is not weak. The emperor wants order and security to be restored as soon as possible. So, there is no time to lose. Now the frontier between Carnuntum and Aquincum is crawling and infested with these barbarian war-bands. The whole province of Upper Pannonia is being overrun. You will therefore immediately and without delay take your equites Mauri northwards, restore order and drive this hairy, unwashed filth from our territory. Cleanse our land of these barbarians! I want the Quadi shitting themselves just at the thought of Rome. Then once you have completed your task in the north," Aureolus growled, "you are to rejoin my main force in the south as soon as possible for what will assuredly be the decisive contest between us and the Macriani usurpers. And Probus," Aureolus continued in a bullying voice, "you had better not be late in arriving for that battle because I will have your balls if you are."

"Very well Sir," Probus replied dipping his head in acknowledgement of his commanding officer. "But I only have eighteen hundred men. From my experience fighting against these barbarian raiding parties, the Quadi Sir, once they learn of my approach they will simply melt away and withdraw back across the Danube with their plunder and then return once we have left the area. All that I can realistically hope to achieve is a temporary cessation of these raids across the frontier. It would not be long term solution."

“I thought your men were the best in the world,” Aureolus said raising a questioning eyebrow as he glared back at his subordinate. “You have certainly boasted about your Mauri more times than I can remember, Probus. So, what’s this? Now you don’t think you can carry out my orders. Are you scared that you would fail?”

“No Sir,” Probus said patiently with a little cold smile. “It’s just that I have a better and more effective plan.”

“What!” Aureolus exclaimed, his eyes narrowing suspiciously. “You saying that my plan is not good enough for you now, boy!”

“Your plan is excellent Sir,” Probus replied looking unperturbed. “And let me say that if there is one general in the whole empire who I would want to serve under then it is you Sir. You kick arse, you really do. But allow me to explain my plan. Sure, I can take my Mauri and try and drive these Quadi war-bands back across the Danube, but like I said, upon my approach the barbarians will simply withdraw across the Danube and bide their time before attacking us again when my forces have left the area. They know that we are stretched. They know they can simply wait. A better strategy, if we want a long-term solution, would be to inflict a decisive defeat on king Hildimer so that the Quadi will never want to raid our lands again.”

"A decisive defeat," Aureolus said sounding sceptical. "Do you inhabit dream land Probus. We do not have the soldiers to send against the Quadi to ensure that they suffer a decisive defeat!"

"I would not need a large force," Probus countered. "I understand the constraints on our resources, but my men are well trained and eager. And I know my enemy. I have fought against these barbarians before. They may be numerous and ferocious in battle, but they are also greedy selfish men who quarrel among themselves a lot and who care little for their king unless there is something in it for them. Which means they are disorganised and difficult to lead. So yes, I am confident that I can inflict a decisive defeat upon the Quadi. With some modest reinforcements I should be able to achieve this. Will you let me try Sir?"

"Your plan?" Aureolus growled, looking undecided.

"Still working on it," Probus replied smiling coyly. "But I will require some modest reinforcements. My Mauri alone will not be enough. And I will need to be invested with the authority to take command of all Roman forces currently stationed in the province of Upper Pannonia. In return I shall promise you that I shall succeed and will still rejoin you in time for the battle against the Macriani usurpers."

"You cannot promise anything! Authority you say. It seems to me Probus that you look like you are more interested in trying to make a name for yourself than winning a decisive victory," Aureolus said glaring back at him. "And by modest reinforcements, what exactly did you have in mind?"

"Give me the new boys," Probus said coolly. "The equites foederati Germanica. Together with them I can get this done."

"The German horse!" Aureolus exclaimed with a frown as Corbulo quickly glanced at his friend in surprise. For a moment Aureolus remained silent as he mulled upon the request like it was a piece of raw meat, his mind working. Then at last the ugly general lifted his chin as if he were issuing a challenge.

"The emperor wants the Quadi driven back across the Danube and order to be restored along the frontier," Aureolus said. "And I am not going to agree to anything until I have heard your plan Probus. And once I have heard it, I will decide whether you are bat shit crazy or whether your plan has some merit. So, speak. What do you have in mind?"

For a moment Probus hesitated as he and Corbulo glanced at each other. Then Probus spoke.

"It will involve crossing the Danube using the pontoon bridge at Carnuntum and taking the fight into the Quadi's own territory," Probus replied breezily. "A risky operation I know but risks will need to be taken. The governor of Upper Pannonia, Regalian is dead, murdered by his own troops I hear but despite the chaos his failed rebellion has caused, our latest intelligence claims that the city of Carnuntum is still in Roman hands."

"If it is still in Roman hands," Aureolus retorted, "then it is barely so and there is no guarantee that the pontoon bridge across the Danube remains in existence. The same intelligence reports also say that the Quadi have surrounded the city and that all the roads to the south have been cut and that the countryside is swarming with barbarian raiding parties."

"Carnuntum has strong walls Sir," Probus countered, "and the Quadi lack the necessary siege equipment to take such a fortified city. I am confident that the place is still in Roman hands."

“Mighty walls did not protect Regalian,” the prefect of the equites Promoti exclaimed coming to Aureolus's support. “And the garrison will only hold out if they have enough food. And what if in their despair they decide to stage another rebellion against the emperor? If Carnuntum is lost again to us - what is left of our defences in the north will collapse. Morale among our men is already at a low point following the rebellions of Ingenuus and Regalian. And now you Probus wants to send the few trained soldiers we have still got left on some adventure north of the Danube? I must argue against this insane plan. The risks are too high."

"What about the Fourteenth Gemina," the commander of the equites Scutari called out in a hopeful voice. "The legion is based at Carnuntum. They are tasked with defending that stretch of the frontier. I know they recently supported Regalian in his rebellion against the emperor, but Regalian is dead and since then the soldiers have returned to their old allegiance to Gallienus. Would they not be able to support Probus's actions?"

"Have you seen their latest strength report," the prefect of equites Promoti snapped raising his eyebrows with an incredulous look. "Well, I have. I did the count straight after Regalian's rebellion was crushed and we regained control of the city. The Fourteenth have been reduced to just a shadow of what they used to be. There were just a few hundred men left from that legion who were fit for duty when I was last with them a few months ago. There were plans to rebuild the legion, but they had not begun before the Quadi attacks put an end to that idea. No. The Fourteenth will not be in any position to offer any support."

As the council chamber fell silent all eyes turned towards Aureolus as the Roman officers waited expectantly for their commander to decide. Mulling over what had been said Aureolus kept them waiting. Then at last he turned to peer at Probus, his eyes narrowing suspiciously.

"I cannot really spare the men you are asking for," Aureolus called out. "The Macriani usurpers already outnumber my own army, and they are bound to pick up more support as they advance through Thrace and into Illyria. And it is against them that we must fight a decisive battle, not these annoying unwashed barbarian raiders in the north. But having said that,"

Aureolus voice abruptly trailed off as he reached up to stroke his chin with a sudden thoughtful look. "Alright Probus," Aureolus said at last nodding carefully. "You are a persistent little fucker aren't you, but Gallienus thinks you are a good soldier. So, I shall give you the German horse. They have something to prove after all. But if you fail me, I will make sure that you never again hold high command. I will ensure that this will be the end of your career. I know you are ambitious. Fuck with me and I will ruin your name and reputation."

***

As Corbulo emerged from the imperial palace, his plumed helmet tucked under his arm, he quickly spotted Probus standing by the side of the street beyond the gate. His friend appeared to be waiting for him and to his surprise at his side was Claudia, his sister. Sporting an amused grin Probus raised his hand in greeting as Corbulo came up, but Claudia did not move - remaining where she was. Her expression strangely cold and subdued. As if something had changed. The young blond woman keeping her distance from him. Saying nothing in contrast to her brother who stepped forwards to greet Corbulo warmly.

“You see now why I hate Aureolus's guts,” Probus exclaimed with a grin as the three of them turned and began to walk back towards the barracks in the morning light. “He's a bully who likes to make threats. That is his style. But he is not stupid either. Underestimate him at your peril. You know they say that no one has ever seen him smile. I don’t think he knows how to smile. But Aureolus is a brilliant general. He knows how to win a battle. Emperor Gallienus is lucky to count him as an ally. Aureolus is going to destroy the usurpers. I know he will and so does the emperor. Macrianus and Balista have no idea of what is coming their way. Aureolus is a one man shit storm when he gets going."

"Let's hope so," Corbulo said nodding politely. "So, I see I am now to report to you," he added glancing at Probus. "The war against the Quadi. We are to work together to defeat king Hildimer. You could have warned me that you had this in mind. It came as a surprise."

"Yeah, I should have," Probus replied with a shrug. "Our fates appear to be entwined. So, it begins. Are you happy that I asked for you and your men? I did not make that choice lightly."

"Soldiering is what I do, war is my business," Corbulo replied. "I go where they tell me to fight. But now you ask, yes I am happy with it."

"Good," Probus replied looking pleased. "The reason I asked for you Corbulo and your ala is that you are a good soldier, and I am no tyrant. You and I are going to do great things together. That is my wish. Today marks the start of a great partnership between us. The world will witness it, and the gods will approve. Out of all those men inside that chamber today it is you who I would want fighting at my side and trust me - I am good judge of character."

"I have not always been a good man," Corbulo murmured looking away with a wistful expression. "You do not know me as well as you think you do. I have done shameful things."

Ignoring Corbulo's comment Probus chuckled.

"Aureolus thinks that he is retaining his best men for the march south," Probus said, "but he is wrong. In fact, he is sending his best troops north. I know what you and your men accomplished last year in the East," Probus continued giving Corbulo a respectful look. "I have heard the talk among the soldiers. So, you and I Corbulo shall work together as equals on this task," Probus added reaching out to grip Corbulo's arm. "Together your Salian Franks and my Mauri can get this done. I have little doubt, my friend. And once we succeed the whole empire will know of our names. Aureolus was not wrong to say that I am doing this to make a name for myself. He knows because he is after the exact same thing. If we get this right Corbulo, our fame and reputation will spread and you know what comes with fame, power!"

Looking hesitant Corbulo lowered his gaze as he walked. "Fame," he murmured at last. "Maybe. But it is a double-edged sword. Fame may lead to power, but it also incites jealousy."

"I am an ambitious man!" Probus said his voice filled with sudden determination. "I have plans. Great ambitious plans."

"Plans?" Corbulo said glancing at his friend and raising an eyebrow. "You never mentioned anything about this before?"

"Yes," Probus said calmly turning to look around at the people in the street as he walked along, "I have plans. I will tell you about them some day. Do you think that I am the only one with ambition around here. All those officers you saw attending the council earlier today will have their own agendas and ambitions for the future. Friends one day, rivals the next. Enemies the day after. A man must be prepared for when the unexpected happens. He may have to choose a side at short notice. Power shifts. I think you know what I am talking about."

"Fame will lead to jealousy which can get a man murdered," Corbulo replied. "Fame can become a death sentence."

"You are my friend," Probus said coming to an abrupt halt and turning to look at Corbulo. "And an ambitious man needs loyal friends whom he can trust and rely upon. Who can help him achieve his ambition. Who can offer him sound advice when he asks for it. Together you and I Corbulo we can achieve great things, and like I said it starts now, here today. This war against the Quadi. It's a first test. If we succeed Gallienus will notice and either reward me or start to see me as a potential rival. Or both. Either way things will start to change. Power will start to shift. A rising star must make friends but also enemies. And if a star does not rise then it must fall. You are with me on this are you not Corbulo?" Probus added with a sudden look of apprehension. "You are in my camp. I can rely on you right to always have my back?"

Gazing at his friend Corbulo hesitated conscious that both Probus and Claudia were suddenly watching him closely.

"Yes, I have your back," Corbulo said at last. "Of course I am on your side. You can rely on me Probus. I will support you."

"Swear it," Probus said gently. "Swear it on the honour of your forebears. The men whose names you recite before going into battle. Swear that you will side with me and no other. I need to know."

"You do not have to ask me to do swear it," Corbulo said looking grave. "We are friends. But if it makes you happy, I shall swear it - on the honour of my ancestors."

Studying Corbulo Probus remained silent for a moment. Then he raised his hand and clasped Corbulo lightly by the shoulder, like a father would do with a son.

"This is good," Probus announced. "And I appreciate that you do not share my desire for fame. But don't you see, that is precisely why I need you Corbulo. Because you will never fear to tell me what I don't necessarily want to hear. You will be no sycophant. And in exchange I promise that I shall never ask you to become something you are not or do something that will make you look dishonourable in the eyes of your ancestors. I know what motivates you Corbulo. I know what you live for, and I know that the advice you will give me will be true and honest."

“Then listen to me now," Corbulo said quietly. "Be careful Probus. I have seen other ambitious men fall into dust. All like you expected to succeed only to learn that the gods did not favour them. My advice would be to hide your ambition from those that may come to see you as a rival."

“I do not intend to make the same mistakes as those who have come before me," Probus sniffed. “I intend to go right to the top Corbulo. That is where you and I are heading. To the very top of the fucking pile!"

Saying nothing Corbulo starting to walk again before glancing at Claudia who was keeping her gaze firmly on the street ahead, suddenly puzzled by her strange unresponsive silence and changed demeanour. Was she still angry that he had rejected her? It had been several months since he had last seen her, but their parting had been amicable. Probus having made some excuses that she had been away in Rome visiting relatives in the capital.

“Your Salian Franks," Probus asked oblivious to Corbulo's quiet concern. “They are ready for war?"

“More or less," Corbulo replied turning his attention back to Probus. “I would like to have had more time to train them, but things are what they are. We'll manage. My men are as ready as they are going to be."

For a while the three of them strode on in silence before Corbulo again glanced across at Claudia, increasingly puzzled by her coolness towards him and the strangeness with which she was treating him. The woman had not said a word to him. As if she was refusing to acknowledge his very existence. This was not like the Claudia he had known before who had liked to chat. Especially after the two of them had been apart for such a long time. The old Claudia would have been keen to tell him everything that had befallen her in Rome or at least check up on what he had been doing. But today nothing, not a single word. As if she were unhappy with him. She was acting like a woman who had been betrayed. Then just as Corbulo was about to confront her, as if anticipating him, Claudia rounded on him, the young woman coming to an abrupt halt in the middle of the street.

"So, I shall say goodbye now Corbulo," Claudia said lifting her chin and staring him straight in the eye as if she were challenging him and as she did Corbulo caught a glimpse of something that startled him. Rage! Her voice however was formal as if she were addressing a servant of no consequence. "I wish you all the best and hope that I shall see you again when this is all over. Look after my brother if you can. Goodbye Corbulo."

And then without another word, without even a farewell kiss, Claudia turned and walked off leaving Corbulo staring at her in confusion.

"Ah," Probus said in a gentle voice as he watched his sister depart. "Don't read too much into that. She has just returned from Rome and must be tired. My sister is just a little bit upset that we are going to war. She worries like all women do. She thinks we are going to get ourselves killed."

"Well, she is right to be worried," Corbulo said as he watched Claudia go. "There is always a chance. We have chosen a dangerous profession after all. But she seemed angry with me, not sad."

"Well," Probus said raising his eyebrows. "I believe she may be a little disappointed with you for turning her down earlier. Claudia is a proud woman. She does not take rejection easily. She is eligible. She has money. She is beautiful and she likes you," Probus added with a little chuckle as he reached up to pat Corbulo on the shoulder. "She really does like you and maybe she is offended because you prefer whores. I will say it again Corbulo but if you were to ask her to marry you, she would say yes, and I would give you, my permission. You would be marrying into a family that is on the rise. Think about that."

Chapter Ten - Chaos at Carnuntum

Leading his Salian Franks and Batavian cavalry down the road at a canter accompanied by Crastus, Tobias, prince Gummar and Probus's Moorish liaison officer assigned to his command, Corbulo swore out loud as he saw the locals ahead of him fleeing in panic across the rolling fields that they had been peacefully working just a few moments ago. The men, women and children racing for the cover of the forest. The peasants abandoning their mules and heavy farm equipment. Men yelling in alarm. Women swooping up their infants in the mad, frantic rush to safety. Babies wailing. Dogs barking. Oxen bellowing. While on the horizon to the east columns of ominous black smoke were towering into the blue summer sky.

"Why do they run from us?" Tobias called out in Latin as he rode beside Corbulo. The imperial accountant's civilian cloak covered in dust; his forehead lathered in sweat as he gazed at the fleeing populace with a perplexed frown. "Do they not know that we are Romans come to protect them? Can they not see our banners? What is this madness."

"Ah you have not been to the frontier then," prince Gummar exclaimed in a resigned voice as he too gazed at the panic created by the appearance of the Roman troopers. "But I have. I warned you that it is fucking chaos up here. No one knows whose side anyone is on anymore. Raiders. Usurpers. Deserters. Bandits. Troops loyal to Gallienus. They are all here and they do as they please. They take what they want. There is no authority. No law except that of the power of the sword. It's not just the Quadi raids. It's also the repeated rebellions against Gallienus by the usurpers Ingenuus and Regalian. They in their quest for power have ruined this stretch of the frontier. And now just the sight of armed men is enough to send the farmers fleeing. You can't blame the people. It's even worse up along the river and in the towns. You will see."

"Come back! We are Romans! We are yours! We are here to protect you!" the cries went up as a few Roman officers broke away from the main column and rode out into the fields as they tried to rally the fleeing populace but to no avail. Their efforts just inspiring more panic. Surveying the scene from his horse Corbulo, clad for battle in his short red cloak, mail body-armour and wearing his splendid, plumed helmet, reduced his horse's pace to a trot before hurriedly turning towards prince Gummar and addressing his deputy.

"Join Harald and the 2nd cohort at the rear of the column," Corbulo said with a concerned look, "and get the men into their battle formations. See to it that a strong guard is posted to protect our supply wagons. We cannot afford to lose them. We are entering a warzone. See that smoke on the horizon. The enemy raiding parties must be close by. From now on we proceed with caution. We may have to fight at short notice. So, see to it that the men are ready and that they remain alert."

"Sir," Gummar said dutifully as he quickly started back down the road towards the rear of the column of Germanic cavalry. Sat upon his horse, ignoring the fleeing populace in the fields, Corbulo watched his deputy go. Then quickly he turned to Crastus, the big man looking awkward and ill at ease in the saddle. "Crastus do the same with the 1st cohort," Corbulo ordered. "Get them ready to fight at short notice. We continue down the road as planned." Turning to peer at the towering columns of black smoke on the horizon to the east with a guarded look Corbulo's concern deepened before a sharp warning cry from one of his bodyguards alerted him to more immediate danger directly up ahead.

Riding straight towards him down the road, a solitary horseman armed with a spear and a large round Germanic style shield had appeared. The man's face was half concealed by a scarf, leaving just his eyes free and he had no body-armour, not even a protective coat of leather. He looked like a barbarian. Clad in the simple, coarse and rugged clothing of the people beyond the imperial frontier. A linen tunic. A long woollen chequered jacket and short trousers that came up to his knees. While on his feet he was wearing a pair of long black leather boots. And as the man calmly headed straight towards the Roman column, without slowing his pace, he showed no sign of fear or alarm. As if he was here on some purpose.

With excited cries two of Corbulo's bodyguards were just about to charge the lone barbarian and finish him off when Corbulo's sharp command called them back. Frowning at the lone barbarian as the man drew nearer Corbulo slowed his horse's pace to a walk. Then abruptly his expression changed, and his eyes narrowed.

"Atlas!" Corbulo roared. "Goddamn it! Is that you?"

"Indeed, it is Sir," the barbarian cried out cheerfully, speaking in good Latin and as he came up to Corbulo the man lowered his scarf revealing a broad amused grin. "Although in these parts I call myself Wilfried," Atlas continued. "That was after all my father's name. You like my disguise Sir? I am trying to grow a beard like these barbarians, but it is going to take some time before its mature. Fooled your bodyguards though. Bunch of fucking muppets as always. Blind as bats. Stupid as dogs. Oh, hello boys! So, you wanted to kill me did you," Atlas added subjecting the bodyguards milling around Corbulo to a mocking smile. His taunt eliciting sharp angry intakes of breath from the mounted soldiers.

"Took me some time to find a new set of clothes and boots that actually fitted me," Atlas continued shifting his attention back to Corbulo and allowing him no chance to get a word in. "In defence of your guards though - they were not the only one who were fooled. So was the enemy. I was able to infiltrate them. No one suspected that I was a Roman spy. Everyone always underestimates me which is a good thing I suppose. But then again, I am fucking good at my job. I took these clothes and weapons from a Vandal," Atlas said gesturing at his shield. "He was drunk and on his own. Had to cut his throat. I know. Not a very honourable thing to do," Atlas added with a shrug, "but I was cold, and I needed a better disguise. Stole his horse too. You should try these barbarian boots Sir. Soft and warm. Really good quality. Better than the kit the army issues."

"I have no time for your games Atlas," Corbulo said as he eyed his speculatore, intelligence officer. "What have you got for me? What news? The road ahead - Is it clear? What about Carnuntum? Is the enemy besieging the city?"

"I have just come from the direction of Carnuntum," Atlas replied. "The good news is that the city still stands as does the nearby legionary fortress. There is no siege as such, and both the civilian town and legionary fortress are still in Roman hands but there are problems inside the town. Big problems with the soldiers."

"Problems?" Corbulo said raising an eyebrow.

"Yeah," Atlas replied evasively. "You will see when we get there. The road leading towards the city is clear for now but it is menaced by Quadi and Vandal war-bands lurking in the nearby forests. Most of the smaller settlements in the surrounding countryside have been abandoned or destroyed. Supplies are scarce and there is plague reported in some of the army camps to the west. There are also roaming groups of Roman army deserters from the Fourteenth Legion who have turned to banditry to make a living. No one is stopping them. It's fair to say Sir," Atlas continued with a sigh, "that it is utter chaos. The enemy are attacking anything that moves along the main road. They have been raiding every farm and settlement. They are taking everything. Most of these groups however are small and fight separately and I doubt they will dare threaten a column of our size Sir. But there is a larger group of Quadi over to the east, maybe two days march away. They are raiding south of the Danube, apparently amassing a vast amount of loot," Atlas said gesturing in the direction of columns of smoke on the horizon. "This larger group is apparently being led by King Hildimer. They appear to be around several thousand strong. And they seem to be better organised and more disciplined than the others. I would call them an army, not a war-band."

"So, the enemy King is to the east of us, downstream!" Corbulo said frowning with sudden concern. "With a few thousand men you say."

"Probus is going to have his work cut out for him," Atlas said with a shrug. "He will have to deal with the king."

For a moment Corbulo gazed to the east in the direction of the distant columns of smoke as Atlas hurriedly fell in alongside and Corbulo continued down the road walking his horse. The plan he and Probus had worked out was simple enough Corbulo thought. Probus would take care of the country south and west of the Danube and he would be responsible for getting his men across the river to raid and attack the Quadi homelands to the north and east. While between them they hoped to corner King Hildimer in a trap.

"What about the enemy warbands between us and Carnuntum - do they have cavalry?" Corbulo asked.

"Mainly infantry - spearmen. But don't be fooled. They can move fast. Some horsemen too Sir and some Roman rebel cavalry from the Fourteenth," Atlas replied with a shrug. "The Romans are the die-hard remnants of the usurpers armies who refused to return to serving Gallienus after the failure of the Regalian rebellion. They have unfortunately been joined by some of our Salian Franks and Batavians who were posted to the border camps along the Danube. The barbarians are mainly Quadi but also include bands of Vandals, Roxolani and some Marcomanni. Opportunistic bastards. They think that they can get rich quickly while Rome is preoccupied by civil war. That appears to be their main concern - that they are going to miss out on all the riches that are suddenly up for grabs along the frontier. It's like a mad scramble that is attracting war-bands from afar. Gathering wealth appears to be the enemy's main motivation."

"Our brothers from the Rhine have joined the enemy!" Corbulo exclaimed looking shocked. "Batavians and Salian Franks have abandoned their posts for this! I don't believe it. Is this true?"

"So, it appears Sir," Atlas replied lowering his eyes.

"Great god," Corbulo murmured as he turned to Crastus who having carried out his orders had returned. "So, it has come to this. Did you hear that. Our own brothers have sided with the very same men who happily attack our settlements and people. I did not think I would see the day. This is betrayal."

"An oath once made cannot be broken," Crastus said, his face darkening with contempt. "That is how it has always been. An oath is sacred and to break it will anger the gods. But these young kids today are soft, and they have forgotten the old ways.

I can understand what motivates the barbarians," Crastus continued, "but that our own brothers - Salian Franks and Batavians - abandon their posts and join in the rape of a province is an utter disgrace. It is infamy! Those traitors are nothing but scum! I mean - where is the honour and loyalty. Where is their pride as men, as warriors?"

"Like I said it is chaos Sir," Atlas continued in a resigned voice, "and by the looks of things there is nothing to stop these barbarian hordes from crossing the frontier and advancing deep into our territory. Hell, I reckon they could go all the way to the city of Rome without encountering any serious resistance. The frontier barely exists anymore. It's wide open."

"There is us," Corbulo said turning to look at his intelligence officer with a reproachful look. "You forget. They will need to get past us first and we are not going to let them pass. We are going to destroy these raiders. We are going to destroy these traitors and anyone else who gets in our way. We are going to remind them all that Rome is to be feared."

"Damn fucking right Sir," Crastus said, awkwardly shifting position in his saddle.

"Sir," Atlas said quickly looking away, chastened.

"What else?" Corbulo continued as he led the column down the road. "What else did you learn Atlas?"

"We may have an advantage over the Quadi if we handle this the right way," Atlas said in a tentative voice. "You see the enemy are operating in small independent warbands Sir. They may be numerous, but they are not very well organised, nor do they seem to be coordinating their actions. They just do what they please. Each band does its own thing. They appear not to have any clear strategic plan other than to steal, fight and rape.

Sometimes they even fight each other. It means Sir that we have an opportunity to defeat each war-band we come across separately. The only properly organised band of men are those with King Hildimer. The war-bands who operate alone should therefore not be a threat to us, but the King and his men most certainly are."

For a moment Atlas paused before a little colour shot into his cheeks.

"It's fucking insane Sir," he continued. "The barbarians are slaughtering anyone who resists. They are hanging people from trees - burning them alive, tearing them apart with ropes and horses while feeding others to starving pigs. As if it were sport to them. Nothing is sacred to them. Nothing is out of bounds. All kinds of terror and cruelty is being inflicted upon their victims. I have seen it with my own eyes. In their homes across the river these raiders may act like normal men do - but here - once they have crossed the river into Roman territory - it is as if they are no longer men, but wild beasts. It is as if they have forgotten who they are. It is as if they have been seized by a crazed blood lust. As if they have been freed to do what they like without fear and inhibition. Without guilt. Without morality. As if - here - anything is allowed and there is no law, not even the moral laws normally respected by every nation. These raiders," Atlas sighed, "they have taken many slaves. I have been into one of their forest camps. It's filled with our people. With slaves. It's terrible. And once these raiders have gathered enough loot and slaves, they intend to re-cross the river. They intend to go back home."

"We have to do something to help our people," Crastus growled, his expression darkening again as he glanced across at Corbulo. "Probus can't handle everything on his own. We cannot allow these barbarians to take our people Sir. Once they are across the river, we will never get them back."

"You said there were problems inside Carnuntum," Corbulo replied, ignoring Crastus as he fixed his gaze upon his intelligence officer. "What problems? What about the pontoon bridge across the Danube. Is it still there?"

"Ah yes," Atlas said with another shrug. "Problems. There are many. You will see Sir what I mean when we get there. Carnuntum is a shit show right now and that is putting it mildly."

"We need to do something for our people Sir," Crastus repeated in a quiet determined voice as once again he turned towards Corbulo. "We can't just abandon them. Let Atlas guide us to these forest camps and let us attack these raiders. Let us free the captives."

"No," Corbulo said finally glancing at Crastus, "we need to cross the Danube and get to the northern bank as soon as we can. There is no time. Probus and I have worked out a plan and we must stick to it."

***

Sitting on his horse, occupying the high ground that rose above the city just to the south of the settlement, Corbulo gazed at the civilian town of Carnuntum nestling against the banks of the Danube. The war banner of the equites foederati Germanica proudly held aloft by his mounted standard bearer. The battle-standard displaying four newly added battle honours to the existing four. Idistaviso. Mons Graupius. The wall of Hadrian. Danube frontier. While Harald and prince Gummar together with Probus's liaison officer, a dark-skinned Moorish officer with coal black hair and long straight sideburns were sitting on their horses nearby. The party of Roman officers and soldier's gazing at the city in contemplative silence.

Carnuntum was larger than Corbulo had been expecting with many of the houses spilling out into suburbs beyond the protective inner-city walls. It must have once been a lively, bustling place he thought but now the suburbs appeared to be still and abandoned. Some of the houses burnt and ruined while he could see no one moving about. Shifting his attention to the city walls he could see that they still appeared to be intact but along the battlements he could make out no imperial banners and the main gates leading into the settlement were closed. While the wide, majestic waters of the river directly to the north cleaved the land in half. The mighty river dotted with small tree covered islands and muddy sandbanks. And there - starting from inside the city - boldly pushing out across the water in a straight impudent line - was a magnificent pontoon bridge. The row of boats neatly bound and buttressed together. The bridge vanishing from view beyond a tree covered island.

For a while Corbulo remained where he was before at last, he shifted his attention to the legionary fortress, home to the Fourteenth, which had been built on the high ground above the river a mile or so to the east. Peering at the camp he tried to discern any activity. Any sign of a welcoming committee. But here too he could see few people about and no one coming out to meet him. As if everyone was doing their best to hide from him and his command.

"So, the bridge still stands Sir," one of his officers called out at last in a hopeful voice. "This is a good start."

"And so does the city," Harald exclaimed.

"We shall see," Corbulo replied cautiously, "prince Gummar," he said turning to him, "you will hold the 2nd cohort back in reserve and guard our supplies while I will take the 1st cohort towards the city gates. Harald you will go with him and once you are there send Crastus back to me. I want you to post a guard on this hill. If we run into trouble inside the town I will signal you with three blasts from our trumpets. Alert me if you spot any signs of trouble."

"Sir," Gummar said nodding. "Sir," Harald said smoothly. "Are you expecting trouble? The city looks peaceful."

"Looks can be deceptive and if all was well, they would have sent out a welcoming party by now," Corbulo growled before with a last look at the pontoon bridge, he turned away and accompanied by his bodyguards he urged his horse down the slope in the direction of the city.

Approaching the main gates of Carnuntum Corbulo's expression hardened as he saw what lay ahead along the last stretch of the road. The suburbs around him were deserted, abandoned and there was no one about. The silence adding poignancy. The afternoon air still as if in shock. The summer heat stifling as if in glee. While high above in the blue sky the scavenger birds were circling in anticipation. Strung out along the road, partially blocking the way, a convoy of wagons sat abandoned. The vehicles had been looted and some still contained the bodies of their owners together with a few dead horses and oxen still attached to their harnesses. Their blood staining the paving stones. Spilling out onto the ground around the wagons were the unwanted contents that the carts had been carrying. Chairs, tables, clothing, rotting food and a mass of broken and shattered pottery.

But as he and his men from the 1st cavalry cohort carefully picked their way past the convoy heading towards the gates, Corbulo could see that the worst was still ahead. It was clear that the convoy had been ambushed within sight of safety and that the attack had been recent. On the road leading to the gates of Carnuntum lay a mass of bodies. Men, women and children. Civilians. At least a hundred. Their lifeless bodies bloated in the heat. The sickly-sweet stench of death lying heavy and oppressive upon the land. Finding themselves under attack the refugees appeared to have made a final mad frantic rush towards the city gates, hoping perhaps to reach safety of the city for their bodies lay concentrated in a narrow arc that pointed straight at the gates. The people had been cut down as they had run. Their bodies peppered with arrows, sword and spear wounds. The heaps of dead growing denser closer to the gates as if this was the place, in the very shadow of the mighty walls, where they had made their final, desperate stand.

Bringing his horse to a halt, staring at a baby that had been impaled on a spear and left out beside the edge of the road, Corbulo remained silent. Several other corpses appeared to have been mutilated and defiled. Their heads cut from their bodies and placed on spikes. Their penises cut off and stuffed into their mouths. Then at last he shifted his gaze towards the gates and walls of the Roman city of Carnuntum. The refugees could have made it into the city. They could have been saved. The distance was not that far. But they had all died, trapped, because the inhabitants of the city had refused to open their gates to them. The townsfolk appeared to have refused to let them in. And no one since had ventured out to give the corpses a decent burial.

Slowly starting out again Corbulo advanced towards the gates as behind him the four hundred- and eighty-men men of the 1st cohort of the equites foederati Germanica followed him in silence. The stamp and clatter of the horses' hooves and the nervous whinnying of the beasts breaking the eerie silence. Up ahead Corbulo could see that the gates leading into the city were firmly shut and as he looked up at the battlements, he could see figures peering back down at him. At last, seeing that the inhabitants were not going to open for him Corbulo raised his fist in the air and brought his horse to a halt.

“Who are you? Identify yourselves,” a voice speaking in Latin suddenly shouted from the battlements. “Which emperor do you serve? Who pays you?”

“There is only one emperor and his name is Gallienus,” Corbulo yelled back. “Do you not recognise our banners?”

“Are you responsible for this massacre,” Crastus roared angrily glaring up at the men on the wall from his horse. “Did you murder these people? They are lying right in front of your fucking gates! They are civilians. Our people. Why did you not let them in?”

“Enough Crastus,” Corbulo said hurriedly rounding on his subordinate. “Accusations like that are not going to help us.”

“They are guilty,” Crastus muttered shifting awkwardly in his saddle. “I know it. You know it. They could have helped these civilians, but they chose to do nothing. Fucking scum. All they had to do was open their gates.”

“No more from you,” Corbulo growled before hurriedly turning his attention back to the men up on the wall. “We serve emperor Gallienus,” he cried out to them in a loud voice. “So, open your gates and let us in. We mean no harm. We are here to protect you!”

“No!” the voice shouted back defiantly. “We have heard that before! We are not fooled by your tricks or ruses. Once you are inside the city you will just plunder what we have still got left and sell the rest of us to the highest bidder. Go away and leave us in peace! This is our city now. You are not coming in. We do not want your help! You speak Latin but you look like Germans! And it was Germans who did what you are looking at."

As a ripple of disquiet and anger swept through the ranks of his men at the unexpected refusal to open the city gates to them, Corbulo bit his lip as he patiently peered up at the soldiers upon the wall. For a moment he did not speak. Then at last he raised his hand as if greeting an old friend.

"Alright I promise you that I shall speak only the truth," he called out. "Yes, my men are Salian Franks, Batavians. We are the equites foederati Germanica. Newly raised to restore order across the empire. We serve the emperor Gallienus and he has sent us here to help you. I repeat, we come as friends and allies. Now you need to let us into the city."

"The equites foederati Germanica! Never heard of them," came the defiant reply. "You are lying. Now fuck off before I put an arrow in your chest!"

"We saw your pontoon bridge from the hill over there," Corbulo called out refusing to move and gesturing to the high ground to the south. "Does it still extend all the way across the river? I need to use your bridge to transport my men to the northern bank of the river and as you know there is no other bridge like yours for hundreds of miles."

But from atop of the city walls there was no reply and as the silence lengthened the tension started to grow. Quickly Corbulo's bodyguards began to move in closer to protect their leader with their shields.

"We need to move you back Sir," an anxious looking officer said hurriedly turning to Corbulo, "at least out of missile range from the walls. I don't think they are bluffing. You are exposed if we stay here Sir."

"No, not yet, we stay put. I need to hear what they have to say," Corbulo snapped shaking his head and refusing to move.

"No!" came the sudden sour and pissed-off sounding reply from the battlements. "We dismantled part of the bridge earlier this year to stop the Quadi from using it. We have been under a loose siege for months now. The enemy come and go. First the fucking barbarians and then your lot battling with Ingenuus and then Regalian and then the Quadi returned once more. There is no peace here. So, we have had enough of strangers and usurpers claiming to be the one and only emperor! Claiming they are here to protect us. They all lie! No one gives a shit about us. This fighting has destroyed the amber trade!"

"Who are you?" Corbulo shouted back, his eyes fixed upon the battlements. "Who am I negotiating with? I told you who we are. So, who are you?"

Once again, the walls remained silent. Then at last the lone voice cried out, the man unable to hide his pride.

"We are the marines from the naval HQ of the Pannonian Fleet or what is left of them. We and a few of the townsfolk have been defending our city for months now. On our own! Against everyone who thought they would have a go. We do not need any imperial help. We are doing just fine. Gallienus was only interested in crushing the usurpers. He has done nothing to drive back the Quadi and the Vandals. The emperor has abandoned us!"

"No Gallienus has not abandoned you!" Corbulo shouted back. "He has sent me and my men to your relief, and you are not fine. We are here to help drive the barbarians back across the river, but I really need to use your bridge, so you need to let us into the city. I promise you that my men will not take to looting once we are inside. We are friends! You have my word as an imperial prefect!"

"We do not need your help!" came the sullen answer from high up on the walls. "We are doing just fine."

"Yes, you do," Corbulo retorted. "You need all the fucking help you can get. If the Quadi king Hildimer and his army turn their attention to you - you will not be able to hold him off for long. You know this to be true. So, open your gates and let me do my job. We are wasting time."

Corbulo's words however were met with silence. Peering up at the battlements he tried to see what was going on.

"There is something else," the voice cried out again. "If we agree to let you into the city then we want something from you in return."

"Name it," Corbulo shouted back.

"Some food would be nice," the voice shouted. "Some fresh supplies. We are all hungry here, but we will settle for getting paid. We haven't been paid our wages as marines for months now. So, pay us - prefect - or else fuck off to where you came from!"

"How many of you are there?" Corbulo called out but his question was met with a burst of derisive laughter.

"Oh, I bet you would like to know that wouldn't you. So that you can judge how strong we really are. No! First you pay us our wages. Five months' worth and a bonus for holding out even after the emperor abandoned us. That is fair. We deserve that - prefect."

Staring up at the marines on top of the wall Corbulo remained silent.

"How many ships have you still got?" he called out at last. "Carnuntum is the HQ of the Pannonian Fleet so surely you must still have some left."

"Three galleys will float," came back the sullen reply. "The rest of the fleet has been burned or vanished downstream during the rebellions. The ships are down in the harbour."

"Alright," Corbulo cried out sounding encouraged. "So, say if I were to agree to pay you your salaries. Then you will do something for me in return. Like I said I need to use your bridge to cross to the barbarian side, but I could also use your support and your ships. I need your help. The marines that I knew when I was posted to the Rhine were first class. They were loyal men. So, what do you say marines. Will you help me drive back these barbarian scumbags from your city? Will you help me free the land from this scourge?"

From the walls there was no immediate reply as if his interlocutor was consulting with his comrades.

"Pay us - prefect," the reply came at last, "pay us our salaries and our bonus and we will give you what support we can."

Looking pleased Corbulo quickly turned to Tobias the accountant who was sitting on his horse nearby observing the exchange with growing horror. The man's face suddenly pale as he realised what was about to happen. His whole expression screaming no.

“Tobias,” Corbulo called out lowering his voice so that the men up on the wall would not be able to hear him. “Do we have the funds to pay these men? If so, I am going to need you to hand them over.”

“Funds!” Tobias exclaimed turning to stare at Corbulo in growing panic. “We have the money but the fiscus has assigned these reserve funds to be used strictly for our own needs. For the success of this campaign. We can’t just pay off some random men who may or may not be who they say they are. That would be an insane thing to do, and I cannot agree,” the accountant added shaking his head. “Don’t ask me to hand over our reserve funds. The answer is no.”

“I need you to hand over the reserve funds right away,” Corbulo said patiently gazing back at the accountant. “The money is needed right now. If we don’t pay, they will never let us into Carnuntum and I could really use their support too. They have warships.”

“No!” Tobias called out in protest, his cheeks colouring. “I am the guardian of Rome’s fiscal rules. I will not yield. Find another way to cross the bloody river. Find some other ships. I am not surrendering our fiscal reserves to a bunch of thieves. No way. This is madness!”

“You want me to kill him now or later,” Crastus said calmly turning to Corbulo. “Sounds like he is disobeying a direct order Sir.”

“I report directly to general Aureolus,” Tobias cried out rounding on Crastus. “I don’t take orders from you. I am a civilian and I am employed by the fiscus, and the rules are clear. I oversee all financial matters in this unit, and I say no!”

"Fuck the rules," Crastus said gleefully urging his horse towards Tobias, the big man looking murderous. "You are with us now. And out here with us your shitty civilian rules mean nothing."

"Listen," Corbulo said sharply as he studied the accountant. "I understand your reluctance to part with the funds but today they are needed. So here is what we are going to do. You Tobias will agree and hand over our reserve funds at once and you will make no record of this in your ledgers. In return I shall promise you that when we get the opportunity, we shall replenish our coffers with loot that we take from the enemy. And once we have done so no one will be wiser as to what we have spent the money on."

Staring at Corbulo Tobias tried to speak but then hesitated before at last licking his lips. His cheeks burning with indignation.

"But I would know," the accountant exclaimed mustering a last-ditch defence. "It would be most improper. We must stick by the rules. Don't you see. The rules exist for a reason. To protect us from financial decline. And this is exactly how decline sets in - it starts with the abandonment of the rules one little innocent step at a time. And if we start now by bending the rules ever so slightly it will lead to more rule breaking later and before we know it, we will discover that we have abandoned every prudent fiscal rule that we have got. And then our financial credibility will be in tatters and chaos will follow."

"Maybe you are right," Corbulo said as a little smile crept onto his lips. "But if we don't get into Carnuntum and across that bridge my plan is going to fail, and good men will die for nothing. And I cannot allow that to happen. So today we are going to bend the rules ever so slightly. I don't care what you record in your ledgers if the accounts match in the end. And no one would need to know except us. Do this and Crastus here will even stop threatening to kill you. Sounds like everyone will end up with something. Maybe he and you will even become friends."

Gazing at Crastus Tobias appeared to squirm. Then taking a deep unhappy breath, he reluctantly nodded.

"Fine," the accountant whined, "but I want it noted that my agreement was made under strong protest. My purpose is to protect the rules! This is what I am here for, and you are stopping me from doing my job!"

Chapter Eleven - With the Marines

It was evening as the troops from the equites foederati Germanica began to pass through the gates and into the city of Carnuntum. The silent, sombre faced soldiers slowly filing into the town in a long column. The soldiers walking their horses, their shields and spears slung across their backs, their marching packs placed across their saddles. Their helmets adorned with two Batavian feathers. The men's iron studded boots and horses' hooves rasping and clattering across the paving stones as the column headed towards the forum, the central square. Next came the supply wagons, trundling into the settlement. The teams of oxen bellowing as they pulled the carts along. The arrival of the Salian Franks and Batavians was being closely watched by parties of armed marines and a crowd of anxious, nervous looking civilians. The Roman inhabitants and defenders of the city lining the street on both sides or peering at the procession from windows and doorways. Few people speaking. Many of the children looked hungry and malnourished while the pong of unwashed bodies and sewage hung over the city like an invisible and stifling cloak.

Leading his men into Carnuntum Corbulo at last came to a halt at the entrance to the forum and as he did so he took a deep breath. Packed into the open central space, the heart of the Roman city, which should in normal times have been filled with traders and market stalls, was a makeshift tent city. The refugees having taken over the entire market square. The people camped out in the open or huddling under little temporary shelters and around small campfires. Their worldly belongings gathered around them. And as Corbulo surveyed the miserable scene the refugees turned to stare at the newcomers in turn. The fear and anxiety among the populace palpable. A few dogs barking accusingly at the soldiers.

“There are more refugees camped down by the harbour,” Mattis the centurion in command of the city garrison called out as he came hurrying over accompanied by a few of his marines. “I’m afraid your men Corbulo will have to camp out in the streets tonight. We just don’t have the space to accommodate you all, but I shall entertain you and your officers myself tonight. I believe we still have some casks of beer left,” Mattis added with a weary grin. “I am sorry that we cannot do more than that for you, but supplies are really scarce and as you can see the city is swamped with refugees from the countryside.”

Turning to the small, stocky centurion with closely cropped hair, a round face and green snake tattoos that disappeared up his brawny arms, Corbulo quickly reached out to grasp the officer’s proffered hand, nodding politely. The two commanders shaking hands in a very public manner as if to show to everyone watching that all was well between them. That the newcomers were friends.

Mattis was in his forties and had introduced himself earlier at the meeting, where the marines had been paid their wages, as the senior surviving officer of the Pannonian fleet, the Classis Pannonica. The months long fighting and the two failed rebellions against Gallienus had wiped out the senior military and provincial civilian authority he had explained together with half the marines of the Pannonian fleet and so he Mattis had assumed command of the city. Rallying the badly diminished marine garrison and inspiring and cajoling them into fending off the enemy attacks and continuing to hold the city for Rome. The centurion’s selfless and unsung efforts to do what he could to defend Carnuntum and its people convincing Corbulo that he could do business with Mattis.

“How many refugees?” Corbulo asked surveying the scene.

“Two thousand so far,” Mattis sniffed as he turned to gaze at the refugees camped out in the forum with a resigned look. “We do what we can but there is not enough food. I have ordered rationing but it's hard to enforce. People hide what they have got and then complain that they do not have enough. There is a lot of stealing. Some violence. The people are on edge. It won’t take much to panic them. My marines maintain order as best as we can, but we are running out of everything including hope. A few more weeks and we will all be starving and then,” Mattis continued a sombre, distant look appearing in his eyes, “I am going to have to tell everyone that they must leave the city. And out there,” Mattis added gesturing at the country beyond the walls, “these people will not stand a chance against those roving bands of raiders, and they know it. They are going to be massacred.”

“Plague? Has there been an outbreak in the city or among the refugees?”

“No thank the gods,” Mattis said quickly shaking his head with relief. “We have not seen any of that but there is an outbreak of plague reported in the camps along the Danube to the east. They say that the barbarian raiders brought the plague with them when they crossed the river. It has come from the east.”

“Good. We cannot share any of the supplies that we have brought with us,” Corbulo said coolly. “I have only enough for my own men. But what I can do is offer you hope centurion. There are now two Roman battle-groups, cavalry, operating along this section of the frontier. Together we are going to restore order and destroy the barbarian threat. Now that we have arrived your situation and that of this city is going to improve.”

“I am glad to hear it,” Mattis replied in a tight voice. For a moment longer Mattis gazed at the mass of miserable humanity camped out across the forum. Then he turned to Corbulo.

“My apologies Sir,” Mattis said lowering his voice. “About what happened outside our gates. The murdered civilians that you saw. It happened a few days ago. The refugees were caught by raiders. I eh, I wanted to let them into the city. They could have made it,” Mattis added with a pained look, “but my men and the townsfolk, they would not let me open the gates. They said that we could not take any more refugees. That we did not have the food. Others said that there would be spies among the refugees. So, we kept our gates shut and watched them being slaughtered. We fucked up. Not our finest hour Sir.”

Studying Mattis, Corbulo remained silent, his expression giving nothing away as to what he was thinking. Then quickly he turned to Crastus, switching to German. “Set up our command post beside the main gate and then see to it that the men are billeted as best as you can. And post a strong force to guard our supply wagons. Tell the men to be alert. I do not want the townsfolk trying to steal our food. Prince Gummar. Harald. Atlas. With me. Let’s take a walk, centurion, “Corbulo said switching back to Latin and gesturing for Mattis to lead the way. “I want to see the state of your defences, starting with your walls.”

“This way then,” Mattis replied as Corbulo accompanied by his officers and bodyguards left their horses behind in Crastus’s care and started to follow the marine commander through the crowds of refugees.

Pushing on through the forum, the refugees respectfully moving out of the way, Mattis his head down, headed for a section of the city walls that faced the Danube. And as the party of Roman officers emerged up onto the battlements of the massive walls, Corbulo turned to look out across the city, taking in the fine view of the rectangular inner city. The straight streets and neat city blocks. The forum, the baths complex and temples with their brick walls, majestic white columns and sloping red tiled rooves. Further along the walkway that ran along the walls, a picket of armed civilians were eyeing him in curious silence. The men and boys were armed with a motley assortment of knives, axes and spears. None of them possessing any form of body armour or shields.

"My men and I will not be staying with you for long," Corbulo said as Mattis joined him, the two officers gazing out across the city from their vantage point. "I need to cross the river using your pontoon bridge as soon as I can. But before we leave," Corbulo said glancing at the marine officer, "I need to reassure myself that Carnuntum will hold if you are attacked again. It is vital that the city holds out and that your men secure my line of retreat. So, can you give me an assessment on the security situation, centurion? Starting with a strength report."

"I have three hundred and twelve marines left from the original naval garrison," Mattis replied sounding tired, "plus eighty trained rowers. That is all that is left of the Pannonian fleet. Then there are about thousand-armed townsfolk, civilians Sir. Most of them are however untrained in warfare. They are not soldiers. They lack training, equipment, discipline and leadership. They have no idea how to fight in close quarters combat and their morale is low. The only reason that we have survived so far is because of our walls," Mattis continued, "which are in a good condition. We are however short of everything. My marines are well trained and equipped Sir but the armed civilians as you can see have barely anything. If the enemy were able to get over our walls in large numbers it would all be over very quickly and then," Mattis added his face revealing a glimpse of the strain he'd been under, "the civilians will panic and there will be a massacre."

"Cometh the hour, cometh the man, centurion," Corbulo gazing out at the city. "Will you be able to hold the city for a little longer?"

"Yes, for a few more weeks Sir," Mattis replied. "But once we run out of food it will be over. When that moment comes, I am going to move the people out of the city, but I and my marines are going to remain here. This is not only our base Sir, but it is also our home, and this is where we should die. At our posts. Faithful to our vow. Faithful to the very end."

For a moment Corbulo said nothing.

"And the Quadi and their Vandal allies, where are they?"

"Out there," Mattis said gesturing at the rolling and forested countryside beyond the city suburbs to the south. "They do not, thank the gods, have the siege equipment to get over our walls so they leave us alone. The enemy appear now and then just to let us know they are still here but there has been no serious assault for weeks now. There used to be fifty thousand people living here in this city at one point," Mattis added in a resigned sounding voice as he turned to look around. "But now we are down to just a fifth of that number. If we survive this, it's going to take many years before we recover from this disaster."

"And the legionary base," Corbulo said pointing in the direction of the fortress to the east. "Do they not help you?"

"The Fourteenth!" Mattis exclaimed contemptuously. "Don't make me laugh Sir. There are less than a thousand of them left and they do fuck all to help us. All they do is stay inside their base. They claim that Gallienus has ordered them to hold their fortress and that is what all they are going to do. It's these rebellions Sir, first Ingenuus and then Regalian. It fucked the Fourteenth up. Their discipline and self-respect are shattered, and their leadership is gone. They are not what they used to be. You cannot rely on them Sir. They will do nothing but defend their base and loot the surrounding country for supplies. And maybe it is best," Mattis added sounding resigned, "that they remain inside their base for we do not want them coming here and taking what little we have got left."

Pausing Mattis quickly glanced at Corbulo, his cheeks colouring with sudden embarrassment. "When Ingenuus was first proclaimed emperor by the Fourteenth Sir," the marine centurion said carefully clearing his throat, "none of us within the Pannonian fleet had a choice but to join in the rebellion. And after Ingenuus we all supported Regalian. It's not that we had any great love for these commanders or believed that they would succeed and in hindsight it was a mistake to support them but at the time both our generals promised us that they would defeat the barbarian raids when all emperor Gallienus could promise was empty meaningless words. This city is our home, and an emperor ought to be able to protect it Sir. Or else what good are they to us."

"You are right," Corbulo said solemnly, "an emperor ought to be able to defend his people. Which is why Gallienus has sent me here. The rebellions have been crushed, centurion. It is time to move on. I am not here to seek revenge for what has happened. My job is to defeat the barbarians."

Turning around to gaze out across the Danube to the north, Corbulo's eyes settled upon the pontoon bridge and for a moment he peered at the gaping hole in the line of buttressed boats that extended out into the river.

“You said you dismantled your bridge,” Corbulo said staring at the pontoon. “Did you keep the boats?”

“We did Sir,” Mattis replied gesturing at the pontoon bridge out on the water. “The bridge Sir is the start of the amber road which leads from here all the way to the shores of the northern sea where the amber comes from. The amber trade and our bridge are what made our city wealthy. In more peaceful times we would get a lot of trade and merchants passing through. But when the Quadi raids started to grow in intensity we decided to dismantle the bridge for the security of the city. The amber trade too had stopped by then because of the threats of attack and the army rebellions. The boats are valuable, so we kept them. They are down in the river harbour but during the fighting we lost all the engineers who know how to put the damn bridge back together again.”

“That will not be a problem,” Corbulo said quickly. “I have engineers among my command who can fix the bridge. If your men can show us where your boats are and your warships, we will set about repairing the bridge at once. Like I said I need to cross the river as soon as possible.”

“They are down in the harbour, follow me Sir. I will show you,” Mattis said gesturing for Corbulo to follow him.

Striding through the open gate in the perimeter wall that surrounded Carnuntum’s naval harbour Corbulo quickly turned to look around at the impressive stone marine barracks that lined the waterfront and the wooden jetties that poked out into the Danube. The small group of Roman officers and bodyguards taking in the purpose-built bays where the great warships and galleys of the Classis Pannonica once used to have their births. Most of the moorings however were empty, the still water filled instead with floating debris and garbage.

While the waterfront was packed with refugees camped out in the open with all their belongings. The smell of many unwashed bodies lingering. The people looking up and staring at the Roman soldiers as the party passed on by and made their way along the quay. At last arriving at a quieter stretch of the river Mattis gestured at a group of small fishing boats tethered to the quay by sturdy ropes.

"Here they are," the centurion said. "The boats we took from the bridge. Your men will need to get them out into the river without losing them to the current and then successfully attach them to the bridge. I warn you it will not be easy. The current is strong. I should know. I have had to row upstream against it for longer than I care to remember."

"Harald," Corbulo said quickly turning to him. "I want you supervising. Get our best engineers onto this right away. How long do you think you will need to repair the bridge?"

"Well, I am going to need building materials, wooden planking, iron nails, rope and some sturdy poles to anchor the boats in the riverbed," Harald said turning to inspect the tethered boats with a critical eye before shifting his gaze to the river and the gap in the existing section of the pontoon bridge. "And I am going to need some civilian labour to help. If this is all forthcoming," for a moment Harald paused as he thought it through, "tomorrow at sunset," he replied at last. "I should be able to repair the bridge by then."

"We kept the original building materials when we dismantled this section of the bridge," Mattis said helpfully. "And I will round up a party of labourers who can help you. Some men too who know the river."

"Good. Get it done," Corbulo said laying a hand on Harald's shoulder. "Get it repaired, and we will cross the river tomorrow night under cover of darkness."

Leaving Harald behind with the pontoon boats Corbulo started to move on down the quay. His gaze settling on the solitary watch tower that guarded the start of the pontoon bridge. The entrance to the bridge was barricaded and fortified with a hastily erected dry-stone wall guarded by two marines.

"I need that wall removed at once," Corbulo called out pointing at the defences.

"I will see to that," Mattis replied hurriedly as he kept pace.

Moving on Corbulo at last came to a halt as his gaze swept across the harbour and as he did, he suddenly frowned.

"I thought you said that you still had three warships," Corbulo said sharply. "But I can see only one in the harbour. Where are the others?"

"Ah," Mattis replied with a sudden sheepish look. "I said that we had three warships that would float. Not three warships that were fully operational. The other two are over there," the centurion said gesturing at two naval galleys still attached to their moorings but sitting half sunk in the river. Their bows submerged in the Danube. The ships abandoned.

"So, you actually have only one warship that is capable of action," Corbulo said sounding annoyed as he rounded on Mattis.

"That's right Sir," Mattis said breezily, gesturing towards the sole remaining naval galley that was sitting in its bay. "That is the Nemesis Sir and what a beauty she is. Fully manned she can take sixty rowers and a company of eighty marines. See that deck artillery Sir. We can lay down a devastating barrage on the shore from the middle of the river. The Nemesis is a beast Sir. We can even set the whole river on fire if we had enough supplies of Naphtha."

"Great, that's just fucking great!" Corbulo snapped as he stared unhappily at the solitary warship tied to its moorings. "One warship. Not three!"

"I am sorry Sir," Mattis replied sounding apologetic. "The rest of the Pannonian fleet was lost in the fighting or just vanished downstream. We do not know what has become of some of our ships or their crews. It's a mess I know. But the Nemesis is a good ship Sir. She was my command, and she has never let me down or been bested when we were on patrol out on the river. She scares the shit out of the barbarians. They have nothing that can compare. They have no answer. What do you want to do with her?"

For a moment Corbulo said nothing as he took in the long narrow hull of the naval galley with her rows of oar ports, the open deck and the central mast with its furled sail, the deck artillery, scorpion bolt throwers, harpoons and ballistae catapults and finally the gracefully curving prow that rose up out of the water and ended in a large wooden carving of the god of vengeance - Nemesis.

"You said that she has never been bested before," Corbulo said turning to look at Mattis with a displeased look. "That the barbarians fear our ships. Do you have the crew to fully man her?"

"I have the trained rowers Sir," Mattis said quickly, "but not the marines to man her. A warship like that can take eighty marines and I just can't afford to spare that sort of numbers from the city garrison. My men are needed to defend Carnuntum Sir. So, we can row the Nemesis up and downstream, but she will have no marines with which to fight."

Studying the warship Corbulo paused, his mind working. Then coming to a decision, he turned to Mattis. "Nemesis, it's a good name," Corbulo said quietly, his earlier disappointment melting away. "Good for what is coming. I want you to get her ready for action. Gather your rowers and assign the best of them to the ship. The Nemesis is going to help us defeat the Quadi," Corbulo added. "And as for the marine contingent. I am going to leave one of my officers and a few of my men behind with you. My man will take command of the Nemesis and he and his soldiers will serve as marines. I can use the ship to maintain contact with my colleague Probus who will be operating along the southern shore. I want her ready for action the moment we have crossed to the northern bank."

***

The baths complex of Carnuntum had seen better days Corbulo thought as he sat on the stool in the tepidarium, the warm room, a mug of frothy beer in hand, gazing at the peeling light blue wall and ceiling paint that depicted fish swimming in the ocean. His helmet and sheathed spatha sword were carefully placed on the tiled floor beside him. Not only was the paint peeling from the walls and ceiling, but the walls were spoiled by a mass of rude graffiti while the water in the bath was cold, and the underfloor heating was not working. Nor did it look like the baths had been cleaned for ages. To make matters worse the finely crafted and colourful mosaic floors around him were missing stones and there appeared to have been an attempt to chip away at the faces of some of the depicted people as if the images were no longer fashionable.

Gathered around the edge of the large basin of greenish water in the centre of the hall, sitting on their three-legged stools, Harald, prince Gummar, Tobias and Atlas were listening to Mattis as the centurion recounted the events of the last few months in a sombre voice. The Roman officers sipping beer from their mugs and now and then making a comment or reaching out to dip their pieces of bread in a bowl of vinegar. The group were alone in the grand deserted bath hall while Corbulo's bodyguards waited outside in the frigidarium, the cold room. The night air seeping into the room from holes in the roof.

"To the west by contrast, we are more fortunate," Mattis continued," that the Alemanni remain quiet after Gallienus defeated them and that the Marcomanni are riven by civil war. It is a great relief to the communities over in that direction but still none of the frontier garrisons are willing to help us. These days everyone just cares about defending their own settlements. The Marcomanni civil war however is really heating up. A man named Crocus has raised a rebellion against king Attalus. It is the usual struggle for power among the warrior elite who rule these tribes, but it could spell trouble for us too. The dispute seems to revolve around the peace treaty that Gallienus concluded with king Attalus. The king wishes to honour the treaty while his rival Crocus wishes to renew the war with us. The Marcomanni lands are to the north-west," Mattis concluded fixing Corbulo with an earnest look, "so you should not encounter them, but I thought I should warn you none the less."

With the conversation petering out Corbulo stirred.

"The land to the north of the Danube," Corbulo said turning to Mattis, "the homelands of the Quadi. I am not familiar with the country in which I am going to operate so I am going to need scouts. Men who know the land and its people. Men who will be able to act as guides to my troops. I was hoping you would be able to help me with that. Are there men among the city garrison who know the lands to the north. Who are willing to act as scouts? If so, I need them, and we will pay."

"Yes," Mattis replied with a nod, "there are such men within the city. The amber road provides us with many local contacts and knowledge of the Quadi and the barbarian lands beyond. In the past we have had good relations with the Quadi. That was before emperor Valerian got himself captured in the East and the world went to shit. I can find a group of such men and if you pay them, they will come." Then Mattis hesitated and Corbulo saw that something else seemed to be weighing upon the centurion's mind. "But to what end Sir?" Mattis asked turning to him with a slight air of puzzlement. "You have not told me what you intend to do once you cross the river. If I recruit these guides for you, they will want to know what they are going to be used for and how long they are going to be away. It will no doubt be dangerous work. They have families here in Carnuntum and they will not want to be away from their loved ones for an extended length of time. Especially now. So, if I may ask - what do you intend to do once you cross the river Sir?"

Corbulo was about to reply when there was a sudden commotion from the direction of the frigidarium. Turning his head he frowned as he heard raised Roman voices crying out in alarm. Moments later a woman burst into the grand bath hall, clad in a stola dress. Hurrying towards the group of Roman officers relaxing by the pool she was moving swiftly on her bare feet with Corbulo's bodyguards in hot pursuit. The soldiers rushing into the tepidarium as they sought to catch the impudent intruder, their hobnailed boots clattering across the fine mosaic floor. Their hands resting upon the pommel of their swords.

"Mattis!" the woman called out sounding harassed as she hastened up to the centurion, "will you please tell these soldiers who I am and that they should allow me to pass."

Hastily scrambling to his feet from his stool as he caught sight of the woman, Mattis hesitated as the bodyguards caught up with the woman and seized her. Then quickly Mattis turned to Corbulo.

"It's alright. I know her," Mattis said hurriedly. "She is no threat. Your men can let her go. Let her speak."

Quickly shifting his gaze from Mattis to the woman Corbulo hesitated. The lady was in her thirties, quite pretty and certainly high-born judging from her attitude, clothing and appearance. For a moment no one spoke, his bodyguards looking at him with inquiring looks as they held onto the woman. Then at last Corbulo gestured to his men to let the women go free.

"What do you want Sulpicia?" Mattis said turning to the elegant woman with a resigned look as she broke free from the soldiers and came towards him. "The hour is late, and I have important guests. Can it not wait?"

Coming up to the centurion the woman lightly ran her fingers across Mattis's shoulders in an affectionate gesture, before with one hand resting upon his shoulder, she turned towards Corbulo. The woman and Mattis giving the impression that they knew each other with and without clothes on.

"I heard that you were entertaining Gallienus's friends my dear Mattis," the woman said speaking in a posh accent of the higher social classes. "The city is talking of nothing else but their arrival. Which is why I have come to see these men for myself. I would like to speak to the prefect here as he and his men now seem to control Carnuntum."

"And you are?" Corbulo said sharply, meeting the woman's gaze.

"Forgive my unexpected and rather rude intrusion, prefect," the woman said her expression softening, her eyes gleaming in the light cast by the oil lamps that hung from the ceiling of the hall. Her voice calm and composed. Businesslike. "My name is Sulpicia Dryantilla and I am the wife of Regalian, the late governor of the province of Pannonia Superior."

"You are Regalian's wife!" Corbulo responded looking surprised. "The usurper!"

"I am Regalian's widow," Sulpicia replied inclining her head in a graceful and respectful manner. "If you were expecting someone older, I am afraid that I must disappoint you, prefect. My husband was twenty years my senior. Here," she said fishing for something in the pocket of her inner tunic and calmly handing Corbulo a single Roman coin. "He even made me Augusta, empress, when he rebelled against Gallienus. My husband had coins struck here at our mint in Carnuntum that bore the image of both our heads. We were to be joint rulers of the empire. There. See. That is my likeness on the coin."

Staring at the head on the poor-quality coin Corbulo remained silent. Then quickly he looked up at Sulpicia, frowning.

"Unfortunately, the mint was looted months ago," Sulpicia said with a polite smile. "In case you were thinking of inspecting it yourself. All the gold and silver that was once stored in there is long gone. Carnuntum and the province of Pannonia Superior are broke."

For a moment Sulpicia paused to study Corbulo.

“Let us get this out of the way right now shall we. You are Gallienus’s man,” Sulpicia continued, “and I know that the emperor sent you here to Carnuntum to restore order which makes this all rather awkward as you will no doubt be aware that Gallienus and my late husband had a falling out. They had a disagreement about who should rule the empire which got out of hand. But such matters are in the past now. My husband is dead and Gallienus still rules. I do not want any more trouble. There has been enough of that already. It is time to bury the pain from that time and move on with our lives.”

“A falling out, a disagreement,” Corbulo exclaimed. “Is that what you call rebellion. Your husband was a usurper. He was proclaimed emperor by rebellious troops. Your husband wanted to challenge Gallienus for the imperial crown! You have got some nerve coming here lady!”

“Corbulo,” Mattis interrupted speaking in a gentle voice. “I know Sulpicia. She means it when she says she does not want any more trouble. Regalian is dead. The rebellion has been crushed. No one here in Carnuntum wants a repeat of what has happened. Instead, she is right. We must look to the future. We must rebuild and restore order along the frontier. You said yourself that now that you are here things will start to improve.”

“Prefect,” Sulpicia said eyeing Corbulo solemnly. “I am not here to plead my case or excuse what has happened. What my husband did was wrong, I accept that. Gallienus is the one and only emperor and I have already sworn my allegiance to him. If you are not already aware of the circumstances of my husband’s death you should know that he was murdered by a band of Roxolani raiders who managed to slip through our defences and get to him. Assassins! They killed him within these very walls when he was bathing. When he was supposed to be safe. But I have already dealt with the men who murdered my husband. The barbarians are dead. I have had my revenge; blood has been satisfied with blood."

"So why are you here?" Corbulo said guardedly, shifting his gaze from Mattis to Sulpicia. "What do you want?"

"I have come to offer you my services, prefect," Sulpicia replied coolly raising her head. "I wish to help you in the task that has brought you and your men here to Carnuntum. To rid our province of the Quadi. To restore order. That is why you are here are you not?"

"You wish to help me?" Corbulo said raising his eyebrows with a dubious look. "Why?"

Quickly Sulpicia exchanged a look with Mattis, her hand still resting on the centurion's shoulder.

"You ask why," Sulpicia said turning to Corbulo with a sombre look. "I come from a prestigious senatorial family, prefect. I am of senatorial rank. My father served with distinction under Caracalla and when I came of age my family arranged my marriage to Regalian. My husband was not a bad man, prefect. He was trying to do right for his people, to exercise his responsibility for the safety of the province. He made me Augusta, empress as you can see from the coin I gave you. But now my husband is dead, my family's name is ruined and our estates in Italy have been seized by imperial decree, and I am left with the task of trying to restore the reputation and status of my family. That is why I offer you my services, prefect. As a gesture of good will and reconciliation. So that emperor Gallienus will have cause to listen to my petition. For I have nothing left," Sulpicia said extending her arms in a sudden hopeless gesture. "I must find a way in which to restore my family's reputation and fortune. I owe that much to the rest of my family who have suffered because of me."

Staring at the woman Corbulo's frown deepened.

"Say I agree to this," Corbulo said at last. "Say I agree to accept your offer of help. How exactly can you be of use to me?"

"You are planning to cross the Danube are you not," Sulpicia exclaimed jutting out her chin as the Roman officers stared at her in silence. "To take the war into the Quadi's homelands. To force the Quadi king Hildimer to sue for peace? Is that not why you have come to Carnuntum. Well, I can help you achieve your objective. For I know where king Hildimer hides his treasure. I know his secret hideout. I can take you to his lair and once you have captured his wealth you can use it to buy peace from the king and end these raids."

Studying the woman Corbulo hesitated, looking sceptical.

"And how would the wife of the Roman provincial governor know where the barbarian king keeps his gold?" Corbulo exclaimed.

"The wife knows," Sulpicia shot back, "because before the rebellions I met the king and spent time with him and his entourage - beyond the Danube. For a while I was a hostage of king Hildimer," Sulpicia added with a smile. "A willing hostage - part of an exchange of hostages that was arranged between my husband and the barbarian king, to guarantee peace between Rome and the Quadi. And while I was there in his home, I discovered the king's secret."

"Is this true?" Corbulo said turning to Mattis.

"It is true," Mattis replied. "Governor Regalian and king Hildimer came to an agreement before the rebellions. Both wanted peace at the time. So, there was an exchange of hostages to guarantee this peace and Sulpicia volunteered to go. But the deal ended when emperor Valerian got himself captured at Edessa and our weakness became obvious to all."

"The king's personal wealth is substantial, prefect but it is also his weakness," Sulpicia said as a little excited colour shot into her cheeks. "Hildimer has been busy amassing quite a fortune over the years which he uses it to hold onto power and see off his rivals. Without his wealth his patronage and power however would be much diminished. He would be weakened. The Quadi, like all the barbarians are a very independent minded and egalitarian people who choose their leaders based on merit and the king is only one of several leading men in their society. There are others who wish to take his place. His position is never secure for he must constantly prove that he has the right to lead. Which is why he needs his wealth to prop up his position among his fellow tribesmen."

Pausing, Sulpicia's eyes gleamed with mounting excitement. "I know the King," she continued. "Steal his gold and he will panic. He will prefer making peace with us to losing his status among his countrymen. So, there lies your opportunity, prefect. Steal his money and use it to buy peace from the King. Steal his gold and the king will fold like a pack of cards! And I," Sulpicia said clapping her hands together, "can take you to where the king has hidden his wealth!"

"So why have you not done so already?" Corbulo replied. "If you know where this treasure is hidden then why have you not stolen it yourself?"

"It is not so easy, prefect," Sulpicia said smiling sweetly, "the place where the king hides his gold is guarded. You need a strong military force to seize it and until today I lacked such a force. But now," she added, "with your arrival and your help, prefect, such an endeavour becomes possible."

Hesitating Corbulo eyed Sulpicia with an uncertain look.

“Prince Gummar,” Corbulo said at last switching to German as he glanced at his deputy, “Your thoughts?”

Sitting on his stool at the edge of the pool of greenish water Gummar was watching Sulpicia and Mattis with an appraising look.

“You wish for my opinion Sir. She has courage. She and the centurion are fucking each other,” Gummar said speaking German in his thick Frankish accent. “And she has lost everything. This I believe. I also believe her when she says that she wishes for reconciliation with Gallienus and I believe her when she says that she knows where we can find the king’s treasure. But she is a fool if she thinks that the emperor will return her Italian estates to her family. Gallienus told me that he will not be lenient with the families of usurpers. He cannot afford to show mercy, for that will be interpreted as weakness. So sure, give her a chance to prove her worth and use her to get to that gold, but she is not going to get what she wants. She is going to be disappointed, and she doesn't realise that she is just a tool. But that is her problem. I say that we accept her offer of help."

“I agree,” Harald said quickly. “Let's use her. If what she says is true, then we could recover a fortune. But fuck using that wealth to buy peace. No one buys peace. Peace is maintained by wielding a big stick. You promised the men Sir that you would make them rich. This could be how we do it. Take that wealth for ourselves I say. This would do wonders for morale.”

Mulling it over Corbulo hesitated again.

"It would be cruel to lie to her Sir," Atlas said gently speaking in German. "It would be cruel to let her think this is going to help her cause when we know it will not. Maybe we should be honest with her instead."

Glancing across at Atlas Corbulo said nothing, his mind working. Then at last he took a deep breath.

“I need local guides and scouts for when we cross the river,” he said switching back to Latin and turning to address Mattis. “At least a score. Men who I can trust and who are familiar with the Quadi and who have a good knowledge of the country beyond the river.”

Then to Sulpicia. “If you as a civilian are willing to serve under my command and take us to where king Hildimer hides his treasure then in return I shall include your contribution to our campaign in my report to my superiors and to emperor Gallienus. I cannot promise you that the emperor will grant you a full reconciliation, but I promise that I will make a case for you.”

“Wonderful!” Sulpicia said looking pleased, clapping her hands together. “Thank you, prefect.”

Then Corbulo turned to Atlas, who was watching Sulpicia with a mixture of sadness and growing interest.

“Atlas,” Corbulo said coolly switching once again to German. “I do believe that we have found your new apprentice at last. I am assigning her to your care. Stay close to her and learn what you can from her. I want to know everything that she knows about our enemy.”

Chapter Twelve - In the Land of the Quadi

Night had come and so had the rain as the Roman cavalry began to cross the Danube. Clad in their poncho's, Corbulo watched his troops moving on by, the Salian Franks and Batavians quietly leading their horses on foot across the narrow pontoon bridge in a long, single file. The driving rain was lashing the river and the bridge, muffling the clatter and stamp of the beasts' hooves across the wooden deck. While the current tugged at the tenuous rows of boats making them sway and groan. The bridge was illuminated by a series of flickering torches that stretched away into the darkness, creating a tenuous and eerie path across the wide river. The fleeting moonlight dancing across the dark, rain-swept waters. The soldiers had slung their shields across their backs and the men were gripping their spears. Their poncho hoods drawn down over their heads concealing their faces and helmets, their bad weather cloaks glistening with streaming water while their horses and mules were laden with their packs and equipment. The men concentrating on maintaining their footing on the slippery deck.

"Was it really necessary Sir," Gummar said at last, speaking in German as he stood beside Corbulo observing the troops, the tall Frankish prince a head taller than his commanding officer. "To leave Crastus and the Moor with a company of my men behind here at Carnuntum? I understand that you wish to use the galley to keep in contact with Probus Sir, hence assigning the Moor to the ship. But I have also noticed that you are keeping Crastus away from me. You are Sir. You are deliberately making sure that he and I are not alone together. Perhaps you are afraid that it will lead to trouble in which case I must protest for it implies that you do not fully trust me to handle my subordinates."

"Oh, am I?" Corbulo replied lightly as he kept his eyes on the troops moving on past.

"Yes, you are Sir," prince Gummar said. "And I must protest. It is not right. Crastus is my subordinate, and he needs to learn his place and accept my command or else it will be bad for morale. It borders on insubordination. My men too have noticed. Some may start to question why Crastus is getting away with this. He needs to accept my command and to do so publicly."

"Crastus is your subordinate, as you are mine," Corbulo replied. "And I do trust you prince Gummar, or else you would not still be here. Crastus is an experienced officer like yourself and I need a good man to take command of the Nemesis. That is why Crastus, the Moor and eighty of our men will remain behind at Carnuntum. To man that warship. We are going to need naval support and yes you are right I need to keep open our communications with Probus too."

"Very well Sir," prince Gummar replied. "I understand that. But keeping me and Crastus apart is not going to work forever. This battle-group Sir, it will work more effectively if everyone of its officers knows their place. If we all respect each other. I believe that you understand this also."

"You wish to propose a solution?" Corbulo said in a tight voice, keeping his eyes on his men, the hood of his poncho hiding the look on his face.

"I do Sir," prince Gummar responded. "Give me permission to fight a duel with Crastus and if I win, he will publicly acknowledge me as his commander."

"Single combat!" Corbulo exclaimed. "Like a gladiator. And what happens if Crastus wins?"

"He won't win," prince Gummar said in a dismissive tone. "Let me settle this Sir."

For a moment Corbulo appeared to think it over.

"No," he said at last shaking his head. "I will not have my officers fighting among themselves. There will be no duel."

"But this is not right Sir!" prince Gummar said angrily. "I am your deputy! I demand respect. One day I am going to be a king of the eastern Franks!"

"When the time is right there will be a reconciliation between the two of you," Corbulo said in a sharp, decisive voice as he turned towards his deputy. "But right now we have more important matters to concern ourselves with. I need you to focus on the task ahead. Your full attention prince Gummar. We have important work to do. That will be all."

Then Corbulo turned to Tobias who was standing nearby, the accountant looking miserable and sullen in his rain-soaked clothing.

"Tobias," Corbulo called out eyeing him, "you have been very quiet since we arrived in Carnuntum. Is there something on your mind? If so, speak it now for once we are across the river I shall have little time for you."

For a moment the civilian said nothing, his eyes on the troops. Then at last he turned to confront Corbulo.

"Using our reserve funds to pay off those marines was not right," Tobias said his voice quivering with pent-up fury. "It was most improper and don't think that you or your officers can scare me. I am the guardian of the fiscal rules. I too have a job to do, and I will not stand idly by as the rules are broken. I will not walk the path that leads to a loss of financial credibility and chaos. We will win this war through sound finance! So, when we get back, I will be reporting you to the fiscus even if we make up our losses with stolen gold. When we get back, I am going to make a full report! You bullied me into breaking the rules of the fiscus!"

"Suit yourself," Corbulo replied looking away.

"Sir," one of Corbulo's bodyguards called out gesturing and as he turned Corbulo saw Mattis hastening towards him, holding a flaming torch. The centurion's face screwed up against the driving rain.

"Corbulo," Mattis called out as he came up, raising a hand. "It's about Sulpicia. Look after her for me will you. She has had a hard time since she lost her husband. And well the two of us have become close since then. I would hate to lose her. She means something to me."

"We will take care of her," Corbulo said giving Mattis a reassuring nod.

"She is never going to get her estates and reputation back is she," Mattis said with a sudden resigned look. "Gallienus is not going to reconcile with her, is he? She is not going to get what she wants even if she does help you steal that gold. I don't think she realises it yet."

"We shall see," Corbulo replied evenly.

"Then you should know," Mattis said looking grave as he stood on the deck and the rain pelted his face, "that Regalian was murdered by a band of Roxolani barbarians who held a grudge against him. The Roxolani managed to slip into Carnuntum and murder Regalian while he was at the baths, one of the safest places in the city. They should never have been able to get close to the governor. But what few are aware of is that the assassins had help from within the city. The assassins were aided by two of our own. Two high ranking advisers to Regalian. These men betrayed him, they conspired with the barbarians to murder their own commander in chief. They allowed the assassins to slip into the city and afterwards when the deed had been done, they deserted their posts and fled across the river to seek sanctuary among the Quadi. That is what happened here."

"I see," Corbulo said looking grave in turn, "and Sulpicia she knows about this betrayal?"

"She does," Mattis replied with a nod. "There are some unkind voices who claim that she too was one of the conspirators, that she too wanted to see her husband dead, but I do not believe that. I know her better than most and I know that, for all his faults, she did love her husband. She did not want to see Regalian dead."

For a moment Corbulo paused as he took in what had just been said. Then at last he nodded at Mattis. "Thank you," he said.

"Good luck Sir," Mattis exclaimed rapping out a salute. "May you strike terror into the hearts of the Quadi!"

“Hold Carnuntum for me as long as you can, Mattis,” Corbulo said as taking his horse’s reins, followed by his bodyguards and staff, he turned and joined the stream of cavalry troopers moving northwards across the river.

***

It was still dark as the group of senior Roman officers stood in the forest along the northern bank of the Danube. The officers gathered around Corbulo and the ala’s standard bearer who was holding up the banner of the equites foederati Germanica. The mood was expectant. The commanders tense as they listened to Corbulo. Their poncho hoods pulled down across their shoulders. Their bad weather cloaks still wet, some holding flaming torches, while a hundred or so paces away, the moonlight reflected from the placid waters of the Danube. It had ceased raining and the damp and dark forest around them was ominously quiet. The Roman troops waiting for the order to move out. The cavalrymen drawn up in their cohort, company and turmae, squadron formations. The horses stirring and neighing nervously and impatiently in and among the trees as the men gripped their spears and shields. Batavian feathers poking up from their helmets. The soldiers ready and eager for action.

"It is time that we announced our presence. There is a large Quadi village just a few miles from here," Corbulo said his gaze moving from one officer to the next, his voice earnest, his expression grave. "Our guides tell me that the village is an important stop for many merchants who use the amber road. They say that it is a wealthy place. A trade nexus between the empire and the barbarian world. The perfect place to begin our campaign of terror."

"How many people are we talking about?" Harald asked. "How many houses? What about defences, do they have a wall?"

"Perhaps a few hundred people," one of the guides replied speaking in his thick and course eastern Germanic dialect as the Roman officers turned to him. "Mainly craftsmen and specialists servicing the amber trade routes and the merchants who use them. The village has no defences. They have no wall or palisade. The place is a trading post and a repair shop. Its where you can hire local guides or mercenaries to take you further inland. That sort of stuff and slaves. They sell slaves -

blond haired people from the north and the Quadi slaves are cheaper than the ones that you can buy in Carnuntum. The people who live there did a lot of business with us before the war," the guide added with a shrug. "But now there is no business, no slaves, no amber. Nothing."

"We attack them at first light," Corbulo said taking over and turning to his officers. "We move fast, and we surprise them. Prince Gummar you will take the 2nd cohort and attack the village from the south while I will take the 1st and circle around and fall on them from the north. You will launch your attack as soon as you hear our horns. Harald you will take command of a single company from the 1st cohort and hold them back in reserve in case we encounter stronger than expected resistance."

"Very well Sir," Harald said dutifully. "And the fate of the village?"

"Burn it," Corbulo replied harshly. "The village is to be raised to the ground and the populace to be given to the slavers. If the Quadi think they are the only ones who can go raiding across the frontier then they need a reminder that two can play this game. What they do to us we shall do to them! This campaign is going to be about sending a message to king Hildimer and the Quadi. Alright," Corbulo added quickly looking up to check the night sky. "Dawn is not far off. You have your orders. Let's go. First into battle, gentlemen. First into battle!"

As the O group broke up and the Roman officers and guides hurried back to their units Corbulo paused as Atlas quietly reached out to lay a restraining hand on his arm. The intelligence officer appearing to have something on his mind as he waited for the others to leave.

"Well?" Corbulo inquired.

“It’s only been a day Sir,” Atlas replied removing his hand and turning to gaze into the dark forest with a strange, faraway look, “and as you know I am not one for handing out compliments but working with Sulpicia is proving to be a true delight. She is quick and eager to learn. We are getting on well. She would make a fine intelligence officer if she were not a woman.”

“You trust her then?” Corbulo said. “She has not given you any trouble?”

“No trouble at all,” Atlas replied, “and yes, I trust her. She is funny. She makes me laugh. I think she speaks the truth when she says she knows where the Quadi king has hidden his wealth. She is certainly eager to get her hands on it as soon as possible. She keeps going on about it like nothing else matters. The poor lady really believes that the emperor is going to reconcile with her if only she helps us steal that gold. It's rather sad to watch but she seems to genuinely bear no grudge against Gallienus. No hostility to the emperor. The only time I have noticed her get angry was when she mentioned the Roxolani assassins who murdered her husband. But here is the odd thing," Atlas said before pausing with a frown. "When I brought up the subject of the two Roman advisers who conspired with the Roxolani and betrayed her husband to the barbarians, she had nothing to say and now come to think of it, neither did she mention them at the baths when she first recounted to us what had happened to her husband."

***

Reaching out Corbulo blew on his curved bone horn and as the deep, humming noise rang out it was swiftly joined by other horns. The treeline coming alive. The haunting sound shattering the peaceful dawn.

“Let’s go! Ride!” Corbulo bellowed leading the attack, the Roman cavalry bursting from the forest in a wide battleline as they thundered towards the Quadi village sitting out in the fields a couple of hundred yards away. The horsemen sweeping across the fields like an incoming tide. The men’s spears lowered. Their shields catching rays of sunlight. Their feathered helmets gleaming in the strengthening light. The horses' hooves pounding and shaking the earth.

Sitting beside a pond at the edge of the village a solitary old man was fishing while a couple of women were busy grinding grain using a round millstone. Further away a boy was returning from the stream carrying two large buckets of water suspended from a piece of wood that was delicately balanced across his shoulders. While next to one of the thatched long houses a gaggle of infants too young to work were sitting about playing, watched over by a girl of around eight. The villagers were clad in a mix of traditional linen clothing and imported Roman cloth. Most of the children were going barefoot. The forty large, long houses and workshops with their daub and wattle walls, thick wooden beams and steeply sloping thatched rooves that nearly touched the ground were arranged in a rough circle around a grander looking building that occupied a rise in the centre of the village.

But as the Roman cavalry burst from the forest and came charging towards them the inhabitants stopped what they were doing to stare at the newcomers and for an insane second nothing happened. Then pandemonium broke out. The old man shot to his feet, bolt up-right, dropping his rod to the ground, jabbing his arm in alarm at the Romans. The women grinding the grain into flower screamed and abandoning their work they fled. The boy carrying the buckets of water came to an abrupt halt, rooted to the ground and unable to move. While more people appeared in the doorways of their homes to see what was going only to vanish back inside as fast as they had appeared. The village suddenly a hive of frantic activity. A couple of old men hurriedly arming themselves with spears. A boy running out of a house armed with a hunting bow. Three panic-stricken mothers rushing over to snatch their infants from the ground. Dogs barking. A forgotten baby wailing as it lay alone outside in its wooden cradle.

Racing up to the first of the barbarian houses Corbulo slowed his horse's pace as a man suddenly appeared, half-dressed and wielding an axe. The lone man bravely rushing towards the Romans intent on attacking them, but he did not get far before he was impaled by a spear, the axe dropping from his hand as he slowly sank down onto his knees. Then Corbulo was past the first houses and into the centre of the village and as the Roman wave came crashing into the barbarian settlement the panic and pandemonium increased. The Roman cavalrymen were everywhere, pushing on past the houses and driving groups of fleeing people before them. Bringing his horse to a halt Corbulo hurriedly turned to look around at the chaos. But it was clear that there was to be no organised resistance. No real fight. The battle was already over. The inhabitants appeared to be mainly women and children and older men who were no longer of fighting age.

Catching sight of prince Gummar's men racing towards him across the fields from the other side of the village Corbulo frowned, displeased with himself. His attack appeared to be overkill. He had overdone it. He could have taken the village with just a tenth of the men he now had with him.

Nearby a screaming woman rushed up to a troop of Romans brandishing a stone in her hand only to be stabbed to death before she could do any harm. Her body collapsing into the mud. Beside the pond the old man was jabbing his fishing rod at a group of Romans who had dismounted and were closing in on him with drawn swords. The man desperately trying to fend them off, his back to the water. While the boy carrying the buckets of water had vanished. The buckets standing neatly abandoned in the field. Turning his head Corbulo looked on as a dog tried to bite one of his men only to be repeatedly stabbed by the outraged soldier, the animal whimpering before dying.

"Where are the men of fighting age?" one of Corbulo's bodyguards called out as the troops of Roman horsemen milled about aimlessly among the houses searching for an enemy to fight. "They are not here. It's just women and old men. Where are the warriors?"

"Orders Sir," an officer cried as he came riding up to Corbulo while at the same time prince Gummar and some of his men appeared from behind one of the houses, the tall man also hurrying towards Corbulo.

"Burn the village," Corbulo called out. "We raise it to the ground. Kill all those who resist and enslave the rest. Destroy their grain and slaughter the livestock. Leave nothing of value!"

As his men set about their task Corbulo coolly looked on from his horse as one by one the thatch rooves of the homes around him started to catch fire. The Romans tossing burning torches onto the rooves and into the buildings. The billowing smoke and the hungry, leaping flames soon spreading rapidly and uncontrollably. The growing inferno, smoke and chaos forcing the remaining inhabitants and their animals from their homes. The people screaming and shouting in panic as they rushed about, trying to escape. Dogs barking. Cattle mooing. Pigs squealing. But there was no place for the Quadi or the animals to go for they were trapped in between their homes. The village was filled with Roman troopers and as the terrified, cornered populace sank to their knees in defeat, pleading for their lives, the Romans eagerly set about slaughtering the village's livestock and relieving the people of their possessions. Pieces of amber, silver and gold coins and jewellery swiftly vanishing into pockets. Knives, axes, cups, earthen-ware, clothing, boots, children's toys and cooking pots vanishing into the men's packs. The Romans taking anything of value in a frenzy of looting. The village suddenly filled with the voices of eager sounding soldiers shouting out to each other. The large round millstone where the two women had been working now stained with fresh animal blood.

Moving among the groups of inhabitants, the civilian slavers from Carnuntum, who had accompanied Corbulo's men, were hurriedly inspecting and pulling people away from their families as they made their selections. The slavers carrying their iron chains, the merchants competing for the most valuable slaves. Their faces flush with excitement, their voices filled with glee at the free bounty they had just been presented with.

At the edge of the village the old man's body was floating face down in the small fishing pond. While a woman was sitting alone on the ground beside her burning home calmly holding her wailing baby in her arms, staring off into the distance as if she was not here but somewhere else. A Roman soldier nearby was casually kicking an empty wooden cradle onto its side. Urging his horse on through the village Corbulo turned to stare at the growing destruction. The roar of the flames and the screams of the desperate people and the dying animals filling his ears. The heat from the flames blasting his face. The smoke invading his nostrils and as he gazed around at the destruction, he had unleashed he suddenly wondered whether the Christian god would approve. Furtively reaching up to his neck Corbulo's fingers touched the small fish amulet that hung there concealed under his clothing. His secret. The dangerous and secret path he had now chosen to follow. But what would the Christian god think of him now. Would the God approve or disapprove of what he was doing? Looking around Corbulo's expression hardened. But who could he ask who would know the answer to such a question?

"Sir," one of his bodyguards suddenly called out alerting Corbulo and as he turned Corbulo noticed a man approaching him through the billowing clouds of smoke. The man appeared to be unarmed and to be richly dressed, sporting a golden torc around his neck. He was dutifully followed by three sullen looking boys aged between eight and fourteen and by two women, one older and one younger. Perhaps the man's wife and daughter. The boys being his sons. The two women were clinging to each other, their faces ashen, their bodies trembling in fear.

Sinking to his knees before Corbulo, the man bowed his head before looking up at him with the pleading look of a desperate man.

"Mercy, prefect," the man called out in Latin. "I am Gunderic, the leader of this village. Take what you want but leave my people their village. There are no fighting men here. Just the old, the sick and our women and children. Spare us. We have done nothing to you. We are traders. We do business with Carnuntum. We have always grown fat together with your merchants. Please, prefect I beg you. Spare us! We are just simple peaceful folk."

Looking down at the man from his horse Corbulo remained silent. His face given nothing away as to what he was thinking while his bodyguards and the Roman horsemen around him looked on.

“Tell me. Why are there no fighting men here in your village?” Corbulo called out. “Where are they?”

“They have gone to join king Hildimer,” Guntheric called out raising his hands in a little helpless gesture. “They have crossed the river.”

“You mean they have gone off to raid our land," Corbulo cried out. "You claim to be just peaceful people, but your young men have brought death and destruction to our people. Cut off his head and that of his eldest son,” Corbulo said quickly turning to one of his bodyguards. “And place them on spikes at the entrance to the village. Enslave the younger boys but let the women go free.”

“Corbulo!” Harald called out in protest, the older officer staring at him, not saying anything further, his body doing the talking.

“No Harald!” Corbulo roared back at him, flush with anger. “I saw a baby impaled on a spear outside the walls of Carnuntum. That was done by these people, by the Quadi! By the young men who crossed the river. They are not innocent. If you cannot handle the consequences of a war, then don’t fucking start one. They had a choice. This is justice. Blood for blood. An eye for an eye. What was done to our people will be done to them! This is revenge!”

“This is not you Corbulo,” Harald cried out. “This is not war.”

As a troop of Romans hurriedly dismounted and seized hold of Guntheric and his eldest son forcing the two of them to their knees, the two women collapsed and broke out into hysterical screaming. But sat upon his horse Corbulo appeared not to be listening. For a long moment his gaze remained fixed upon Harald, his friend staring back at him as if the two of them were engaged in a battle of wills. Then Corbulo turned and nodded at his men for the execution to go ahead. And as a soldier chopped Guntheric's head off using an axe and quickly pocketed the chief's golden torc, Harald turned his horse around and rode off. Watching the executions Corbulo looked grim but resolute. And as the eldest boy was beheaded in turn the older of the women broke down and before anyone could stop her, she had slashed the throat of her daughter with a little concealed knife, before doing the same to herself. The two dying women collapsing on top of each other with blood pouring from their throats.

“Sir,” Gummar said urging his horse up to Corbulo, the tall Frankish prince taking in the gory decapitated bodies. “The village is gone. We carried out your orders. What next?”

“Find Atlas and Sulpicia and bring them to me,” Corbulo said addressing one of his bodyguards. Then he turned to prince Gummar, observing him with a cool, calculating look. “This is the plan," he said. "We are going to devastate the Quadi homelands. We are going to set this land on fire just like they have done to us. We are going to raid their settlements just like they did across the frontier. We are going to make them feel the war. This place," Corbulo growled gesturing at the burning village, "proves what I suspected. King Hildimer, in his arrogance and overconfidence, has left his people unprotected and without adequate defences. All the fighting men appear to have crossed the river to raid our land. But the king made a mistake. He was clearly not expecting us to cross the Danube and raid his land in turn and now we are going to make him pay for that mistake.”

“So, it seems,” Gummar said with a little weary grin. “We have caught the king with his pants down.”

"In that direction lies the Morava River," Corbulo said pointing across the pleasant, rolling countryside to the east. "It's not far from here. We will head over there now. The Morava is a tributary to the Danube, running north to south and I am told by the guides that there is a ford across the river just a few miles from where the river flows into the Danube. We will cross the Morava at that point and set up our base camp on the eastern bank."

"And then what?" prince Gummar said as he turned his eyes to the east.

"I am going to split up our command," Corbulo replied, "to increase our effectiveness and so that we can do maximum damage to the enemy. Our limiting factor is time. We will divide the ala into twelve separate columns each comprising of two turmae, sixty men, led by a senior decurion while the remainder of our force will be assigned to build and guard our camp. The base line will be the Morava River. From there our columns will start moving south-east in a grand sweep as far east as the fortress at Brigetio on our side of the frontier. I intend to devastate the country from the banks of the Danube in the south to the foothills of the Carpathian Mountains in the north. That is where the Quadi's most productive farmlands are located. We are going to hit them where it really hurts."

"Right," Gummar replied.

"So, we move fast. We avoid places that are protected by serious defences or are too strong to attack," Corbulo continued. "We do not have the time to conduct sieges nor the numbers to suffer serious casualties. The plan is to inflict maximum damage and destruction upon the enemy for minimal loss. You prince Gummar will lead the column that will operate closest to the Danube and Harald will oversee the erection of our fort along the Morava. Each column is to act independently. Our officers will need to use their own initiative. They are to employ the guides Mattis recruited for us to show them the way to every Quadi village, homestead and settlement. They are to attack and burn them to the ground. Pay close attention to their food supplies. Destroy all the grain you can find and slaughter their livestock. But leave the people. We do not have the time or the resources to take them all. We will continue to do this for the next six days but by the seventh day after setting out all columns need to report back to the base camp at the ford across the Morava. Understood."

"If we do that the Quadi are going to starve once winter comes," Gummar replied eyeing Corbulo.

"Exactly," Corbulo murmured as he started to urge his horse out of the village to avoid the growing clouds of smoke. "And when the Quadi realise that they will come to regret ever having attacked us. Maybe then they will be willing to discuss peace terms which are favourable to us."

"And what if we encounter serious resistance Sir?" Gummar asked as he followed Corbulo out of the burning village. "Maybe not all the fighting men have crossed the Danube. What then? Is it wise to split up our forces when we are going to be operating so deep inside hostile country? Separated Sir - we will be vulnerable. There is a risk."

"There is always a risk," Corbulo snapped. "We are here to burn their homes and destroy their food supplies," he added before pausing out in the field and turning to look back at the fiercely burning buildings, the flames leaping into the air, columns of black smoke rising high into the sky. "The cold and hunger will then do our work for us over the winter," Corbulo continued. "This is about teaching the Quadi the cost of attacking Rome.

To not fuck with us again. If we are ever to reestablish a successful deterrence the enemy need to be reminded that there are consequences to their actions."

Turning to prince Gummar Corbulo gave his deputy a cool look.

"Instruct your officers to avoid any places that look like they can offer serious resistance," he said. "We do not have time for that. Hit the enemy settlements hard and fast, then move on to the next village. Just keep moving. Our mobility will be the best defence that we have got. If we can keep moving the enemy will be confused and unable to quickly concentrate a force large enough to intercept us. They just won't have the time."

Nodding that he had understood his orders, prince Gummar paused as he too turned to eye the burning village. Then he sighed.

"If we devastate his land, it will bring king Hildimer rushing back across the Danube with his army in order to protect his kingdom," Gummar said. "He won't be able to ignore what we are doing."

"I certainly hope he comes hurrying back. That is the intention. It's all part of the plan that Probus and I worked out."

For a while the two officers did not speak as they watched the village burn. Then at last Gummar stirred as he caught sight of Atlas accompanied by Sulpicia riding towards him.

"And the king's gold?" he asked.

"I am going to go and steal it," Corbulo replied as he turned to eye the approaching pair of riders.

Chapter Thirteen - A King's Treasure

Standing beside his horse, clad for war, his plumed helmet resting on his head, his sheathed spatha sword hanging from his belt, his short red cloak covering his coat of mail body armour, Corbulo watched the column of sixty horsemen as they left the Roman camp and quickly rode off, heading east. The riders vanishing from view into the forest. Then heaving himself into the saddle of his horse he turned to eye the Roman camp that occupied the high ground overlooking the Morava River. The sixty men of his own command already waiting patiently on their own horses for the order to ride. Atlas and Sulpicia too mounted on their horses. Everyone ready and waiting on him. For a moment however Corbulo kept them waiting. Taking in the corralled horses and the work parties busy digging a V shaped ditch and building an earthen rampart that was being topped by a wooden palisade. The small rectangular fort starting to take shape. The sound of trees being felled coming from the nearby forest. The men shouting to each other as they worked. The smell from the soldiers cooking-fires hanging in the still air. While down the slope the waters of the Morava gleamed in the morning sunlight. The ford across the river visible. The summer sky blue as far as the eye could see.

At last, Corbulo turned to Harald and prince Gummar who were standing close by, waiting in silence. Harald looking grim and uncomfortable as if he were trying to figure out a way to make up with Corbulo without losing face. Prince Gummar his usual resigned looking self.

"Complete the fort," Corbulo said tuning to Harald. "I want it finished by the time we return and make sure to protect our battle-standard and the baggage train."

"It will be Sir and of course I will defend the standard and our supplies," Harald replied. "We will be here when you get back."

Eyeing Harald Corbulo hesitated as if he was considering saying something else before changing his mind and shifting his attention to prince Gummar.

"Maybe now is the time to confirm final contingencies Sir," the Frankish prince said with a little smile. "I mean what do we do if it all goes tits up and our plan does not work out?"

"If I am killed," Corbulo replied, "command will fall to you prince Gummar. Your orders will be to extract the ala as best as you can. You will need to try and get the men back to safety. Those are my final instructions. And if you are killed then Harald will take command and do the same. The equites foederati Germanica must survive. That is the only contingency that there is."

"Very good Sir," Gummar beamed looking pleased by what Corbulo had just said. "So, I would be in command. Good," Gummar added eagerly. "Don't worry I will make sure that your final orders are carried out."

"Well, I am not dead just yet, so you are going to have to wait for a while," Corbulo replied giving Gummar a hard look. "You have your orders," he continued glancing sternly from Gummar to Harald, "see that they are carried out. First into battle, gentlemen. First into battle!"

Then as both Harald and prince Gummar rapped out a salute, raising his fist over his head, Corbulo urged his horse on out of the camp and as he did so Atlas and Sulpicia quickly fell in beside him. No one speaking while Corbulo, leading his troop of sixty horsemen, picked up the pace, taking the path that ran parallel to the Morava as he began to head north.

***

To the north the Carpathians looked stunningly beautiful. A vast natural barrier of rock. Some of the peaks on the distant horizon capped by snow. The slopes and deep valleys of the mountains covered in dense pine forests and long narrow meandering valleys. The country painted in a dozen different shades of green, brown and white. The mountains dominating the southern plains like resting giants contentedly looking down upon their domains, secure in the knowledge that they would never be parted from them. The rolling foothills interspersed with meadows and towering rocky crags of white stone that reached for the sky like clawing fingers. The bright summer sun was bathing the country in light and warmth. The mountains unconcerned and dismissive of the small and insignificant party of Roman riders galloping towards them.

Peering cautiously at the mountains Corbulo reached up to wipe some sweat from his forehead while up ahead Sulpicia led the way. The woman practically standing up in her stirrups. Her body bent forwards, presenting him with her arse. Her horse gasping for breath. Her fluttering cloak trailing behind her. Clumps of dirt springing into the air. Sulpicia had set a blistering pace from the start. Her eagerness to get to where they were going as soon as possible eventually forcing him to rein in her enthusiasm. For not all the horses in his small command were in great condition or able to keep up with the pace she had set. And he could not afford stragglers or to lose any of his soldiers and horses. But his attempts to slow down their progress just seemed to have irritated her.

Studying the woman now, Corbulo frowned. He had still not made up his mind about her although it was clear Atlas had. His intelligence officer's enthusiasm and admiration for his new apprentice appeared to be growing by the hour. The two of them giggling together like naughty children. While during the moments when he and his party had rested their horses, he had noticed Atlas and Sulpicia going off alone together into the forest. And on top of that there was a strange smell about Atlas that he could not place.

Not that she had been uncooperative Corbulo thought. Far from it. Sulpicia had told him that king Hildimer's treasure was kept hidden in a cave in the mountains and that the cave was located a hard days' ride from where he had chosen to set up his base camp. Regalian's widow confidently informing him that the cave was guarded by a small encampment but that he and his men should have no trouble in overpowering them if they maintained the element of surprise.

"Tell your apprentice that we will camp as soon as it grows too dark to continue," Corbulo called out in German, glancing at Atlas who was riding beside him. The intelligence officer's face half concealed by his Bedouin keffiyeh. "The men and horses need the rest. Then at dawn she is to lead us to the enemy encampment and the cave, understood."

"I will speak to her," Atlas replied his eyes resting upon Sulpicia's arse. "She certainly can ride Sir. Better than most of our men in fact. In my professional opinion she has the right qualities for my line of work. She pleases me. She would make a brilliant scout and spy. What do army regulations say about female speculatore, Sir? She and I would make a great team going forwards. A woman does not arouse as much suspicion as a man does, you see."

"I have no idea what the regulations on that are," Corbulo said shaking his head, "and I am pleased that you have finally found your apprentice. But don't get too attached to her Atlas. This is just a temporary thing. And keep it professional. I have seen you two sneaking off into the forest alone!"

"I am not fucking her," Atlas replied in German as he turned to look at Corbulo. "If that is what you mean."

"Well whatever," Corbulo growled. "I don't know what she has done to you Atlas, but she has got you wrapped around her finger."

"Hardly," Atlas said looking away with a secretive grin.

"Yes, she has," Corbulo persisted as he started to reduce his horse's pace to give the beast a rest. "All she has to do in fact - to get you to do what she wants - is to flatter your massive ego, Atlas."

"Why are we slowing?" Sulpicia called out turning to look back with a frustrated expression as she noticed Corbulo and his men starting to fall further behind.

But Corbulo was not listening and did not answer as the Romans slowed their horses to a walk.

***

Leaving their horses tethered to a tree Corbulo, accompanied by a few of his soldiers, followed Sulpicia as she led the way, the party quietly creeping through the darkened forest. The cold, blueish moonlight breaking through the gaps in the thick tree canopies. The heavens covered in a mass of beautiful tiny stars. The forest was silent, apart from the soft call of an owl and the occasional snap of a twig as the Romans moved on by. The scent of rotting tree trunks and the earthy smell of pine filling Corbulo's nostrils. At last, Sulpicia came to a stop along a rocky ridge and squatted, pointing.

“There,” she whispered as Corbulo quickly crouched beside her, the woman pointing at a small cluster of campfires that were burning in the valley below. “That is the encampment that I was telling you about. The cave entrance is up there,” she whispered pointing at the dark outline of a steep mountain on the other side of the narrow valley. Its slopes covered in thick pine forest. “From the encampment there is a path that leads up the slope. I shall show you how to get to the cave tomorrow when it is light. Unfortunately, it is impossible to do so in the darkness. We would never find it at night.”

Peering at the encampment in the valley below Corbulo remained silent. Then he lifted his gaze towards the forested mountain slope across the valley as far-off a wolf howled. The animal's solemn, mournful cry answered a few moments later by another wolf.

“How many men are in the encampment?” he whispered.

“The king keeps ten handpicked men there at any one time,” Sulpicia said quietly. “Their task is to guard his treasure.”

“And the cave entrance?”

“It’s concealed,” Sulpicia said. “But I know what to look for. If you and your men can take care of the encampment, I will find the cave entrance and take you to the king’s treasure. We both win, prefect.”

Squatting Corbulo shifted his gaze from the campfires back to the silent mountain and then back again. His mind working.

“Prefect,” Sulpicia said as to Corbulo’s surprise she suddenly placed her hand on his arm. Her grip gentle but strong. “I think you and I have got off on the wrong foot. I sense that you do not approve of me.”

“No,” Corbulo whispered, shaking his head and keeping his eyes on the encampment. “That’s not true. We made an agreement. This is business. I don’t know why you would think that.”

“Because it is true,” Sulpicia said quietly. “But you are wrong prefect. You and I - we could be friends. I was an empress once. I can help you at the imperial court if Gallienus ever forgives me. I know important senators. I could be an ally to you and your men. You judge me too quickly.”

Shifting his gaze back to the dark forested mountain Corbulo paused.

“Why did those two Roman officers betray your husband?” he whispered glancing at her. “I understand they were Regalian’s friends, your friends.”

Squatting beside him Sulpicia did not immediately answer, the darkness hiding the look on her face, the question appearing to catch her off-guard. Then at last she stirred.

“They had their reasons,” she whispered. “But they are gone now. Together with the assassins. My husband is dead, and I must move on without him now. What good does dwelling on the past do?"

"Betrayal like that is no small matter," Corbulo said quietly. "It is not something that is so easily forgotten."

But as he glanced sideways Corbulo saw that Sulpicia had silently risen to her feet and was already heading into the forest, back the way they had come.

***

To the east up the narrow, forested valley the sun had just appeared, strengthening the dawn light, when with savage yells the Roman cavalry came charging into the small Quadi encampment that occupied the valley floor. The horsemen catching the tribesmen by complete surprise as they swept through the encampment clutching their spears and shields. The barbarians stumbling to their feet in confusion from where they had been sleeping around their campfires. Some struggling to arm themselves while one man rushed at the Romans only to be impaled on a spear point while another man was knocked to the ground by a horse. The rest hurriedly surrendering as they saw how outnumbered and hopeless their position was. Slowing his horse to a walk as he entered the camp Corbulo hurriedly turned to look around at the tribesmen who were now crying out in desperation. Their hands raised in the air as some of the Romans dismounted and started to kick the prisoners down onto their knees.

"Bind their hands and feet," Corbulo shouted at the decurion in command of the troop. "And post three pickets, one up there and one down the valley and one up on the high ground over there. Tell the men to stay alert. I want to have advance warning of any possible trouble."

Dismounting Corbulo quickly handed the reins of his horse to one of his men and turned towards the makeshift shelter that dominated the camp. The low, sloped roof made from clumps of grass and tree branches. The doorway covered in a grimy cowhide that hid what was inside the hut. The whole crude structure appearing more fit for animals than humans. Pulling his spatha sword from his belt Corbulo approached the entrance before cautiously pushing aside the cowhide and peering into the darkness beyond and as he did so he nearly gagged on the stench coming from inside. Holding his hand pressed to his nose and mouth his eyes slowly adjusted to the darkness and he saw that the roof of the shelter covered a large hole in the ground with steps cut into the earth, which led downwards into what appeared to be a single chamber.

Suddenly Corbulo sensed movement in the darkness beyond.

"Romans!" a voice suddenly called out in Latin from the darkness, the voice sounding astonished.

Shuffling into the light a man appeared. He looked around fifty with a full beard, wearing clothes that were dirty, torn and soiled. His face was unwashed and one of his eyes was swollen shut, the skin around it bruised as if someone had hit him hard. While his hands were tightly bound together by a piece of rope, and he stank like a sewer on a hot day.

"Romans!" the man cried out again as he came to a halt at the base of the steps and stared up at Corbulo with his one good eye.

"Who the fuck are you?" Corbulo growled, frowning.

The man however was unable to answer right away, seemingly stunned by Corbulo's unexpected appearance. His one good eye blinking in rapid, uncontrolled succession before a massive smile lit up his face and his shoulders sagged with relief.

"My name is Clement of Antioch," the man said raising his chin and gathering what dignity he still had left, addressing Corbulo in good clear Latin. "Grandson of the famous Clement of Alexandria. Scholar and amber merchant to the great house of Ulpia Severina. I was on my way back to Carnuntum from the shores of the Northern Sea with a load of amber when the political situation changed and the Quadi decided to take me prisoner. They have kept me here in this wretched place for months! I thought I was done for."

“You are a Roman,” Corbulo said taken aback, still holding one hand to his nose against the stench, as he studied the dirty man.

“A humble merchant Sir,” Clement replied gracefully inclining his head. “In the service of the house of the lady Ulpia Severina. I work for her. The amber was to be delivered to her.”

“Amber,” Corbulo said raising his eyebrows. “And where is your amber now?”

“I don’t know,” Clement said with a shrug. “The Quadi took it, I think. They took my mules away and fuck knows what they did with the men and guides I hired for the journey. They have told me nothing. They have kept me a prisoner in this hut for months, rarely letting me out. The only thing my captors told me was that my fate would be determined by king Hildimer once he returns from his raiding. You do not fight for the Quadi king, do you?” Clement added with sudden apprehension his smile vanishing.

“No. I am the prefect of the equites foederati Germanica. The king is not here,” Corbulo said beckoning for Clement to come on out. “Can you walk? Come on out into the light. We can take you back to Carnuntum but not right away.”

“Bless you Sir,” Clement exclaimed. “Yes, I can walk.”

Emerging from his semi-subterranean dungeon Clement blinked again as he tried to adjust to the sunlight. The Roman soldiers pausing what they were doing to stare at him. The dirty man groaning in soft delight as he felt the warm sun on his face and skin.

“I am sorry that I smell so bad,” Clement said at last with a good-natured smile, turning to Corbulo. “The Quadi would not untie me, so I was forced to piss and shit myself for weeks on end. These rags that I wear are the same clothes I was wearing months ago."

"Find him some new clothes and take him down to the stream so that he can get a proper wash," Corbulo called out quickly turning to a couple of his men. "Then keep him here until I am back. He is not to leave the camp." Then to Clement. "You and I will talk when I get back. You are safe now with us. My men and I will take you with us when we leave."

"You are here for the king's gold aren't you," Clement said in a sharp voice as he eyed Corbulo. "I heard the Quadi talking about it. The gold. That is why they are camped out here in the wilderness. But if you take his treasure prefect, you will be unleashing the king's rage."

Studying Clement coolly Corbulo remained silent. Then without answering he turned to Sulpicia and Atlas who were waiting for him, holding a bundle of unlit torches. The pair eager and impatient to leave. "Show me the way to the cave," Corbulo said nodding at Sulpicia.

Following Sulpicia as she confidently led him and his three companions up the steep and narrow forested path Corbulo glanced around at the forest, but all was quiet except for the soldier's army boots crunching across the ground and the men's laboured breathing. Shifting his gaze from the forest towards the higher slopes of the mountain he could see nothing untoward. No sign of trouble. The valley below was covered in thick tree canopies while further away a long white stream of water was crashing down the side of a cliff.

"You say that you got to know king Hildimer when you spent time at his court as a hostage," Corbulo said catching up with Sulpicia as she slowed her pace and prepared to scramble over a large boulder. "So, what else can you tell me about the king? About what kind of man, he is?"

"He's a king, a man," Sulpicia shrugged. "He likes to drink too much. He sleeps with other men's wives. He brawls. He has a son who nearly killed me once. He loves Roman gold and silver, and he has a soft spot for me because I make him laugh. Why? Why do you ask?"

"Because I have been thinking about what you said," Corbulo replied. "About having an ally at the imperial court, an ally with connections to the Senate. Maybe you are right, and I and my men could do with such a friend. It never hurts to have friends in high places."

"I see that you are warming to me at last," Sulpicia said flashing Corbulo a quick smile as the small party continued up the path. "And you are not wrong. These are dangerous and unsettled times prefect. Friends you think are friends will stab you in the back one day if you are not careful."

It was sometime later when Sulpicia cried out in triumph and pointed at something a few yards ahead.

“There it is,” she exclaimed.

Leaving the mountain path, she stepped out onto a natural rocky balcony that protruded outwards over a sheer hundred feet drop. The platform offering stunning views of the forested valley below. Looking excited, Sulpicia turned towards the rock face and as she started to remove some branches and debris the narrow entrance to a cave suddenly appeared. The dark opening just large enough for a man to slide through.

“We go in single file,” Sulpicia said turning to Corbulo unable to hide her growing excitement as Atlas and the two soldiers quickly prepared to light the torches they'd brought with them. "I will lead the way. The treasure room is some distance into the mountain. Watch out that you don't hit your head on the low ceilings," she added with a mocking smile. "And don't get curious about the side passages. Stay close and follow me. I know the way. You don't!"

Following Sulpicia into the cave, clutching a burning torch Corbulo peered into the darkness ahead. The air was suddenly cold and damp. The passage ahead narrow and straight. While from somewhere up ahead he could hear rushing water, the noise growing louder the further they went. Then abruptly Sulpicia came to a halt, her torch casting shadows across the rock and as he raised his own torch Corbulo saw that they had entered a large, cavernous hall. And flowing through the midst of the cave was a narrow stream, a river! The gushing water vanishing off into the heart of the mountain.

"The river Styx, "Atlas exclaimed as Corbulo was joined by his three companions. The torch bearing Romans turning to gaze about in awe at the mass of stalagmites and stalactites that adorned the cavern. "What is this place?" Atlas continued. "It looks like the entrance to the underworld."

"The king enjoys his secrets," Sulpicia called out over the noise of the flowing water as she moved her torch around. "Few know about his treasure room. He does not want anyone to find it, but I will show you where it is. Follow me. We need to get our feet wet. But be careful that you do not lose your footing and get swept away. For if you do you will most likely sweep the rest of us along with you. The current is strong, and the floor is slippery."

Then before anyone could react Sulpicia had boldly plunged into the middle of the stream. The rushing water coming up to her waist. Gasping from the cold she hesitated before with sudden determination she was off, wading downstream before promptly vanishing into a dark tunnel through which the water appeared to be escaping. Exchanging a quick look with Atlas, Corbulo took a deep breath before following Sulpicia into the underground river. His boots scraping across the uneven, stone strewn bottom of the channel as he reached out to steady himself against the rock wall while holding his torch in the other hand. Then ducking his head, he too vanished into the narrow water-logged tunnel. Fighting back the sense of claustrophobia as the rock closed in on him, he pushed on. The mountain water was ice cold. The sound of the river filling his ears. The current tugging at his legs as he followed Sulpicia's flickering torchlight.

"Fuck me," Corbulo heard Atlas swearing behind him as the speculatore nearly lost his footing. "What a place to hide your gold."

Moving on down the passageway Corbulo suddenly noticed that ahead Sulpicia had come to a stop and as he came up behind her, he saw that they had entered another large cave filled with stunningly beautiful, coloured rock formations. The crystals gleaming in the torchlight like pillars made of diamonds. For a moment Sulpicia did not move, blocking the way as she caught her breath. Her eyes roving about as if searching for something. Then raising her torch, she took a couple of steps deeper into the cave before illuminating a small sandy beach. Emerging from the stream and onto the pure white sand she paused and once again carefully raised her torch and as she did so, on a rocky shelf high above the water, two large iron chests suddenly hove into view. The iron strong boxes gleaming metallically in the torchlight. The chests resting on the shelf of rock. Both beautifully decorated and reinforced with rows of small iron buttons running along their sides. The handles were crafted to look like imperial Roman eagles and as he stared at them Corbulo saw that one of the boxes had a silver engraving - the dusty letters spelling out the name of the B&M Banking house of Londinium.

“The king’s treasure!” Sulpicia exclaimed turning to Corbulo with a wild, triumphant look. “Shall we take it?” she added with a mischievous grin.

***

Emerging from the cave and back into the bright sunlight, Corbulo and Atlas carefully placed the heavy iron strong box, which they had been carrying, onto the ground. Straightening up Corbulo looked on in silence as he was followed out of the cave by his two remaining men who were carrying the second strong box. The soldiers gently placing it beside the first chest as if its contents were fragile. The last to emerge from the cave was Sulpicia and as she hurriedly set about concealing the cave entrance Corbulo turned his attention to the treasure boxes, squatted beside them to inspect the chests in the light. Reaching out he carefully ran his finger across the dusty iron surface.

“They are Roman made and designed,” he exclaimed. “Look! That one appears to have come all the way from Londinium. That’s in Britannia. Bankers' guild by the looks of it. Excellent craftsmanship. What the fuck is it doing all the way out here beyond the Danube.”

“I don’t know Sir,” Atlas said as he too crouched beside the chests and turned to inspect them. “But we have a problem. The boxes are locked. They need a key to open them. Do you have the key?” Atlas inquired swiftly rising back to his feet and turning to Sulpicia with an inquiring look.

“No,” she replied as she quickly finished her work covering up the cave entrance before turning to the Roman soldiers. “No, I don’t. King Hildimer has the only keys that can open them. He wears them on a chain around his neck and doesn’t even take them of when he bathes.”

“The king bathes,” Atlas said giving Sulpicia a grin.

“He does indeed, just like a Roman,” Sulpicia said giving Atlas a little fond smile. For a moment she paused. "So now that you have the treasure what will you do with it? Will you use it to buy peace with the King like I said you should?” she added turning her attention to Corbulo.

“We will take it back to our fort,” Corbulo replied squatting beside the treasure chests.

“Maybe you have other another use for this wealth in mind?” Sulpicia said in a sudden and surprisingly seductive voice as she eyed Corbulo. “You are a rich man now prefect. Tempting, isn’t it? The idea that you could just disappear with this fortune and go and live somewhere where no one knows you. You could live like a King for the rest of your days. Or perhaps you wish to use this wealth to proclaim yourself emperor and pay for an army? Or you could just be boring and reward your men like Harald wants you to or deposit the funds with the imperial fiscus which is what that greedy imperial accountant Tobias would want you to do. So many options, prefect, I wonder which you shall choose.”

Saying nothing Corbulo straightened up and turned to gaze at Sulpicia before turning back to the locked iron chests, looking suddenly displeased.

"And what would you do with such a fortune?" Corbulo said quietly. "If you were not buying peace."

"I would buy the imperial throne and declare myself empress," Sulpicia said with a twinkle in her eye. "And I would employ you prefect and your men as my personal guard."

"You mock me," Corbulo said quietly. "My men and I are not for sale."

"Spoken like a true soldier," Sulpicia replied in a changed tone of voice, her expression growing serious. "And I apologise prefect for misjudging you. It was not my intention to insult you or question your loyalty, but I have been here before. I have seen how great and suddenly acquired wealth can change a man. So, are we good now, you and I?" she added. "I kept my promise to lead you to the king's treasure. I did what I promised to do. Do you trust me now?"

"You did," Corbulo replied rising to his feet, "and in return I shall keep my promise to you. Gallienus and the imperial court will hear about the role you played in helping us steal the king's gold! I will make a case to the emperor on your behalf. Whether he will listen I do not know. But you have my thanks. We could not have done this without you."

"So, what now, prefect? What is the next step?" Sulpicia said looking at him with a pleased smile. "We have the gold."

"Now, as you have done what you promised to do," Corbulo said evenly, "you are free to return to Carnuntum. You are a civilian and not subject to military law. For your own safety therefore, it would be best if you returned to the city as soon as possible. Your part in our agreement has come to an end and I have no more need for you. It is time you returned home. So, once we get back to our fort, I will arrange for an escort to see you safely back across the river."

“What! You are letting her go?” Atlas blurted out rounding on Corbulo in confusion. “But you assigned her to me as my apprentice. I don’t understand. We are only just getting started. This is wrong Sir. She should stay. She would make an excellent scout and spy. Sulpicia can still be of use to us!”

“Of course, I shall obey if you order me to leave and return to Carnuntum, prefect," Sulpicia said inclining her head in a respectful gesture. "But I feel that my task here is not yet done and I am perfectly willing to accept the risks. So, if it is all the same to you, I would like to remain with your ala for a little while longer. Atlas is right. I can still be of use to you. I can help you. Let me prove myself to you. I know king Hildimer better than you do and I have to say I find this work quite exciting and refreshing."

For a moment Corbulo hesitated, once again appearing displeased.

“It will be dangerous,” Corbulo said at last with a shrug. “If you stay with us, you will be exposed to much danger. There is fighting coming. Men are going to die. Can you handle that?”

“I can prefect,” Sulpicia said. “I have seen blood and death before. Everyone up here on the frontier has.”

Gazing at Sulpicia Corbulo hesitated again. Then with a resigned look he turned to Atlas and gave him a nod, conceding defeat.

“Fine. But she will be your responsibility. You look after her,” he said, switching to German.

***

Something appeared to be going on in the encampment where he had left the rest of his men Corbulo could see, as he and his companions, carrying the two heavy iron chests between them, descended the path into the valley. Alarmed Corbulo peered at the tumult as he hastened through the forest and down the path towards the valley floor. Outside the solitary hut a group of his soldiers had gathered around Clement who was semi-naked from the waist up and on his knees in the dust. His head bowed, the man crying out in pain as if he had just been punched. The soldiers appeared to be angry. Furious! A few of them having drawn their pugio knives from their belts as they circled around the prisoner. The men arguing aggressively with each other. Shouting. The insults coming thick and fast. Some threatening more violence against Clement.

"What the hell is going on here!" Corbulo bellowed as he hurried into the camp. "What is the meaning of this? Why is he down on his knees and half dressed? He is one of us. He is a Roman."

"Is he Sir?" one of Corbulo's men cried out in a mutinous sounding voice. "I am not so sure. When we took him to get washed as you instructed us to," the soldier continued, "we found this on him," the man added holding up a little chain from which dangled a small silver cross. "You know what this means Sir. He is one of them. He is a fucking Christian!"

"And all Christians must die!" another soldier cried out angrily giving Clement a shove that toppled him onto his side. "That is the law. That is Valerian's imperial decree. Christians must be persecuted. Their God is the God of outlaws. They deny the imperial cult. Let us kill him now Sir and be done with it. This piece of shit is not worth taking back to Carnuntum."

"What?" Corbulo cried out turning to stare at Clement in shock and for a moment he could not move. "Is this true," Corbulo called out as he started towards the amber merchant. “You are a Christian?”

“It is true,” Clement said gasping in pain as another soldier savagely kicked him in the ribs. “I am a Christian. I will not deny it. And I am not afraid to die for my lord - so you and your soldiers will have to do what you must. I will not abandon God,” Clement cried out struggling back up from the ground, his voice gaining in strength and conviction, as if he was unburdening himself before his imminent death. “You cannot change my mind! I am a priest of the one and only true God and will go gladly into his eternal embrace. For there is only one God. And his rule will be for all eternity. Glorious and just! And all those who refuse to follow the one and only true God will be cast into the fires of hell. For you worship false idols. The Christian god sees into the hearts of all men!”

Swearing out loud Corbulo stared at Clement as his men prowled around the Christian like a pack of starving wolves, the soldiers in a murderous, rebellious mood. Biting his lip Corbulo made a hissing noise as he struggled to decide on what to do.

“Give the word Sir and we will butcher him right here and now,” one of his soldiers cried out angrily brandishing a knife.

“I will not ask for mercy!” Clement shouted defiantly. “I will not deny the existence of God. I will not convert. I do not fear death!”

Staring at Clement who was gazing straight back at him Corbulo groaned unable to speak or move. The Christian, now that he had unburdened himself, appeared to be calmly awaiting his fate; the tension rising before at last Corbulo broke free from the spell that had bound him.

"No," Corbulo cried, turning to his soldiers and holding up his hand. "The Christian will not be harmed. Maybe he does deserve to die for being a Christian but that is not for us to decide. We will take him back with us and let the proper civil authorities decide what to do with him. He is still a Roman citizen. He should be given a fair chance to defend himself. So, no one is to touch him until he has been put in front of a magistrate and convicted."

Chapter Fourteen - Clement of Antioch

Standing up upon walkway behind the ramparts of the unfinished Roman fort that occupied the high ground overlooking the Morava valley and the ford across the river, Corbulo peered at the column of horsemen who had emerged from the distant forest to the east and were trotting towards him. The sentries manning the nearby watchtower were crying out in excited voices as they pointed at the approaching riders with their spears. While a Roman trumpet was still blaring in warning from one of the advanced pickets. Spread out around the fort armed with shovels, axes and saws the work parties who were still labouring to complete the fort's defences had paused to see what was going on. The men gazing in silence as the horsemen. It was the morning of the seventh day since Corbulo had sent his soldiers out to devastate the Quadi homeland.

“That’s Berthold and his men,” Harald said quickly as he stood beside Corbulo, the older officer gazing at the troop of riders with a serious expression. “Looks like he has got some wounded with him Sir. Looks like they ran into trouble.”

“I see them,” Corbulo replied. “Decurion,” he shouted hurriedly turning to the watch commander. “They have got wounded. See that the doctor and his staff are ready to receive them.”

“That makes ten Sir. With Berthold’s return - all columns have now reported back to camp,” Harald said glancing across at Corbulo. “All except for prince Gummar and his men.”

“Good,” Corbulo replied.

“You think he and his men are alright?”

“Yeah,” Corbulo said in a resigned voice. “Gummar will be back. He will stay alive just to piss me off. He won't want to miss this fight.” For a moment Corbulo watched as the wooden gates into the camp swung open and the band of weary, dust covered riders hurried into the fort.

“Debrief young Berthold and then come and find me,” Corbulo said turning to Harald and giving him a little, curt nod.

Watching Harald as he dutifully hurried off to carry out his orders Corbulo's expression quietly changed. Harald was old school and his closest friend within the ala. A strict disciplinarian who was not afraid to speak his mind when he thought something was not right. The two of them had known each other for years. From his earliest days as a young officer in the army. Their respect for each other was genuine and had survived numerous disagreements. Harald was a man he could trust. Harald should have been his deputy Corbulo thought. He should have made Harald his second instead of Gummar, but he could not undo that now."

Shifting his gaze to the unfinished Roman fort, his temporary base of operations north of the Danube, Corbulo frowned. His eyes taking in the deep V shaped ditch that ran around the rectangular perimeter. The tree stumps that littered the cleared forest beyond. The steep earthen embankment that protected the camp and the wooden palisade of tree trunks that ran along the top. The four tall watch towers in each corner of the fort. Sheltered within the defensive works the camp was a hive of activity. The men under his command moving about busying themselves with the horses, cooking, resting and tending to their equipment and repairing their clothing and boots. The camp alive with the soldier's boisterous voices and the smell of woodsmoke coming from the campfires. While tucked away in one corner a few barbarian women, men and children were plying their trades. The soldiers camp inevitably attracting a small following of Quadi civilians with something to sell.

Spotting Clement and his escort entering the camp from the direction of the river; Clement weighed down carrying two heavy buckets of water; Corbulo observed the Christian in sudden thoughtful silence. Then climbing down the ladder and back into the camp he made his way over to where Clement had just finished pouring the water he'd fetched from the river into a large barrel. The old man straightening up with a weary, resigned look as he prepared to repeat his task.

"It's alright," Corbulo said gesturing to Clement's solitary escort. "I will take over from here." Then to Clement. "Let's take a walk."

Studying Corbulo with his one good eye Clement hesitated. His bad eye covered by a black eye-patch that was strapped around his head and which made him look like a pirate. His once filthy beard had however disappeared leaving him cleanshaven. His stinking rags replaced by a surplus white woollen army tunic that was slightly too small for him. Without saying anything Clement stooped and picked up the empty buckets and joined Corbulo as he headed towards the gate that led down the slope to the riverbank.

"Your eye - will it heal?" Corbulo said as the two of them left the camp and started down the forest covered slope towards the Morava.

"Hard to say. Perhaps," Clement replied staring straight ahead. "But the prefect of the equites foederati Germanica does not walk me - his prisoner - down to the river because he is interested in my eye," Clement added. "Just say what you have come to say, prefect."

“I must debrief you. I should have done it earlier,” Corbulo said with a shrug. “You are an amber merchant. An important man working for an important Roman family. You travel the amber road. You will have knowledge about the barbarian tribes that could be useful to me. You know their world. You must hear and see things on your travels that not many other men do. If there is something that you think I should know - some danger that I should be made aware of - then now would be the time to tell me. It will help your cause, I promise.”

Coming to a halt along the slope Clement turned to look down at his surplus army boots and for a moment he appeared to be thinking. Then he turned to Corbulo with a little amused smile.

“My cause is fucked, prefect. I think we both know that. I confessed to being a Christian and publicly refused to convert in front of many witnesses. Society will not accept such defiance, such an affront to the old gods. They are going to crush me. Not even my mistress the lady Severina will be able to save me this time. Even though she is a good friend of emperor Gallienus. I know what fate awaits me when we get back to Roman controlled territory. I am finished.”

“But we are not back there yet,” Corbulo said evenly, “so answer my question. Is there anything of value that you can tell me? Anything that could help your cause. If you help me then maybe I can help you.”

Once again Clement hesitated.

“No, I have nothing useful to tell you prefect," Clement replied. "I am sorry. All I can tell you is this. I am fifty-two years old. I was born in Antioch; I am from the East. As a child I grew up listening to my grandfather preaching the Christian message and so I became a Christian like him. We were a wealthy family and among our slaves was a German. He was a good storyteller. A good friend. As a boy he filled my head with stories of his native land. Imbuing me with a desire to go and see these lands and peoples for myself. Then when I was eighteen my father sent me to Rome to work for a business acquaintance who was active in the amber trade. And I have worked for the house of lady Ulpia Severina ever since. I have been travelling across the Germanic world for over thirty years now."

"You preach the message of your Christian god to the barbarians?" Corbulo inquired as the two of them resumed their journey down to the riverbank.

"No, I may be a priest, but I am done preaching," Clement said shaking his head. "It just brings trouble, and I am getting too old for that shit. Now I only act as a priest when someone asks me to."

"And your mistress, lady Severina," Corbulo asked frowning, "she is aware that you are a Christian? She tolerates this?"

"Yes," Clement said nodding. "Lady Severina is not a Christian, but she is a good and just woman. Which is why I have worked for her and her family all my life. So, if you want to help me prefect," Clement said turning to gaze at Corbulo with sudden determination, "you will make sure that her name is not brought up in my forthcoming trial. For I do not want her reputation damaged by association to me. She should not suffer because of my Christian faith!"

"I cannot make that promise," Corbulo replied. "When we return to imperial territory, I am going to need to hand you over to a magistrate who will determine your punishment. I cannot go against the law."

"Yes of course," Clement said looking disappointed. "For we Christians are all traitors right. I get it! The world is filled with prejudice. It was ever so." Then taking a deep breath Clement gathered himself and turning to Corbulo his expression appeared to change. “I must thank you for saving my life back at that Quadi encampment, prefect,” Clement said quietly. “I am sorry that we have not had a chance to speak since, but your men have kept me busy hauling water up from the river to the camp. And I am not in the mood to give them another excuse to beat me up.”

“We all have our tasks,” Corbulo said evenly. “But don’t thank me just yet. Maybe all I have done is bought you a stay of execution. Once I hand you over to the magistrate, they may decide to impose a fine on you or maybe if you are unlucky, they will hang you."

“Yes,” Clement said sounding resigned. “The pagans hate Christians because we deny the existence of all their gods. We refuse to accept the imperial cult. We are seen as traitors. But you prefect,” Clement added again glancing across at him. “You are a good man. I can sense that you have a just and noble heart. So, you must do what you must do but nevertheless you shall have my gratitude for the kindness that you have shown me.”

“I may be able to do more,” Corbulo said as the two of them reached the shores of the Morava and Clement squatted at the water’s edge and started to fill his buckets. “I can speak to the magistrate on your behalf and urge them to show clemency if you were to agree to renounce your Christian faith. A deal could be agreed that would save you. I know you will refuse,” Corbulo added quickly raising a hand to prevent Clement from interrupting him, “but all you must do is pretend. It may be the difference between life and death.”

Pausing in his work Clement turned to look up at Corbulo.

“Why?” the Christian exclaimed frowning. “Why would you be willing to do that for me. Why help me? I am an enemy of Rome in the eyes of the law, by imperial decree and you are a soldier sworn to protect Rome and the emperor. We are not friends; we are on opposite sides!”

"I have a question for you," Corbulo said quietly as he turned to look out across the river. "Can a man believe in the Christian god and at the same time also believe in the old gods? Can he believe in both?”

Hesitating, taking by surprise, Clement did not immediately offer an answer. Then at last he resumed filling his bucket with water.

“I am not a perfect man," Clement replied looking serious. "Far from it in fact. I am weak. I have my vices, my temptations which I find hard to resist. I like pretty women too much to retain a wife, and I like to drink too much. I like money too, amber,” he added. “Oh yes. I stray. I sin. I sin a lot. But at the end of the day, it is my faith which gives me strength. It is my Christian faith that always leads me back to the right path like a torch in a dark night. And I hold onto my faith lying a drowning man holds onto a piece of flotsam. But to answer your question. Yes. It is possible to believe that the Christian god is just one of many gods. But those who think like this are only just starting out on their path to becoming true Christians. Those of us who are further along that path understand the truth better.”

“The truth?”

“That there is only one god,” Clement said with a sad smile. “For that is the truth that lies at the end of the path. If you wish to become a true Christian at some point you will have to abandon your faith in false idols, in the imperial cult, in everything that has come before. Revolutionary isn't it!”

Staring out across the river Corbulo remained silent as he took in what had been said.

"And what would your Christian God think of what we are doing here?" Corbulo said at last gesturing around him. "About the war that I have brought to these lands. Would he approve of what I am doing here? How does a soldier who willingly kills and destroys gain the respect of your God?"

Finishing filling his buckets Clement slowly rose to his feet and for a moment the two of them remained silent as they stood on the bank staring out across the peaceful river.

And as they did it was as if something subtle and unspoken had been exchanged between them.

"You wish to know what God thinks of war," Clement said at last stooping and lifting his buckets as he prepared to return to the camp. "That is an odd thing for a Roman military prefect to ask me but now that you have, I shall try to offer you an answer. God does not condone war, prefect. He disapproves of going to war, but men will do it anyway. We are all sinners," Clement said glancing across at Corbulo with a sudden mischievous look as the two of them started on back towards the camp, "but if you wish to gain god's respect, a good place to start, prefect would be for us to become friends."

Chapter Fifteen - War Council

Once again, the distant Roman trumpet rang out as if the signaller's purpose was to summon more soldiers up onto the ramparts of the fort. It was morning and standing among his men up on the walkway, peering out over the top of the tall wooden palisade of tree trunks that was embedded into the earthen embankment, Corbulo watched the band of horsemen who had just emerged from the forest. The riders were heading straight towards him across the clearing, the ground studded with tree stumps and the remnants of freshly chopped down trees, and they were making a proper racket. The urgent trumpet ringing out incessantly but following no established military signal that Corbulo could understand. And as he lifted his gaze to the edge of the forest Corbulo could see no sign of a hostile pursuit. No evidence that his men were being chased or in danger. But they were all there he thought in relief as he silently and quickly finished counting the number of horsemen.

“Prince Gummar returns!” Harald called out as he came hurrying down the walkway towards where Corbulo was positioned.

“So, he does,” Corbulo replied.

“He’s a day late,” Tobias said darkly, speaking in Latin, the accountant standing a few feet away, a leather satchel slung across his shoulder as he too stared at the band of horsemen. “By my count he has got all the men with him who he started out with. It doesn’t look like he has suffered any casualties. So, either he avoided fighting, or he was very lucky indeed.”

“I hope you are not calling prince Gummar a coward, Tobias,” Corbulo replied without taking his eyes off the approaching riders.

“No, just making an observation,” Tobias muttered sourly.

Drawing closer to the fort, leading his men at a brisk pace, prince Gummar suddenly raised his spear in the air, pumping it up and down as if he were returning in glorious triumph, the gesture provoking a smattering of cheering from the Roman soldiers lining the walls of their fort.

“He is showing off Sir,” Harald said looking unimpressed. “Looks like Gummar intends to make a grand entrance. Good thing Crastus is not here. He would have something to say about that.”

“Open the gates and let them in,” Corbulo cried out ignoring Harald as he turned to the soldiers down in the camp beside the gates. Then he was off to join them, swiftly followed by his bodyguards and Tobias, the party of men clambering down the ladders that led down into the camp.

“You are a day late, what news?” Corbulo called out as he hurried over towards the Frankish prince who had come to a halt just inside the gates, still mounted upon his horse. His men were clustering around him catching their breath. Their cloaks and faces stained with dust. The flanks of their horses heaving from exertion as if they had been riding hard for a long time. The relief to be back among their comrades however was palpable.

“Apologies Sir,” Gummar replied as he caught sight of Corbulo. “It was unavoidable.”

“Prince Gummar!” Harald cried out interrupting and unable to hide the frustration in his voice as he came marching up accompanied by Atlas and Sulpicia. “I do hope that you have not forgotten that army trumpets are to be used strictly for signalling purposes only. That display just now, out there, was gibberish. We are not boys playing trumpets for fun. This is the fucking Roman army. Trumpets are to be used only in the correct, authorised manner!"

"Good to see you too Harald," Gummar replied forcing a tired smile. Then turning back to Corbulo the smile abruptly vanished.

"You ask for news Sir, well I have some," Gummar said hurriedly, trying to stifle his excitement. "I took my men east and south sticking to the bank of the Danube as you instructed me to. Seems your plan is working. The enemy appears to know that we have been attacking their homes. The Quadi war-bands are returning home. We saw them crossing the Danube. Many, many war-bands, small and large Sir. They are flooding back across the river to defend their homes. We took a prisoner who told us that King Hildimer is also hurrying back with his army. Seems our presence here has put an end to their raiding."

"Good," Corbulo said looking pleased. "Good! Then our plan is working. The enemy war-bands who you saw crossing back over the river," he continued, "they are burdened with their loot and slaves?"

"Yes, they are - heavily burdened!" Gummar replied with growing excitement as he understood where the conversation was going. "We saw them crossing the river with our own eyes. We are lucky that the Quadi are greedy bastards. Instead of dropping everything to defend their families they are trying to ferry all their spoils and slaves back across the river. It has made them slow and vulnerable. They appear most reluctant to abandon their loot."

"Good," Corbulo repeated quickly coming to a decision. "Then the time has come to attack. We must ride at once. Harald," Corbulo said turning to him. "I am leaving you here with a company of men to guard the fort. You will switch Gummar's sixty riders for sixty of your own fresh men so that these riders here can get some rest. And you will hold this fort until we return." Then to Gummar. "You are right. If the Quadi are returning home with their loot and slaves that will make them slow and vulnerable. They will be disorganised while crossing the Danube. So, you and I," Corbulo said pointing at Gummar, "are going to take advantage of this and cause them some trouble. Now is the time. We will start our sweep downstream in the direction of Aquincum. With luck the enemy will have no time to organise themselves or to support each other. If we move fast, we should be able to destroy their war-bands one by one. And I want king Hildimer dead or alive! Our main objective is to try and catch the king as he crosses back over with his army. When he is at his weakest and most vulnerable. That is what Probus, and I planned to do. So, prepare the men and horses. We ride within the hour."

"Sir," Gummar gasped," there is something else. The prisoner we took, he told us that there is a second Quadi army over in the north guarding their border with the Marcomanni. He told us that this army is ten thousand strong and commanded by the king's uncle."

"What!" Corbulo said, his face darkening abruptly. "A second army! Are you sure?"

"Yes Sir," Gummar said nodding. "I had the man's story independently corroborated by a second prisoner. I believe they were speaking the truth. They told me that the king sent his uncle off to guard the western border. The Quadi are worried that the civil war among the Marcomanni will spill over into their territory. The good news is that this second army, according to our prisoner, is made up of very young and very old men. While most of the quality fighting men accompanied King Hildimer on his raid across the Danube. The bad news Sir is that it seems King Hildimer is not as stupid as we hoped he would be. He appears not to have left his realm completely undefended after all. We may have underestimated the king."

"This second army, where are they now?" Corbulo barked.

"Hard to say for certain," Gummar replied. "The prisoners weren't sure."

"And where are these prisoners now?

"They are dead Sir, they…they tried to escape," Gummar said with a sheepish look.

"The border between the Marcomanni and the Quadi is about five or six-days march on foot to the north-west from where we are now," Sulpicia interrupted raising her chin. "But if the King's uncle has got cavalry, his riders could be here within two or three days. Maybe even sooner."

"Maybe they are already on their way here Sir," Atlas said turning to Corbulo with a sudden concerned look.

Silence followed. Sulpicia and Atlas's intervention bringing forth sullen, dissatisfied looks upon the faces of the Roman officers.

"Why the fuck were you not aware of this earlier?" Corbulo said angrily rounding on Atlas who was suddenly looking uncharacteristically embarrassed. "Your job is to gather intelligence on the enemy is it not? So how can you miss the existence of an enemy army of ten thousand men! We have Quadi civilians approaching our fort every day to sell their shit. Did you not think of asking them if there were any threats to our position which we did not know about? Did you not try to interrogate those civilians about what they knew. It's basic fucking stuff!"

“I am sorry, Sir,” Atlas replied lowering his gaze. “I have been busy with other things.”

Glaring at his intelligence officer Corbulo paused looking angry and troubled, before quickly shifting his gaze to Sulpicia who simply looked away as if the matter did not concern her. Something appeared to be going on with Atlas he thought. He appeared to have changed since he had taken Sulpicia on as his apprentice. His usual cockiness, arrogance and confidence had gone. Even the practical jokes had ceased although that was not a bad thing. And it was not the only thing that had changed Corbulo with mounting concern. Atlas smelled. Every time he had encountered him there had been a strange smell about him that he could not place. Which was troubling Corbulo thought.

“So, we have an enemy force ahead of us of unknown strength and potentially another Quadi army to our rear,” Harald said taking a step towards Corbulo, his expression grave. “If the troop numbers are correct, we could be outnumbered anywhere between fifteen and twenty to one Sir. In such circumstances do you think it is still wise to attack? If the King’s uncle moves swiftly against us, he could cut off our line of retreat to the bridge at Carnuntum. We would be trapped against the Danube and annihilated. The existence of this second army changes the calculation.”

“No,” Corbulo replied turning to his friend, “we’re not going to retreat. We are going to finish the job we came here to do. The odds are still doable. We may be outnumbered but we still have the initiative, and we are mobile. We need to make a show of strength. If we need to get out of trouble we can always move fast. Gummar, prepare the ala. We ride as planned."

"We have the king's gold," Sulpicia blurted out turning to Corbulo. "Your presence here has already caused the Quadi to abandon their raids across the Danube. You have achieved what you set out to do, prefect. So why fight? Why not use the gold to buy peace with king Hildimer. Is that not why you came here. To put a halt to the raids and restore order along the frontier?"

"Is she really part of this conversation?" Gummar said pointing an irritated finger at Sulpicia as he turned to Corbulo, "for I don't recall that she, a civilian, a woman, was ever invited to join this discussion!"

"She helped us steal the king's gold," Corbulo replied evenly. "She knows things about king Hildimer which can prove useful so on that matter, for now, she is entitled to voice her opinion. But you are wrong," Corbulo said turning to Sulpicia, "we have not yet achieved what we came here to do. Our purpose is to inflict a decisive defeat on king Hildimer. One so decisive that he and the Quadi will not dare invade the empire again. So yes, we need to fight. We need to draw blood from the king before there can be peace."

"So why steal the king's gold if you refuse to use it," Sulpicia shot back defiantly, her eyes blazing. "That wealth could buy peace for this part of the frontier without the need for fighting. I know the Quadi king, and he knows me. I have a good relationship with the king. He has a soft spot for me. I could help set up the negotiations. I could be your go-between. Allow me to go to see the king with one of his treasure chests and act as your emissary. The treasure chest would be an act of good faith. To prove that we are serious. We could have real peace. Is that not what everyone wants," she called out turning to look around at the Roman officers.

"Sulpicia," Atlas said hastily turning to her and speaking before anyone else could. "You are a woman and a civilian. You don't understand. This is not about peace. These men here, they are professional soldiers, and they want to fight because destroying the enemy will make them rich. Think of all the loot they can take from their enemies. They want to fight because, well, they just want to fight," he added with a shrug. "So don't try and stop them."

"Shut her up Sir!" Gummar cried out in an angry voice. "This is not the place or time for a woman to offer advice."

"Alright that's enough!" Corbulo cried out. "Get the men ready to ride," Corbulo said to Gummar. "And as for the king's treasure and your proposal," Corbulo went on turning to Sulpicia, "the answer is no. The king will not see that as a gesture that we are serious. He will see it as weakness. No, I am not letting you go and see the king. Instead, we will take the treasure chests with us. They will be safer with us than left behind here in the fort. Tobias," Corbulo said quickly turning to the imperial accountant, "I am going to need you to accompany us and as before, you will be responsible for looking after the treasure chests. See that they remain secure. Atlas," Corbulo continued turning next to the intelligence officer, "you too are coming with us. I am going to need you and Sulpicia to scout ahead of the main force. Follow the course of the river downstream and let us know what you find. Harald," Corbulo said finally turning to his friend, "guard the Christian prisoner and hold the fort until we return but if you see that you are about to be attacked by a superior force then you are permitted to withdraw and retreat. Got that."

“Nah,” Harald said in a resigned voice, shaking his head. “I will hold the fucking fort for you Sir. We will be here when you return.”

Chapter Sixteen - The Fight Along the Danube

Charging across the fields towards the enemy, their horses' hooves thundering and pounding the ground, the squadrons of Salian Franks and Batavians were doing their best to stay in their V shaped attack formations. The wide Roman battleline sweeping in towards the banks of the Danube. The placid waters beyond glistening and beckoning to them in the fierce afternoon sunlight. But here and there the soldier's inexperience and lack of horse-riding skills was showing. The charge revealing their hasty and incomplete training and rushed conversion from infantry to cavalry. Some of the riders were falling behind their officers. While some squadrons were in danger of getting in each other's way. The wild charge stretching the Roman formations to breaking point. The mad sweeping assault in danger of losing crucial momentum and coherence.

"At them! Finish them off!" Corbulo bellowed leading the assault, clutching his long thrusting spear under his arm while his ovoid shaped cavalry shield was strapped to his other arm. The white emblem of a wolf adorning the dark wood. His torso protected by a coat of finely crafted chain mail. His head covered by a plumed cavalry helmet with close fitting cheek-guards. The ground around him was shaking with the pounding of hooves. The fields alive with the wild, savage battle-cries of his men as they closed in on the enemy.

Directly ahead the Quadi war-band appeared to have been caught completely off-guard. The tribesmen screaming and yelling to each other as they frantically rushed to arm themselves and form a shield wall. Barbarian horns ringing out. The riverbank in chaos as people rushed about. But it was already too late.

Punching through the flimsy, incomplete enemy line the momentum of the Roman charge broke the barbarians in just a few seconds. Driving his spear straight into the face of a tall man who tried to block his path, Corbulo knocked the warrior to the ground. The savage blow sweeping the man clean off his feet and onto his back. Then Corbulo was through the enemy position and into their rear. Slowing his horse he hurriedly turned to look around as the fighting around him descended into a chaotic melee and hand to hand combat. Nearby a screaming Roman rider was pulled from his horse by two tribesmen armed with Roman spatha swords but just as they were about to finish him off, they were in turn impaled in quick succession by the man's comrades. Groups of Roman horsemen thundering past. The enemy warriors sinking to the ground, their swords dropping from their lifeless hands.

Their line broken by the initial assault, the Quadi suddenly found themselves surrounded by Roman horsemen to their front and behind them. The surviving warriors were milling about in confusion and growing panic. And sat upon their horses, moving about, frantically jabbing at the enemy with their long thrusting spears the Roman troopers had set about killing them. Their spears and long cavalry swords thrusting and sliding into exposed flesh as if they were spitting pigs.

"Finish them off!" Corbulo roared. Then abruptly Corbulo found himself under attack. Rushing towards him a huge warrior wearing a coat of looted Roman body armour and armed with a spiked club suddenly appeared from out of the chaos of struggling, snarling men. The man's intent clear as he leaped towards Corbulo and caught hold of his spear trying to wrestle it away. Grimacing, Corbulo struggled with the man. Then with a savage yell the warrior struck Corbulo's horse with his club, the iron spikes driving deep into flesh, the ferocious blow bringing down the screaming horse and throwing Corbulo to the ground. Landing with a painful thump Corbulo gasped for breath. But there was no time to accept the pain. Looming up over him the warrior had raised his club as he prepared to finish him off, the man's face contorted in rage and hatred. Rolling away just in time Corbulo pulled his spatha sword from his belt and wildly slashed at his opponent and missed. Staggering back to his feet he nearly stumbled backwards over a corpse as the big warrior came at him again. The man screaming, spittle flying from his mouth, as he wildly swung his club. Blocking the attack with his shield Corbulo cried out as the tremors from the powerful blow shot through his body.

Once again, his opponent lunged and once again Corbulo caught the blow on his shield as he danced away. Then seizing his chance as the man was momentarily distracted by another Roman horseman, Corbulo charged at the warrior and catching him in a tackle the two of them went crashing and rolling backwards over the ground in a mass of flailing legs and arms. The man losing his club. The world suddenly reduced to just this one fight. All pain and fear forgotten. The two fighters only aware of their primal life impulse, to win and to survive.

Ending up on top and having lost his spatha, Corbulo snarled like a starving wolf as the two men furiously grabbled with each other. Struggling to gain a killer grip on their opponent. But the warrior was strong. Hissing, the man tried to gouge out Corbulo's eyes with his thumbs but in response Corbulo furiously sank his teeth into his opponent's hand eliciting a shriek of pain. Then managing to momentarily break free from the warrior's grip Corbulo yelled as he swiftly drew back and headbutted his opponent, breaking the man's nose with a sickening crack that elicited another howl of pain. Seizing the advantage Corbulo once again headbutted his opponent, bone smashing into bone. The blow momentarily stunning the warrior, his grip loosening and weakening. Staggering back onto his feet, his face covered in blood, his head ringing, Corbulo hurriedly turned to look around for a weapon but not finding one in time instead he lunged at his opponent, stamping his iron studded boot down on the man's face. The blow cracking more bones. Again and again with furious energy Corbulo brought his boot down on the man's face until the warrior had been reduced to bloody pulp.

With a roar the world seemed to return and Corbulo was once again aware of the furious fighting around him. The field covered with the dead and the dying. Wounded men trying to crawl away. The blood staining the grass. The ground littered with abandoned weapons, dead horses, broken shields and helmets. With a whirring noise a throwing axe whistled past Corbulo's head, missing him by just inches. The attack making him cry out in shock. Then abruptly he was surrounded by three of his dismounted bodyguards. The men rushing to his aid and protecting him with their shields as they started to drag him backwards and out of the thickest and fiercest part of the fighting.

"What the fuck do you think you were doing Sir!" one of his bodyguards roared as he turned towards Corbulo. The soldier looking beside himself with fury. "We nearly lost you. Did you not hear me calling you! That was a most stupid thing to do. You are not going to help anyone by getting yourself killed like that. The ala needs you to stay alive Sir. You need to stay alive! So next time listen to me, for fucks sake!"

Staring at his bodyguard Corbulo said nothing before shrugging off their restraining hands and hurriedly turning to look around. Out in the fields and along the river bank the fighting was starting to come to an end as the Romans closed in on the few remaining Quadi tribesmen, dispatching their outnumbered and overwhelmed enemies with increasing impunity.

"They are done!" one of Corbulo's bodyguards cried out as he too observed what was happening down by the riverbank.

Corbulo was just about to speak when a sudden and frantic cry of alarm made him abruptly turn around. The Roman cry was swiftly followed by a hurried trumpet blast signalling - *enemy attack*! The sound and the signal sowing confusion among the Roman horsemen who were milling about across the battlefield. And as his eyes turned in the direction from which the warning had come Corbulo swore as he suddenly spotted a new Quadi war-band charging downhill towards his position. The fields that had been empty just moments before now filled with a mass of running men. The barbarian warriors brandishing their weapons and shields as they came charging to their comrades help. Their unexpected appearance drawing forth gasps of dismay from the Romans gathered around Corbulo. And as they came charging into the attack the enemy warriors began to yell their barbarian battle-cries. Horns blaring. The terrifying sound sending an involuntary chill straight down Corbulo's spine.

But there was no time to waste. Mastering his shock at the appearance of this new band of enemies, Corbulo hurriedly sized up their strength. Then his gaze quickly settled upon the forest a quarter of a mile away. The trees and thick undergrowth presenting a dark impenetrable wilderness in sharp contrast to the open sun-kissed fields in which he found himself. For a moment he hesitated. Then he was on the move. Rushing over to where his standard bearer, clad in his splendid wolf's head and pelt was sitting upon his horse, holding up the proud banner of the equites foederati Germanica. Snatching the battle-standard from the man's hand Corbulo started to run away.

"Fall back! Fall back! With me!" he yelled holding the precious banner up above his head for all to see. For a moment nothing appeared to change. The chaos along the riverbank continuing.

Then abruptly the Roman cavalry abandoned what they had been doing and began to follow him, some of the men moving on foot, having lost their horses. The retreat swiftly gathering momentum and eliciting howls of triumph from the pursuing Quadi tribesmen who were closing in fast. The tribesmen now sprinting to catch their retreating quarry.

“Sir,” one of Corbulo’s bodyguards shouted as he came racing up before hurriedly dismounting, “take my horse!”

Swiftly Corbulo swung himself into the saddle of his new mount, still clutching the ala’s battle-standard, as around him the mass of Roman cavalry surged past, intent on getting away from the enemy. The squadrons and companies now hopelessly mixed up and disorganised. Hurriedly turning to survey the pursuing Quadi as his staff and bodyguards hastily regrouped around him, Corbulo grimaced as he wiped some blood from his brow. Then once again he turned to cast a quick look in the direction of the forest.

“Fall back!” he cried setting out again. “Retreat! With me!”

And as the Roman cavalry retreated along the river bank the Quadi continued their bold pursuit. The tribesmen’s battle-cries turning into yells of triumph. Some of the Quadi starting to scream insults at the Salian Frankish troopers, believing they had them on the run. The barbarians oblivious to the trap and the unseen and silent threat that lurked among the forest along their flank. Leading his men onwards Corbulo once again turned to check on the enemy pursuit. Then judging the moment to be right he slowed his horse and reached for the curved horn made of bone that dangled around his neck.

“About turn!” he yelled as he turned his horse around. “First cohort will face the enemy!”

Then as the Roman troopers slowly began to obey his order Corbulo placed his German horn to his lips and started to blow. The deep, humming sound ringing out across the fields and the nearby forest. Pausing for breath Corbulo stared at the enemy infantry who were still advancing towards him. Confident in their numbers. Eager for battle. Confident they had him on the run. Once again, he blew on his horn and as he fell silent for a long tense moment nothing happened before suddenly from the forest an answering horn rang out, swiftly followed by the blaring of Roman trumpets.

Bursting from the wood where they had been waiting, concealed in reserve for just such an emergency, the 2nd Cohort suddenly appeared. The Roman troopers led by prince Gummar sweeping gleefully into the enemy flank. The ambush catching the Quadi tribesmen by complete surprise. Leaving them with no time to organise a proper defence. Looking on from his horse Corbulo grunted in satisfaction as the massed squadrons of his second cohort went charging straight into the exposed flank of the enemy infantry. The Roman troopers hammering into the Quadi with brutal and merciless force. The momentum of the charge mowing down the tribesmen like harvesting wheat. Men tumbling to the ground. The horses trampling them underfoot. The once confident and insulting enemy cries abruptly transformed into horrified, panic-stricken shrieks.

“Now we have them Sir!” an excited voice yelled.

Raising the battle-standard of the equites foederati Germanica Corbulo pointed the banner at the enemy. “At them!” he bellowed. “At them. Finish them off!”

His men did not need any further encouragement. With wild, savage howls of triumph they broke into a charge, thundering towards the hapless tribesmen. The riders of the 1st cohort lowering their spears as they went crashing through the foremost ranks of the enemy. The cavalry assault deciding the fight in just a few seconds. Assailed on their flank and now from the front the Quadi broke. The surviving tribesmen turning and fleeing. The frantic, terrified men who had been so confident just moments before now running for their lives while others turned to the river and in desperation flung themselves into the Danube where the weight of their clothing and body armour swiftly pulled them under. Following his men but staying out of the fighting, his mounted staff and bodyguards sticking close, Corbulo looked on with growing satisfaction as the battle swiftly became a rout.

The Quadi had no chance of escaping on foot and as parties of enemy warriors started to try and surrender, pathetically dropping their weapons and raising their hands, desperately pleading for their lives, one of his officers turned to Corbulo with a silent, inquiring look but in reply he shook his head.

"Kill them all!" Corbulo said grimly. "We have no time or the capacity to take prisoners. They are all guilty men."

At last, the fight was over and as Corbulo picked his way across the field littered with the debris of battle and the dead, the dying and the wounded he saw Gummar riding towards him. The tall Frankish prince looked elated; a massive smile plastered across his face.

"We destroyed them Sir," Gummar cried out speaking in German in his thick Frankish accent. "Not one but two war-bands in one day! That's not bad. Tonight, we should make an offering to Magusanus for giving us this great victory. How about we make it a human sacrifice. One of the Quadi prisoners would do. We could burn him. What do you say?"

"Well done prince Gummar," Corbulo called out looking pleased. "I am glad you obeyed your orders and did not reveal your position until I had summoned you. That made all the difference. But there will be no human sacrifice to Magusanus tonight. If you wish to honour the battle-God, then do so by building an altar to him and offering him the enemy's weapons which we have captured. You may dedicate this victory to him. Then throw the rest of the enemy's equipment into the river so they cannot use it again and let the men know. Tell them that they fought well today."

"Very well Sir," Gummar said his enthusiasm only slightly dimmed. "So, what now?"

Quickly checking the position of the sun Corbulo reached up to wipe some more blood from his brow. Then he turned to look around at the battlefield and the parties of dismounted Romans who has started to move in and among the enemy dead searching for loot and finishing off the enemy wounded. The soldiers stooping to rob their slain opponents of anything of value.

"It's getting late, and the men and horses will need to rest," Corbulo said. "We will camp here tonight. I want you to set a picket up on that high ground over there," Corbulo said pointing. "And another one over there. That should give us advance warning of any trouble. Cremate our dead prince Gummar and see what you can do for our wounded. Then check on the state of our supplies and have your officers prepare their strength reports. Once you have done that come and find me with the final tally. We will push on again tomorrow at dawn."

Leaving his deputy behind Corbulo trotted towards the water's edge where some yelling and screaming had suddenly broken out. Gathered in a tight cluster near to the water's edge were a group of civilians, men, women and children. The people appeared filthy, exhausted and terrified. Their clothes reduced to rags. Some of them were clamped in slavers leg irons. And as Corbulo and his staff approached he could see that a tug of war was going on. Some of his soldiers were trying to pull a young woman away from the group while some of the civilians were hanging onto the screaming woman, refusing to let her go.

"What the hell is going on here," Corbulo barked as he came up. "Can't you see. They are our people! They are not barbarians!"

Letting the young woman go the soldiers retreated a short distance, the men suddenly looking uncomfortable and guilty, refusing to look up at their commander. Glaring at his men Corbulo allowed the soldiers to feel his silent disapproval of what they had been attempting to do. Then from his horse he turned to look down at the group of civilians huddled together in a pathetic attempt at trying to create some safety with numbers.

"Bless you prefect," an old man suddenly called out speaking in good clear Latin. "We are Romans, all of us. Civilians. Taken from our homes to be sold as slaves Sir. The Quadi they took us. But now you and your men have saved us. You have freed us from a fate worse than death. Bless you Sir, bless you..." and as the man spoke more and more of the civilians started to join in, showering Corbulo with frantic, unrestrained gratitude. Some of the people weeping for joy as if a dam of emotions had been allowed to burst. Other shaking and unable to speak. The sheer horror of the ordeal that they had been through written across their pale, haggard faces.

"Alright, alright," Corbulo said at last raising his hand. "You are not out of danger yet. Unfortunately, I cannot take you with me. The best I can do is point you in that direction," he said pointing to the west. “You will have to walk for I do not have any wagons or spare horses. But I will be sending my wounded men back with you. There is a temporary Roman fort along the banks of the Morava River. Head for the fort and you should be safe there for a while. And remember this,” Corbulo said his expression growing stern, “it is the emperor Gallienus who has sent me to rescue you. The emperor has not forgotten his subjects. He fights for you. He is your lord. Remember that!”

Turning away from the civilians Corbulo dismounted and led his horse down to the water’s edge, allowing the beast a drink. Holding the reins for a moment he gazed into the dark waters of the Danube, quietly controlling his breathing, taking a personal moment to settle his nerves. Trying to force the close brush with death from his mind. Accepting a cloth from one of his bodyguards Corbulo quickly used it to wipe the blood from his face but as the army doctor suddenly appeared, hovering nearby, eager to inspect him for wounds, Corbulo silently waved the man away. Crouching beside the river dipping the cloth into the water he finished cleaning his face. Then straightening up he turned his eyes towards the Roman side of the river.

“Congratulations Sir on your victory, that was well done,” Atlas said as he came up to where Corbulo was standing. The intelligence officer appearing strangely subdued. Turning around Corbulo said nothing as he watched Tobias and his small armed escort moving up, leading the two mules carrying the King’s treasure boxes strapped across their backs. While behind them Sulpicia had appeared, riding a horse, her back straight as a plank. Her head held aloft as if she were royalty attending a party that was being hosted in her honour. Glancing at Atlas he nodded a silent thanks before once again turning his attention to Danube as if he were searching for something, first upstream and then downstream. But the wide river remained deserted.

“Something the matter Sir,” Atlas said picking up on Corbulo’s mood.

“Yes, I was hoping that we would have come across Crastus and the Nemesis by now,” Corbulo replied sombrely. “It’s been too long since we have had news from Probus but there is no sign of the Nemesis. I hope they are alright. I need to get a message through to Probus. He is out there somewhere,” Corbulo said gesturing irritably towards the opposite side of the river. “If the Nemesis does not show up soon, I am going to need someone to swim across the river, find Probus and deliver my message.”

“Well, don't ask me because I can’t swim Sir,” Atlas replied looking away.

***

Night had come and sitting beside the campfire Corbulo was still awake. The Roman camp around him asleep. The sound of snoring, the occasional snort and stamp of a horse and the soft hiss and crackle of the burning fire the only sounds. The warm summer air was balmy and filled with the scent of freshly felled wood and smoke. The darkness total except for the mass of Roman campfires concentrated close to the bank of the Danube.

Poking a stick into the flames Corbulo idly watched the hungry flames toying with the wood. The sparks shooting up into the night only to vanish as soon as they had appeared before abruptly, he was aware of movement in the darkness and a moment later Sulpicia and Atlas sat down beside him. The fire lighting up their faces in its reddish flickering light.

“Prefect,” Sulpicia said turning to Corbulo with a purposeful look as Atlas looked on in his strangely subdued and distracted manner. “I really need to speak to you.”

“It's late,” Corbulo said glancing across at her with a weary look. "Can it not wait?"

“It’s regarding the king’s gold that you and I stole,” Sulpicia said quietly pressing on, her voice determined. “I know you said no but I need you to reconsider. Allow me to go and meet with the king and act as your go between. I can help end this war. I am the perfect emissary. Allow me to take one of the chests of treasure with me to prove that I am serious, that you are serious about making peace. The king will not see that as weakness. No. He will listen to me. I know the king, he will be desperate to make peace now. You have already shown him to be weak in his warrior's eyes. That could prove fatal to him, and he knows it. A king who cannot protect his own people quickly loses all respect. What is true for us Romans is also true for the barbarians. Please I beg you, let me go and speak to king Hildimer."

For a moment Corbulo did not reply, gazing instead into the fire. Then at last he turned towards Sulpicia.

“Why are you so interested in making peace,” he said quietly. “When you and your husband Regalian raised the banner of rebellion against emperor Gallienus you knew that this act would cause enormous suffering. What Regalian did was the opposite of making peace. He and you started a war! So why now? Why are you now so interested in making peace? I can’t figure it out.”

“That is a stupid question,” Sulpicia retorted looking away. “Everyone wants peace. It’s obvious. I learned my lesson, prefect, when I lost everything, my husband, my position, my estates and my reputation. And now I have nothing left. So yes peace. If I can help bring it about well then I have gone some way to making up for all the pain and destruction my husband and I caused."

“No,” Corbulo said slowly shaking his head. “Your request is denied. I cannot let you go to speak with the king. The answer is no, and it is final. If you were to go to his camp now, he would simply use you as a hostage against us and besides you have been with us for too long. You know our plans and our numbers. I cannot take the risk. Our enemy may learn much from you."

"I would not betray you!" Sulpicia said sounding outraged at the thought, her eyes blazing. "If you think I would divulge important information to king Hildimer then you clearly do not know me."

"Maybe that is true," Corbulo replied, "but everyone eventually talks when they are tortured. I am sorry but I cannot take the risk."

“This is wrong, prefect,” Sulpicia hissed, growing angry. “Why do you refuse to use the gold that we stole? What was the point of taking that treasure if you don’t use that wealth. You say that you cannot figure me out but now it is I who cannot understand you.”

Gazing back at Sulpicia Corbulo remained silent.

“We had an agreement, you and I,” Corbulo said quietly but firmly, “you would lead me to the king’s treasure and in return I would promote you to the emperor when I make my final report. That is all. Nothing more, nothing less. I never promised to give you a say in how I intend to use the treasure we took from the king. Your part in all of this is now over. You should return to Carnuntum."

Glaring at Corbulo from across the fire, Sulpicia looked livid. Then without saying another word she rose to her feet and vanished off into the darkness. For a moment Corbulo watched her go before his gaze settled upon Atlas, Corbulo considering his intelligence officer with a displeased look.

“You have not been the same, Atlas, since you started working with her,” Corbulo said quietly. "You are a changed man, and I don't know why or how. But she has managed to wrap you completely around her finger. I can see it and so can everyone else. That woman has seduced you and started to cloud your judgement. What’s the matter with you? Where has the cocky, arrogant, confident trickster we all used to love to hate gone?”

“Yeah, maybe it is as you say,” Atlas replied looking away with a tired, distracted expression. “I just find it strangely hard to say no to her. I am sorry Sir. It seems she has managed to find a weakness in me. A flaw in my character. I am not sure what I can do about it.”

“Well, whatever it is stop it! I told you to keep it professional,” Corbulo said throwing the stick into the fire, “and focus on your job Atlas. Get your act together, man. Good men will die if the likes of you and me screw things up. And I cannot have that.”

“I am not fucking her,” Atlas replied sourly looking down at his hand. “It is not true. It's not like that.”

“Well, she is doing something to you,” Corbulo growled, “and I don’t like it. You are not yourself these days. People are starting to notice.”

“Right," Atlas said with a sigh. "So, what do you want me to do?"

“I want you to keep an eye on her,” Corbulo said switching to German as he turned to look at the darkness beyond the fire.

“Make sure she does not do anything stupid like absconding from the camp without permission. And tell her Atlas that if she mentioned this idea of hers again, I will be sending her back to Carnuntum with or without her consent. And you will keep her away from me. There is something not quite right about that woman.”

Chapter Seventeen - To Capture a King

"It's Atlas, Sir," one of Corbulo's bodyguards called out pointing. "But it is too soon for him to return. Something must have happened!"

It was morning and leading the column of Roman cavalry across the fields at a walk Corbulo had turned to peer at the small band of approaching horsemen. His scouts had appeared along the top of a barren ridge and the men were now galloping towards him across the green rolling countryside.

Refusing to slow his pace or change direction Corbulo continued onwards across the fields before glancing at Tobias nearby, riding his horse, the accountant followed by his small escort and the mules carrying the king's treasure chests strapped to their backs.

"Sir!" Atlas cried out as he, Sulpicia and their band of guides came galloping up. "The Quadi King! Hildimer! I think we have found him."

"You sure about this," Corbulo called out. "You sure it is him? The king!"

"I think so," Atlas gasped catching his breath and nodding as he hurriedly fell in alongside. "We came across a large group of Quadi Sir. They are in the middle of crossing the river, returning home. The Danube is filled with boats and rafts. There must be at least a thousand or more tribesmen. They appear to have a mass of loot and slaves with them. Such a large force can only mean that this is a king's war-band. It must be him, Hildimer!"

"A thousand men in the midst of crossing the river you say," Corbulo said before hurriedly turning to gaze in the direction of the Danube which was hidden from view by the rolling countryside. “Where?”

“Less than an hour’s ride from us,” Atlas blurted out, unable to hide his growing excitement. “If we attack them now, we can catch them as they are still crossing the river. When they are still disorganised. When we came across them only a few of their men had made it over onto this side of the river and those were not prepared for battle. They did not look like they were expecting trouble. They appeared to be more interested in securing the loot they have stolen and their slaves. They had posted no pickets. If we move fast Sir, we can rout them! We can destroy them and possibly kill or capture their king.”

“Did they see you?”

“No, I don’t think so. We kept our distance when we first spotted them. I can show you where they are Sir. Less than an hour’s ride away!”

“Did you see if they had any cavalry with them?”

“No cavalry, Sir,” Atlas said quickly shaking his head. “We did not see any. But they are transporting stolen cattle across the river on barges.”

Carefully Corbulo exhaled thinking it through. Then making up his mind he turned to prince Gummar who was riding beside him. The Frankish prince observing the conversation with Atlas in eager, hungry silence.

“Prince Gummar,” Corbulo said quickly, “you will take the 2nd cohort. I will lead the attack with the 1st. Once we approach the enemy, I want you to break away and loop around and fall on them from the rear. But you are to attack only once you hear my signal. Two blasts from my horn. Is that understood. Make sure that you and your men are not spotted while carrying out your manoeuvre. We need to surprise them, and we need to move fast. Go," Corbulo added.

"Sir," Gummar growled looking pleased as he hurriedly wheeled his horse around and started back down the length of the Roman column.

"Take us to where you saw the enemy," Corbulo said turning to Atlas.

***

Out on the Danube under the deep blue summer sky and blazing sun the wide, placid waters were choked with an armada of hundreds of small boats, crude rafts and dugouts. The vessels piled high with a mass of looted possessions and packed with crowds of men, women and children. The people using paddles and their hands to propel themselves across the river. The disorganised flotilla of boats slowly heading for the northern shore. The craft were struggling to maintain their positions against the current. The river alive with shouts, swearing men, barking dogs, wailing babies and the loud impatient mooing of cattle. The nervous, jittery bulls, cows and horses standing marooned upon their barges. While on the chosen landing grounds along the northern shore more boats were already attempting to land their precious cargoes. Warriors were wading ashore waste down in the river, leading lines of slaves who were bound to each by ropes and chains. Some of their colleagues were carrying heavy packs on their shoulders, dumping them along the riverbank where large piles of looted possessions were starting to form. Others were coaxing herds of stolen cattle, mules, pigs and horses, off the rafts and into the shallow water with the aid of barking dogs and the men's spears. The Quadi trying to push the beasts into the temporary animal pens that had been erected along the water's edge. The whole riverbank alive with activity and crawling with people. No one yet aware of the mortal danger that was swiftly approaching.

"First Cohort will attack the enemy!" Corbulo bellowed gripping his spear. "Hear me lads! The man who brings me their king will receive a year's wages! At them boys! Charge! Charge!"

And his men needed no further encouragement. With a great roaring cry the hundreds of Roman troopers broke into a wild charge. The horsemen sweeping in over the ridge and then straight down the slope towards the enemy landing grounds. A mass of fast-moving beasts and eager men. The horses' hooves pounding and shaking the earth. The assault sending a flock of startled birds fleeing into the sky from a nearby cops of trees. The Roman spears were lowered. Their shields adorned with the white wolf emblem on a black background. Their menacing and excited battle-cries ringing out as they sensed another victory.

Following behind his men, accompanied by his staff and bodyguards, but holding back from leading from the front again Corbulo looked on. It seemed that about half the enemy horde had so far managed to cross the Danube while the rest were still stuck out on the water or still on the Roman side of the river. Down by the water the Quadi appeared to be in shock. The warriors coming to a startled halt and ceasing what they had been doing to stare in astonishment at the Roman cavalry before frantic screaming and yelling broke out and panic set in as people began to rush about. The panic swiftly spreading to the river where two rafts went crashing into each other, the collision sending a magnificent horned bull crashing into the water with an outraged bellow.

Along the riverbank swiftly recovering from their shock bands of Quadi warriors were bravely rushing to meet the Roman charge but it was too late for them to form a proper shield wall.

With thundering hooves, the Salian Franks and Batavians went straight through them. The sheer momentum of the Roman cavalry assault scattering their opponents, cutting and tumbling men to the ground with their spears and horses. The riverbank was instantly transformed into a shrieking, chaotic melee. Men stabbing and jabbing at each other in a frenzy of violence. Cantering into the ferocious fighting Corbulo drove his spear into the back of a wounded but running man finishing him off but losing his spear in the process. Hurriedly pulling his spatha from his belt he turned to look around at the hand-to-hand fighting, his bodyguards protectively closing ranks around him. But there was no sign of the Quadi king. No proud battle-standard to give away his position. Where was the bastard?

“A year's wages to the man who brings me their king!” Corbulo roared as he turned this way and then that way.

Storming towards Corbulo two Quadi warriors tried to get close enough to attack him with their spears but as they came at him one of them was quickly knocked to the ground by one of Corbulo’s bodyguards. Moments later the man was shrieking in terror as he was trampled by horses' hooves while his colleague was repeatedly stabbed by two of Corbulo’s bodyguards. The furious Roman blows catching him in quick succession in his chest, shoulder, neck and arm, bringing him down onto his knees with a groan before a glancing blow from another horse knocked him out onto his back where he no longer moved.

Ignoring the attack Corbulo continued to search the battlefield for king Hildimer before without warning a Frankish throwing axe came hurtling through the air and struck one of the men riding next to him. The weapon embedding itself in the Roman's leg and causing the soldier to cry out in agony and shock. Grimacing Corbulo started to move, his bodyguards following as they cut and battered their way through the chaotic fighting. Slashing at a warrior with his sword Corbulo missed. His opponent clutching a spear staggering backwards in response, the tribesman looking wild and out of his head. Then just as the man was about to launch himself at Corbulo a herd of bulls and cows, driven mad by the sound of battle, came thundering and stampeding straight through the midst of the battle. The terrified, panic-stricken animals flattening everything and everyone in their path. And instantly Corbulo's would be assailant had vanished from view his body carried away under the animal's hooves.

Swearing out loud as his horse nearly reared up in panic and threatened to throw him to the ground, Corbulo struggled for control. Then he was out of the danger and charging down a fleeing tribesman, striking him with a slicing blow across his neck that brought the man down to the ground with a sharp cry. Rallying near the edge of the water Corbulo had barely any time to recover before with a low growl a Quadi war-dog, wearing a spiked collar came hurtling towards him, a streak of black fur, before the beast launched itself at him displaying its horrible fangs. But the dog had misjudged his leap and instead of finding Corbulo the beast went smacking into the side of Corbulo's horse sending the screaming horse kicking and cantering away in a frenzy. One of its back legs striking the dog in its head as it fled. Struggling to stay in the saddle and calm his mount Corbulo swore out loud as a woman tightly clutching the hand of a young girl came running past him. The girl's face white as a sheet, her eyes bulging in absolute terror as the pair tried to escape, madly weaving their way through the fighting.

Mastering his horse Corbulo hurriedly turned to look around but the fighting along the riverbank was nearly over. Dead and wounded Quadi tribesmen lay scattered everywhere across the field and along the water's edge. His men were busying themselves with finishing off the remaining survivors and the enemy wounded while Roman civilians were rushing past, trying to escape. The terrified civilian cries incessant. Others were down on their knees begging for mercy unaware that they had been freed. His men appeared to be triumphant Corbulo could see but the battle was not yet over. Catching sight of a band of a hundred or so Quadi warriors further down the riverbank he swore again. This band of warriors appeared to have had time to form a proper defence. The warriors forming a tight circle for all round defence. Their spears wedged into the ground and pointing outwards like the bristles of a hedgehog. And as he stared at them Corbulo could see that his horsemen did not know what to do. The rows of spear points making their horses reluctant to charge into the enemy. The Salian Franks milling about around the edges of the hedgehog position but not being able to break into the formation. The cries of the leaderless Roman cavalry growing increasingly frustrated.

These Quadi appeared to be better prepared and knew what they were doing and as he peered at them Corbulo suddenly noticed an enemy war banner being held aloft in their midst. Some of the tribesmen too appeared to be better equipped with proper looking body-armour and helmets than their comrades. Were they protecting their king! Instantly Corbulo was moving towards them, galloping past a massive pile of looted belongings and as he rode towards the enemy he was joined by a solitary bodyguard. But there was no time to go looking for the rest of his staff and his bodyguards who had got separated from him during the earlier chaos. Slowing his pace as he approached the band of Quadi, Corbulo cried out to the men who were with him, before coming to a halt.

"Dismount! We will take them on foot. With me boys!"

Dismounting and letting his horse go free Corbulo looked grim as he quickly adjusted his shield on his arm and tightened his grip on his spatha sword. Then as he was joined by more and more of his dismounted men, he started to advance towards the band of Quadi. His eyes fixed upon a well clad giant of a man defiantly holding up the enemy banner.

Closing in on the enemy the combatants suddenly fell silent as each side eyed the other with savage determination. This was going to be a fight to the death and both sides knew it. Leading his men at a walk Corbulo spat something from his mouth before raising and drawing back his sword so that it was level with the top of his shield, the point aimed straight at the enemy. Breaking the ominous silence, he suddenly cried out and charged the last few yards towards the enemy position. The soldiers with him joining in with a great, triumphant roar.

Catching and deflecting an enemy spear against his shield Corbulo thrust his sword straight into a tribesman's face. The steel blade punching into flesh and bone with a sickening crunch as to his left and right he was joined by his Salian Franks. The Romans protecting each other with their shields, most of the men having been extensively trained for this type of combat. Their infantry training now revealing itself. The soldiers starting to cut their way into the centre of the circle of enemies with grim resolve. The close hand to hand combat ferocious and brutal. Bodies sinking to the ground. Men being stabbed, impaled, cut and cleaved. Their corpses trampled underfoot. Blood flying through the air. Voices screaming, groaning and yelling in triumph. The relentless thrust, block and counter thrust going on with no let-up, no mercy.

Crying out in shock as a Quadi sword point punched past his shield and into his shoulder Corbulo staggered backwards. But his chain mail body armour had done its work, and the blade had not managed to pierce his flesh. Battering away another spear that tried to stab him Corbulo swore as he felt his arm stiffen with pain but there was no time to check if he had been wounded somewhere else. Parrying another tribesman with his shield, the Roman soldier beside him knocked his opponent of balance and seizing his opportunity Corbulo stabbed the tribesman in his exposed neck. The blade slicing through an artery and splattering Corbulo's face with blood. Then suddenly Corbulo was through and into the centre of the enemy position. Rearing up very close to him was the giant holding the enemy banner. The man surrounded on three sides now by Romans, his position utterly hopeless. But as Corbulo leaped towards him the man was struck by a Frankish throwing axe that hit him square in his back. The blow bringing him down onto his knees with a groan before he abruptly vanished from view under a pile of Romans who leaped onto him. The frenzied soldiers stabbing at him with their swords. Then one of the Romans close to Corbulo picked up the fallen enemy banner and holding it up in triumph he yelled. The man's cry bringing forth howls of triumph from his comrades. Pausing, breathing heavily Corbulo turned to look around at the bloody carnage. The fight was over. All around him lay dead Quadi warriors. Many still lying where they had fought to the last. The circle of once living men turned into a circle of the dead.

"Is he the king?" Corbulo shouted as he pulled one of his men off the fallen giant but in response no one offered a reply. Looking frustrated Corbulo stared down at the dead giant, gripping his bloodied sword in his hand. The pain in his shoulder starting to bite deep. His muscles stiffening and making it hard to move his left arm. Then looking away Corbulo swore. No one appeared to know the answer to whether this was the Quadi king or not.

“Sir,” a Roman voice cried out suddenly pointing at something.

Turning to look in the direction the man was pointing Corbulo frowned. Further along the riverbank, downstream from his position, small parties of surviving Quadi warriors and Roman civilians were fleeing. Running as fast as they could, abandoning anything that was too heavy to carry. The people desperate to get away. Staring at them Corbulo grunted before stiffly and painfully reaching for the curved horn that hung from around his neck. Forcing the instrument to his mouth with a shaking hand he quickly blew on it, before pausing and then repeating himself. The signal to summon prince Gummar into the battle. The deep humming sound ringing out across the riverbank.

But as he shifted his gaze to the direction in which he was expecting Gummar to appear Corbulo swore again as nothing happened. For a long moment he waited but there was no answering horn. No sign of his men from the 2nd cohort.

“Where the fuck is Gummar!” Corbulo cried out in frustration. “He is going to let those bastards escape!”

But among the weary soldiers who were with him no one answered. The men busying themselves finishing off their wounded enemies and moving about looting the dead. Corbulo was about to blow on his horn again when from the direction of the river a new and unexpected trumpet rang out. The long, urgent blast ringing out across the water. Turning in the direction from which the trumpet blast had come Corbulo gasped in surprise.

Out on the Danube the armada of small boats, dugouts and rafts were still stuck in the main channel. The occupants of the boats seeing what was occurring on the northern shore and unsure of what to do. The boats leaderless. The men paddling to keep their position against the current but not moving towards the shore. The Quadi warriors shouting to each other. Their slaves silent. Babies wailing and cattle mooing. But there heading downstream straight into the centre of the flotilla of watercraft was a newcomer. A solitary Roman warship. Her sails furled and stowed. Her banks of oars plying the river in magnificent and practised unison as she gracefully bore down on her enemies. And as Corbulo looked on in in awe he could see the deck of the Nemesis lined with Roman soldiers.

“Holy fuck! Look at that!” a few Roman voices cried out as they too spotted the majestic warship moving calmly and purposefully into the flank of the enemy flotilla. “It’s the Nemesis!”

Rooted to the ground Corbulo could only observe as the battering ram at the bow of the naval galley sliced through a dugout, tumbling its yelling occupants into the river, the craft vanishing completely. Then the Nemesis was in and amongst the armada of little boats and the carnage began. Spitting arrows from her deck the soldiers onboard began to target the small boats and rafts with deadly volley after volley. The Roman arrows sweeping men and beasts from the defenceless boats and into the river. Scything their opponents down. Leaving their enemy with no place to hide or run to. The tranquil river scene instantly transformed into a screaming hell as more and more bodies ended up in the water. The Nemesis leaving a devastating trail of destruction in her wake as she cut straight through the centre of the flotilla. Her bronze headed battering ram crushing and sinking boats. Her swell swamping heavily loaded rafts and capsizing dugouts. Her bowmen tumbling their enemies and beasts into the water. Soon the river was filled with bodies, some dead, some drowning, some trying to cling to the wreckage of abandoned watercraft while others were desperately trying to swim to the safety. The pitiful cries of desperate people and panic-stricken cattle ringing out. The Danube suddenly filled with the corpses of drowned cattle, some of the stronger beasts managing to keep their heads just above water as they frantically sought to reach the land. The terror visible in their bulging eyes.

But there was no let up from the Roman bombardment as suddenly the Nemesis reversed course. Her banks of oars starting to propel her back upstream. Joining the volleys of arrows spitting from the Nemesis's flanks the Roman heavy artillery, bolt throwers and harpoons began to target the Quadi boats that were further away. The missiles hurtling into their targets with incredible speed and force, punching into flesh and through armour with devastating force. Sending their targets crashing and flying into the river like leaves blown about in the wind. The harsh shouted orders coming from the deck of the Nemesis audible as the artillery teams loaded and released their missiles. The Romans working with quick, practised professionalism. The storm of flying projectiles bringing forth gasps from the Roman soldiers gathered around Corbulo.

Staring at the growing carnage out on the river Corbulo suddenly saw several flaming arrows go hurtling high into the sky from the deck of the Nemesis before gracefully curving back down into the river. Moments later a section of the Danube was on fire. The incredible sight bringing forth cries of wonder from the Roman soldiers as if they were witnessing magic. The flames spreading rapidly across the placid waters as they engulfed any watercraft that was unfortunate to be close by. The flames setting fire to the boats and anyone left in the water.

The horrible shrieks and screaming of burning people adding to the chaos.

“Sir,” the one bodyguard who was still with Corbulo called out in warning as the man suddenly pointed at something inland and away from the river.

Hurriedly turning to see what the man was pointing at Corbulo bit his lip as downstream from his position companies of horsemen had suddenly appeared coming down towards the river from over the ridgeline at a gentle trot. The riders appearing to be in no hurry to join their comrades. The men from his 2nd cohort had finally showed up. Spotting prince Gummar among them Corbulo hurriedly moved to intercept his deputy.

“Where the hell were you!” Corbulo shouted angrily as he advanced towards Gummar on foot. “Did you not hear my signal. Because you didn’t attack when you were supposed to attack you let some of our enemy's escape. What the fuck happened to you?”

“We ran into some trouble of our own,” prince Gummar replied, his face sour and unapologetic. “I did as you instructed,” the prince continued as he wearily brought his horse to a halt and as he did, Corbulo suddenly noticed that some of the riders with him were bearing wounds. “We ran into another band of Quadi,” Gummar said looking displeased, the tone of his voice slightly insubordinate as he turned to Corbulo, “and we had to fight them. That delayed me and I lost some good men today! I lost some friends, Sir.”

Coolly sizing up his deputy Corbulo remained silent. Then taking a deep breath he turned towards the massive piles of abandoned Quadi loot that lined the landing grounds along the shore. “Post a guard on that loot,” Corbulo said. “I don’t want the men taking what they want. That stuff is off-limits. We will let the freed civilians take what they want first. It's their belongings after all. The remainder, all that can be easily carried, will be divided up among the soldiers with each man receiving an equal share. Burn the stuff that no one wants, and which is too heavy to carry. And find Sulpicia and get her to identify wherever that dead Quadi giant over there with that war banner is king Hildimer or not. I need to know if we got the bastard."

Turning away Corbulo strode back towards the water's edge. Out on the Danube the surviving Quadi boats and rafts had fled back to the Roman side of the river. The placid water had gone strangely quiet. The Danube filled with floating, burning wreckage and bodies, loads and loads of bodies. The corpses drifting slowly away downstream and out of sight or washing up against the riverbank and getting stranded on the mudflats. But Corbulo's gaze was not on the carnage and debris of battle. They were fixed upon the Nemesis as the solitary warship, job done, steadily approached the landing grounds along the northern shore. Her oars propelling the vessel towards his position and as she drew closer Corbulo suddenly spotted Crastus standing high up on the prow at the very front of the galley beside the figurine of Nemesis the god of vengeance. The big centurion was holding onto a tight mooring rope and cut a dashing figure. Like some conquering pirate. And as the bow of the Nemesis came gliding into the soft mud of the riverbank Crastus started to bellow and beat his chest in savage triumph with his one free hand. His monkey act eliciting a smattering of sniggering and cheers from the Roman soldiers assembling along the bank. Then as the naval galley dropped its iron anchor, Crastus leaped from his perch straight into the water, landing with a great splash but still being able to maintain his footing. A physical feat that brought forth more cheering from the Roman soldiers who were looking on. Wading ashore

Crastus, sporting a huge grin and looking like he was thoroughly enjoying himself, headed towards the spot where Corbulo stood waiting for him. While the centurion's soldiers crowded the deck, the men's arms raised, the soldiers crying out to their comrades ashore. The men in a jubilant mood.

"Did you enjoy that little display out on the river," the big brash centurion called out as he advanced towards Corbulo, his grin splitting his rugged face. "I thought I would try out all the Nemesis's weapon systems. Just to see how they work. Probably won't get a chance to do that again. I liked the Greek fire, but we ran out of naphtha! Still, we ruined the Quadi's day - did we not Sir. Fucking destroyed them! That was what I call a proper massacre."

"You look like you have been enjoying yourself Crastus," Corbulo said smiling, the centurion's grin proving too infectious to resist.

"I have and I am Sir," Crastus said as the two officers quickly embraced before Crastus took a step back and rapped out a smart salute. "You well Sir? The ala - we are in good shape?"

"Yes, we are alright," Corbulo replied.

"Is Harald still alive?" Crastus said with sudden touching concern as he quickly turned to search the officers and men gathered around Corbulo. "I do not see him here."

"Yes, he is still alive. He is back guarding our base camp."

Nodding, looking pleased Crastus quickly turned to some of the officers and men gathered around Corbulo and picking out friends he began to shake their hands but as prince Gummar rode up accompanied by Sulpicia and Atlas, Crastus coolly ignored him. The two officers carefully and studiously avoiding each other. Their intense personal dislike unable to dampen the general euphoric mood of the Romans gathered around the shore.

"Well? Is it him?" Corbulo said hurriedly turning to Sulpicia as she came towards him.

"No," she replied coldly shaking her head, refusing to look him in the eye. "That man you asked me to identify was not king Hildimer. Nor is he among any of the other bodies that I looked at."

Swearing softly Corbulo turned to Gummar who shrugged. "We have not found him on the battlefield," the prince said. "I have tasked some of my men with bringing in the enemy corpses. Maybe he will be among them."

"You are not going to find king Hildimer here," Crastus interrupted. "The king crossed the Danube further downstream two days ago."

"What! Are you sure of this?"

"I am Sir," Crastus replied. "I and my ship have been out patrolling on the Danube ever since you left us at Carnuntum. We saw the king crossing over himself, but we arrived too late to stop him. He has five thousand men with him," Crastus added eyeing Corbulo with a grave look.

"Five thousand men!" an officer standing beside Corbulo exclaimed.

"And cavalry," Crastus continued, addressing Corbulo. "The king can muster at least several hundred horsemen. Maybe more. He has an army with him. Fuck knows where they are right now. But we heard them complaining that their homes were being attacked. Was that you Sir?"

"Who else," prince Gummar sneered gazing at Crastus with a sour, displeased look which the big centurion ignored.

For a long moment none of the Romans spoke. The silence suppressing some of the earlier elation.

"So, this was not the king's warband who we attacked," Corbulo said turning at last to look around at the riverbank with a resigned look. "You were wrong Atlas," he added shifting his gaze to his intelligence officer. "But no matter. This is what we came here to do - to destroy the enemy."

"So, what now?" Gummar growled sounding unhappy. "What do we do now that we have failed to catch the Quadi king. With respect Sir, the plan was to try and ambush the king as he crossed the Danube and that has now failed. So, we are going to have to come up with a new plan and quickly. If the king has cavalry they could attack us at any moment. Our situation is precarious."

"I know," Corbulo replied turning to his deputy with a grave look. "And you are right. We cannot go up against an army of five thousand men, especially one that is supported by cavalry. Alright," Corbulo continued coming to a decision. "There is nothing more we can do. We will have to retreat to our fort along the Morava and regroup there. Crastus," Corbulo added turning to him. "Did you and the Moor manage to contact Probus as I instructed you to? Can you get a message through to him? It's urgent."

"I certainly did," Crastus replied grinning again. "Probus has been busy clearing out the enemy war-bands from our territory Sir and rallying what remains of the Danube garrisons. He's done alright if I may say so. I didn't expect much from him to start with but he's good at making people agree with him. He even had words with those lazy bastards from the Fourteenth whose job we are doing for them. The Moor and I managed to meet up with some of Probus's Africans a week ago. We have set up a system of scouts along our side of river who are able to get a message through to Probus."

"Excellent," Corbulo replied looking pleased. "Well then, I need you to get a message to Probus from me. Like I said it is urgent. This one really needs to get through no matter what."

"Sure. I can do that," Crastus replied cheerfully. "Although these Moors can be a bit funny. They have this strange notion in their heads that they are better than us. I will happily prove to them that they are wrong."

"Good, I will give you the message verbally and also state it in writing just so that there can be no confusion."

"Very well Sir," Crastus replied. "But there is something else that you need to know. Yesterday coming downstream, we spotted another Quadi warband landing on the northern shore upstream from here. They were a sizable force. About the same strength as this one which we destroyed today. But like the king they too had some cavalry. And who knows how many more have now made the crossing into your rear. So, Sir if you are planning to retrace your steps and retreat along the river to your fort you are likely to run straight into them. I think it's possible that the enemy has already cut off your retreat and like I said fuck knows where king Hildimer and his army are right now. There is a danger that you will get trapped between these two enemy forces."

Once again silence settled upon the gathered officers. The men glancing at each other with concerned looks.

“We could build rafts and ferry the men and horses to our side of the river,” one of his officers said turning to Corbulo.

“No,” Corbulo said, “that will not do. It would take too long, and king Hildimer will take such a retreat as a sign of weakness, and I am not done with the king yet. Besides I am not abandoning Harald and our men back at the fort. No. We are going to remain on the barbarian side of the river and see this out to its conclusion. We will just have to rely on our mobility to escape if we run into a superior enemy force. Crastus,” Corbulo turning to him, “we will give you our most seriously wounded so that you can take them back to Carnuntum. They will be safer with you than with us. See that they are properly tended to. But the priority is to ensure that you get my message through to Probus, understood.”

“Sir,” Crastus said quickly saluting.

“Regards our retreat. There is another way,” Atlas said quickly turning to Corbulo. “If the Quadi hope to trap us against the river we could avoid them by heading inland before turning back to the west.”

“That would take us into trackless forests and swamps,” Corbulo responded looking unhappy.

“Yes, it would,” Atlas replied, “but my guides say they know a path through the wilderness. If we move fast, we have a good chance of slipping away before the enemy can catch us. The Quadi will not be expecting us to enter those forests and swamps. If you give permission, I will lead us out of danger. Let me do this. This is what I am good at Sir.”

Chapter Eighteen - The Fork in the Road

It was raining as the column of Roman cavalry trotted across the green, rolling countryside. The rain was coming down at a sharp angle, blowing into the men's faces. The heavens were grey and overcast, the clouds moving restlessly across the sky to the east with no hint that the weather would turn soon. The soldiers were clad in their bad weather poncho's, their hoods drawn over their heads, their shields slung across their backs, the men gripping their long thrusting spears. The rain streaming from their cloaks and hoods, their horses' heads lowered. Few of the soldiers were speaking, bearing their discomfort in stoic silence. Leading his men Corbulo once again glanced across the fields towards the small troop of Quadi horsemen who were stubbornly keeping pace with him. The enemy scouts riding parallel to his men and maintaining a respectable distance. The Quadi riders sticking to the ridge line as they shadowed his force. The enemy had found them that morning but so far, they appeared content to just follow and observe.

“Damn scouts!” an officer riding behind Corbulo called out in frustration, his face crunched up again the driving rain. “Shall I take a squadron and drive them off Sir. They will be reporting our position to their comrades.”

“No leave them be,” Corbulo replied, shifting his attention to Atlas, Sulpicia and the group of guides who were leading the way up ahead. “Save your energy. Those men will not let themselves be caught. They will just return once you have given up the chase. Their orders will be to follow us and see where we are going. There is nothing we can do about it. Ignore them.”

“They will be directing every Quadi war-band they can find towards us, Sir,” Gummar said sounding concerned as he rode beside Corbulo. The Frankish prince gazing across the fields at the group of Quadi riders moving along the ridge. "Those scouts will be calling in reinforcements. King Hildimer and his army must be on our trail by now. The net is closing in on us Sir. The Quadi will be gathering their forces to stop us. I reckon it's only a matter of time before they start to attempt to slow us down so that their infantry can catch up with us. And once that happens, we're in some serious trouble. The Quadi may be just watching us for now, but I expect that when more enemy cavalry arrives, they will start to conduct probing attacks. Well, that's what I would do anyway."

But Corbulo was no longer listening. Up ahead Atlas, Sulpicia and the guides had come to a sudden and unexpected halt upon the top of a low ridge. The party gazing at something he could not see. Urging his horse onwards Corbulo broke into a canter as he hastened towards the spot where Atlas was sitting on his horse, swiftly followed by his staff, bodyguards and the standard bearer holding up the war banner of the equites foederati Germanica. And as he came riding up to his men Corbulo did not need to ask what was going on for suddenly beyond the ridge, across the open grassland, he spotted the Quadi horsemen. The enemy group was small and alone, no more than a dozen riders, and among them was a man holding up a large flag of truce.

For a moment the two groups eyed each other without moving. The tension growing. Then with a grunt Corbulo urged his horse towards the enemy, slowing his pace to a walk as he approached the barbarians before coming to a complete halt when he was just a few yards away from them. His silent companions mustering behind him. The party of Roman soldiers eyeballing their enemies with hard and uncompromising looks. Sat upon their horses the Quadi however appeared unruffled, coolly standing their ground. Their flag of truce battered by the incessant rain and wind. The bearded tribesmen were bareheaded, clad in their long tight-fitting trousers and shirt like gowns made of flax that came down to their knees. Their shoulders cloaked in fur lined capes that were fastened at the neck by brooches.

"Well, we are here, so say what you have come to say," Corbulo called out in German breaking the ominous silence.

For a moment the Quadi did not reply, the men glancing quickly at each other as if they had not been expecting Corbulo to address them in German. As if the use of their language had offended them.

"You are invaders and this is our land," one of the men said in good Latin, gazing back at Corbulo with a look of disgust. "You have attacked our homes and slaughtered our women and children. You do not belong here."

"We have done nothing more than what you have done to our people," Corbulo retorted in German. "If king Hildimer had not decided to go raiding across the border we would not be here, and your villages would not have been burned to the ground. The fault lies with your king. He started this war and now he owns it."

Gazing at Corbulo, the man who had spoken remained silent. Then he smiled, showing a mouth filled with yellow rotting teeth.

"My king offers you terms," the warrior called out in Latin. "You are outnumbered and far from home. Surrender now and he will spare your lives. But if you refuse, we shall kill all of you. We will scatter your remains far and wide so that your spirits will never find eternal peace."

“We are not going to surrender,” Corbulo replied in German. “If king Hildimer thinks he has the upper hand, then he is mistaken. Your king is weak. The time for peace talks has not yet arrived.”

“Does killing us all extend to women too!” Sulpicia suddenly cried out addressing the Quadi as she boldly pushed her horse to the front, showing her face. “Does king Hildimer think killing women will make him a great warrior? The man I once knew was not so cruel. He was my friend once. Tell your king that we have taken his treasure. All of it," Sulpicia called out. "Tell him that if he wants to get it back, he is going to have to negotiate with us. Tell him that I Sulpicia, wife of Regalian is willing to negotiate with him on the return of his gold."

Turning to stare at Sulpicia in surprise for a long moment the Quadi did not respond. Then their leader shifted his gaze back to Corbulo before with a resigned shrug he turned his horse around and followed by his companions he rode off. The band of men quickly disappearing over the next ridge.

Watching them go Corbulo looked grave. Then he turned his gaze towards Sulpicia locking eyes with her. His displeasure apparent. The woman glaring back at him with silent defiance.

***

The rain had ceased, and it was growing dark as Corbulo trotted up to where Atlas and his guides were milling about. The small band of scouts standing about looking undecided and unsure. In the dying light Corbulo could see that ahead lay a vast, dark and impenetrable looking forest. The huge wilderness stretching away to the horizon, to the west, north and south, nothing but trees and more trees. A massive natural barrier with no end. Reigning in his horse Corbulo remained silent as he peered at the forest. Then he turned to Atlas.

“Well?”

“We have come to a fork in the road, Sir,” Atlas said taking a deep breath. His guides watching him as he spoke. “We must decide. We have no choice but to enter the forest if we want to get back to our fort. The guides say that this forest goes on for dozens of miles. They say that is it enormous. If we go that way,” the intelligence officer said turning to gesture to a track to his left that led off into the dark forest, “the path will take us through the forest to a ford across the river which we must cross. If we take that path,” Atlas said gesturing to the track on his right that vanished off into the trees, “we will not only have to pass through the forest but at the end of it through swamps too and then find a suitable place to cross the river.”

Peering at the forest and the two diverging tracks that led into them Corbulo frowned before turning to look back at the column of weary, sodden Roman horsemen who were moving towards him at a walk. Less than seven hundred surviving men remained with him and some of these soldiers were bearing light wounds from the earlier engagements.

“Alright. It’s too dark to continue for today,” Corbulo announced. “We will make camp here for the night. The men need to eat and get some rest, the horses too. But no campfires understood. I know the men are wet, but I don’t want to draw any more attention to ourselves than we already have. The enemy are nearby. Set the pickets as usual. That will be all.”

“Sir,” an officer said smartly before wheeling his horse around and rushing off to carry out his orders.

“Gummar,” Corbulo said quietly as he urged his horse up to his deputy, “with me, you too Atlas.”

Leading his two companions away from the others, Corbulo came to a halt when the three of them were alone and out of earshot. Sitting on his horse as his colleagues gathered around watching him in expectant silence Corbulo once again turned to peer at the vast wilderness that barred his way.

“The paths through the forest,” Corbulo said, “which is the fastest and easiest route?”

“The one on the left,” Atlas replied without hesitation. “The guides say if we take that route, it will take us two days to get back to the fort. One day to pass through the forest and reach the ford across the river. Then another day back to Harald and his men across easy and open country.”

“And if we were to take the other path?”

“Three days Sir instead of two,” Atlas replied. “The guides say we will spend a day in the forest and then at least another half a day crossing the marshes. They say that there is a path through the marshes but that it is narrow, winding and treacherous. They advise that we take the path to the left Sir. It is the easier and faster route, and I concur with them.”

Gazing at Atlas Corbulo looked undecided. “Gummar?” he said at last turning to his deputy with a questioning look.

“I don’t like this forest,” the prince answered quickly. “It doesn’t smell good. Not like the forests back at home. A forest like this would be the perfect place for an ambush. Once we enter this wilderness our mobility will count for shit, and we will be forced to stick to the path. The Quadi will know this. This is their land Sir, and they will know this country better than we do. But as we do not seem to have much choice, I agree with Atlas and our guides. We just must get this done and over with. We should take the fastest and easiest route. We don't have the time. I reckon king Hildimer is only a day behind us."

Lowering his gaze Corbulo made his decision. "All right," he said looking up at Atlas before turning to Gummar, "we will take the track to the left, the fastest and easiest route. Tomorrow, we set out at dawn. You and your guides will lead the way," Corbulo said pointing at Atlas, "and I want patrols guarding our flanks, to warn us of any Quadi ambush," Corbulo added turning to Gummar. "But keep this to yourselves for now. No need for anyone else to know or worry about what we are doing. Tonight, the men need to eat and get some proper rest."

"Sir," Gummar said quickly as Corbulo started back to the spot where his men had begun to set up their camp, "and when we get back to the fort, what then? You are not seriously suggesting we make a stand and fight against an army that could outnumber us ten to one?"

"Yes, we are going to fight," Corbulo growled. "We are going to defeat king Hildimer and end this fucking war on our terms. Why else did we come here for!"

***

Corbulo was asleep, lying curled up in his blanket beside his tethered horse, when a hand suddenly shook him awake. Hurriedly he sat up. Instantly on guard. It was still dark and the camp around him was quiet and peaceful. The night sky dotted with thousands of stars. The Romans were still asleep. Standing over him holding a burning torch were prince Gummar and the camp's watch commander, both officers looking anxious and as he saw their expressions Corbulo felt a sudden chill of unease run down his spine.

“Sir,” Gummar said quietly as Corbulo hurriedly struggled to his feet. “We have a problem, a serious fucking problem.”

“What?” Corbulo growled as he stared at his deputy before quickly shifting his gaze to his watch commander.

“I was doing my rounds Sir,” the watch commander quietly explained, “checking on the sentries, to make sure they had not fallen asleep and so forth. All was well. Then I thought I would check on the accountant Sir. The civilian from the fiscus. As he is tasked with guarding that Quadi treasure. And I found him. Tobias and the two soldiers assigned to him have been poisoned and a mule carrying one of the Quadi treasure chests is missing. It’s gone. Stolen!”

“Poisoned!” Corbulo exclaimed looking startled. “One of the treasure chests has been stolen!”

“Yes Sir,” the watch commander replied shifting uncomfortably on his feet. “The doctor is with the accountant and our soldiers now, but he is pretty sure they were poisoned. I checked again with the sentries but none of them saw anyone enter or leave the camp.”

“There is more,” Gummar said fixing Corbulo with an unhappy look. “Both Atlas and Sulpicia are missing too. I have men searching for them right now. But they cannot be found in the camp.”

Swearing softly Corbulo stared at his deputy. Then snatching the torch from Gummar’s hand he was off, hurrying through the camp towards the place where he had last seen Tobias. Approaching the spot Corbulo saw the army doctor and his apprentice crouching beside Tobias who was lying stretched out in the grass, not moving. The medical team were talking to each other in hushed, urgent voices. But as Corbulo came up they stopped speaking.

Quickly Corbulo crouched beside Tobias and frowned as he gazed down at his still body. The man's eyes were closed.

"He's still alive Sir," the army doctor said quietly. "But barely. He has a one in two chance of making it I reckon. The other two over there," the man added gesturing towards two more bodies lying in the grass, "are dead. It's poison Sir. All three were poisoned. Probably by using Nightshade or Hemlock. Someone must have slipped it into their food or drink."

Saying nothing Corbulo stared at the imperial accountant. Then swiftly rising back to his feet he moved over to the two dead soldiers before turning his attention to the solitary remaining mule.

"Whoever did this," Gummar said quietly as he pointed at the mule and the remaining treasure chest which was sitting in the grass covered by an army blanket, "did it so that they could steal the king's gold. Tobias may be an arsehole Sir, but he took his job very seriously. He was not a thief. He made sure that that gold was well guarded and always watched."

"Why only take one treasure chest?" Corbulo said as he stared at the heavy iron chest. "If you are going to steal the gold, why not take both?"

"Maybe they did not have the time, or they panicked," Gummar replied with a shrug. "Who knows. But what is certain is that one treasure chest has been stolen and two of our men have been assassinated."

Swearing softly Corbulo stared at the treasure chest. Then he turned to Gummar, his expression grave.

“You think Atlas and Sulpicia stole the gold?” Corbulo asked.

“It’s the most likely explanation,” Gummar said taking a deep breath. “Both are missing alongside one of the treasure chests. That is not a coincidence. No, they took the gold and fled into the forest. That is what happened. They must have been planning this for some time. They were always together, those two.”

“But Atlas!” Corbulo exclaimed in a pained voice, his disbelief palpable. “Atlas! I did not see that coming. He is just not that kind of man. He wouldn’t steal from us. He just would not do it.”

“People have a nasty habit of surprising you,” Gummar replied gloomily. “And gold well it has a habit of corrupting men.”

“It’s still too dark to go looking for them now,” Corbulo said quickly turning to stare in the direction of the vast wilderness. “But at first light I want you to organise search parties and see what they come up with.”

“Sir,” Gummar said nodding quickly. “And what about Tobias?”

“What about him?”

“Well,” Gummar said looking away, “this is our chance to get rid of him. Just let him die. No one would know or blame us. It’s not our fault he got poisoned. The arsehole was going to cause trouble for us. He threatened to report us to the imperial fiscus when we got back. If he is dead, he won’t be able to do that. Problem solved.”

“For fucks sake,” Corbulo growled pushing past Gummar towards the spot where the doctor was crouching beside Tobias. “Why does every one of my officers want to kill the man. He may be an arsehole, but we are not murderers. No. We will take him with us. Doctor, do what you can for him," Corbulo added glaring at the doctor. "Do what you can to keep him alive. That's an order and as soon as he is awake and able to talk, I want to speak to him."

***

Dawn had come and sat upon his horse Corbulo was busy directing the ala, the soldiers breaking their camp and getting ready to set out again, when suddenly the watch commander appeared, looking excited as he came rushing up. The man raising his hand.

"Sir, we found something," the officer cried. "You had better come and have a look for yourself."

Hurriedly following the officer as the man led him towards the edge of the wilderness Corbulo frowned. His frown deepening as a little way into the forest he spotted prince Gummar and a few of his men. The Romans had dismounted and were standing around something that lay propped up against a tree trunk. And as Corbulo came riding up he grunted in disbelief as he spotted Atlas lying stretched out, slumped up against the tree. His eyes were closed as if he were asleep. Hurriedly dismounting Corbulo approached.

"He's breathing," Gummar called out as he noticed Corbulo. "He's alive. But he's still completely out of it. We couldn't wake him."

Crouching beside Atlas Corbulo peered at him before gently slapping his face, but Gummar was right. Atlas was out cold and did not react. The only clue to that he was still alive, the gentle rise and fall of his chest. Then Corbulo sniffed, noticing the strange scent again that seemed to stick to Atlas and which he had noticed before. Picking up an abandoned pipe that lay beside Atlas, as if it had fallen out of his hand, the pipe still half filled with what looked like crushed poppies, Corbulo brought it up to his nose and sniffed again. Then he sat back and took a deep breath as he stared at his intelligence officer in dismay.

So that was what Atlas had been doing Corbulo thought as suddenly he understood. Atlas had been smoking opium. Drugs! He had been sneaking out of the camp to smoke opium with Sulpicia. That must be why he had seemed distracted and not been himself of late. That was why Atlas's judgement had been poor. That was what he had smelled on him earlier. Opium! Turning to look up at Gummar Corbulo saw that his deputy had already come to the same conclusion.

"Looks like he took an overdose," Gummar said. "He must have been out here all night. Lucky for him he is not dead. Too much of that stuff," Gummar said guardedly gesturing at the smoking pipe and the crushed poppies, "can kill a man. But at least we now know he did not steal that gold."

"Wake him up!" Corbulo said in disgust, rising to his feet and taking a step back.

As Gummar came up to Atlas and crouched beside him the tall Frankish prince paused for a moment glancing at his men with an amused smile. Then with a loud piercing shriek he started to slap Atlas across the face, his flat hand striking hard and fast until with a scream, Atlas came round and opened his bloodshot eyes. The terror and shock in the intelligence officer's eyes eliciting a smattering of chuckles from Gummar's men who were watching him.

"What have you been doing, bad boy!" Gummar called out as he thrust his face right up to Atlas's. "Your secret is out. You do know that smoking opium is not good for you don't you!"

Pushing Gummar aside Corbulo crouched in front of Atlas.

"What the fuck have you been doing?" Corbulo snapped holding up the smoking pipe as evidence. "What is this, Atlas?"

For a long moment Atlas however appeared unable to respond. Then he groaned, leaned his head back against the tree trunk and closed his eyes.

"It was her idea Sir," he said at last, groaning again. "Sulpicia. She had the opium. That pipe belongs to her. She said it would be fun. We started smoking together soon after you made her my apprentice. We would sneak out of the camp and smoke together. I was not fucking her Sir."

"No, you were not fucking her," Corbulo said sternly, "but she was fucking with you Atlas. How could you be so stupid! Was she here with you last night? Were you smoking together?"

"Yes," Atlas groaned keeping his eyes closed as if the light hurt him. "We came out here together."

"And where is she now?" Gummar asked crouching beside Atlas and giving him another little slap across the cheek. "Where is Sulpicia now? Come on. Out with it, we need to know. It's urgent."

Opening his eyes Atlas blinked and turned to look around him in confusion.

"She was here with me, last night," he gasped. "We smoked. We talked. Then I must have passed out. Why? Has something happened to her?"

Exchanging a quick glance with Gummar, Corbulo leaned in close to Atlas gently seizing him by his throat as if he were about to throttle him.

“Last night Sulpicia stole one of the king’s treasure chests,” Corbulo snapped. “And now she has disappeared. For a while we thought you were in on it. That you were her accomplice but lucky for you that no longer appears to be the case. Now think Atlas. Think carefully. Where could she have gone? Did she say anything that might give us a clue as to where she is going? It’s important,” Corbulo said tightening his grip. “Do you understand. All our lives are at now risk. Two men are already dead because of her!”

“Fuck! She did what!” Atlas exclaimed looking shocked as he stared up at Corbulo with growing horror. Then he groaned and closed his eyes again.

“I am sorry Sir; I have no idea why she would do that or where she has gone. She never mentioned anything about stealing those strong boxes.”

“Ah, you useless bastard,” Gummar said leaning back and eyeing Atlas in disgust. “It’s obvious what happened here Sir,” he continued turning to Corbulo. “The lady has a plan. She sets out to win Atlas’s confidence by befriending him and starting to get him addicted to opium. Then when she is ready to strike, she takes him out here into the forest, just the two of them, for a nice little puff together, while she makes sure that he gets an overdose so that he will be completely out of it when she makes her move on the king’s treasure. And our most brilliant intelligence officer, who is always so full of himself, completely falls for it like a fish hooked to the rod. You are an idiot, Atlas! Your girlfriend just tried to kill you.”

"No, no," Atlas gasped, his cheeks colouring in shame. "That can't be the reason. She did not need to knock me out to get to the treasure chests. They were always in Tobias's care, not mine. I am sorry Sir," he added turning to Corbulo, "I know you told me to watch her, but I got sloppy. I did not always watch her. Last night she could have stolen that treasure without giving me an overdose. There was no need to take me out here. I was not watching her."

"Then why go to all this trouble?" Corbulo said frowning. "Why would she go to all this trouble to give you an overdose of opium and knock you out? It doesn't make sense unless she wanted something from you Atlas. What did she want from you Atlas! Think man!"

"Well, it's not his tiny cock," Gummar said glancing up at his men who chuckled in response.

For a moment Atlas looked confused as he tried to think. Then suddenly he groaned, and his eyes widened in horror. "Oh shit," he gasped. "I remember now. We talked. She wanted to know which path we would take through the forest. She wanted to know the route we would take back to the fort and I told her. I told her which route we would be taking!"

Staring at Atlas Gummar had gone silent as Corbulo leaned back, his mind working. Then softly Corbulo swore.

"She has gone to king Hildimer's camp, to bargain with him," Corbulo said straightening up, his face darkening. "That is where she has gone. That is why she spoke to the Quadi negotiators yesterday, those men who called on us to surrender. That intervention by her was meant for king Hildimer. To alert him that she was here and that she was prepared to negotiate with him. She was sending the king a message!"

"We have been played," Gummar groaned reaching up to rub his hand across his face. "The woman has been playing us all along!"

"This was never about using the king's treasure to negotiate peace," Corbulo said. "That was all a lie! She cares nothing for peace or for reconciliation with Gallienus for that matter. That was just lies to get us to do what she wanted which was to steal that gold for her. This is about revenge."

"Revenge?" Gummar said frowning.

"Yes," Corbulo growled. "Sulpicia never intended to use that gold to negotiate a peace treaty with king Hildimer. No, all along she was planning to use that treasure to negotiate a private deal with the king. That is why she was so keen to go and meet the king once we had his gold. She used us to get what she needed and now she is gone. She has betrayed us."

"But revenge, on who?" Gummar exclaimed.

Leaning against the tree Atlas groaned again as he turned his eyes to the sky. "I think I know," he said. "Oh, why did I not see this earlier. I have been stupid, stupid, stupid!"

"On that we can agree," Gummar replied scornfully.

"Sulpicia is seeking revenge on the men who murdered her husband," Atlas said. "That is what this is all about. That has been her only aim from the very beginning. The assassins, the band of Roxolani who murdered Regalian are already dead. But remember they had help from two of Regalian's advisers, Roman officers. Two close friends and associates of Regalian who conspired with the assassins to murder him. Treachery of the very worst kind. And who is now offering these same two Roman officer's sanctuary and political asylum? King Hildimer!

Sulpicia wants to make a private deal with the king, the return of his treasure in exchange for the two officers who betrayed her husband."

For a moment no one spoke. Then Gummar swore softly.

"You are right, Atlas," Corbulo said at last in a guarded voice. "And in her determination to get her revenge Sulpicia has put us all in danger. I fear that in her quest for revenge she may be willing to sell the whole ala, all of us, to the Quadi. She knows our true strength. She knows our intentions and now she knows which route back to our fort we will be taking. All highly useful information when it comes to negotiating a deal with the king would you not agree."

"You think she is not only going to offer the king the return of his gold," Gummar gasped, "but also serve us up to the king on a plate?"

"It's possible," Corbulo said looking grave. "That woman has become blinded by her desire for revenge. It may not have been her original intention to sell us out to the enemy but if you ask me, I think she will do what she must do, to convince the king to agree to her deal. She will use everything she has got including us. Selling us out would be a small price for her to pay. She certainly did not give a shit about you Atlas did she!"

Once again Gummar swore out loud and as he did Corbulo took a deep breath and turned to gaze into the vast forest that lay before him.

“So,” Gummar said quickly, “as we must now assume that king Hildimer knows which route we are taking back to our fort, maybe it would be wise if we changed our plans and took the other, longer, path back. The one that leads through the marshes. Might save us stumbling into", he continued angrily turning to Atlas, "oh I don't know, a fucking ambush!"

Chapter Nineteen - How the World Turns

Strung out along the forest path the slow-moving column of Roman horsemen were vastly outnumbered by the trees. The forest pressing in on either side. The beech trees and venerable looking oaks standing guard like sentinels. The path blocked here and there by fallen saplings as if the forest did not want the riders to pass. The undergrowth filled with thorns and colourful but poisonous berries and mushrooms as if to remind the horsemen that they should not be here. The sheer scale of their changed surroundings appeared to have dampened the soldier's spirits. The silence and stillness of the woods interrupted only by the solemn thud of horses' hooves, the rattle of the men's equipment and the buzzing insects in the undergrowth and small flocks of disturbed birds that took to flight as the column pushed on by. The plants and flowers turning and bowing in homage to the fierce noon sun. The fresh earthy forest scent was everywhere. The path leading the Romans ever deeper into the beautiful wilderness.

Leading the column, sat upon his horse, Corbulo peered at a deer that had appeared away to his right on a rise in the ground, some distance into the forest. The magnificent animal with its great antlers was standing completely still as it stared straight back at him with its large, inquisitive brown eye.

Shifting his attention to the path ahead Corbulo caught a brief glimpse of one of Atlas's guides flitting through the forest before the man vanished from view. As instructed Atlas and his scouts were screening the main column, watching for any signs that they were about to blunder into an ambush. But since they had entered the forest that morning, they had not seen a soul and they had encountered no trouble. The wilderness appeared to be emptied of people.

“Sir,” one of Corbulo’s bodyguards called out softly as he came cantering up along the side of the column.

“What is it?” Corbulo replied glancing at the man.

“It’s the civilian, the accountant Sir,” the soldier said quickly. “He’s conscious and says he wants to speak to you.”

“Bring him to me."

A little while later two horsemen appeared trotting up the side of the column and towards Corbulo. One of the horses was carrying two men. Tobias looked pale and weak, and his eyes were closed as he leaned back against the doctor who was supporting him and preventing him from falling off. But as the riders reached Corbulo and fell in alongside, Tobias opened his eyes.

“My apologies,” Corbulo began, the tone of his voice formal as he turned to the imperial accountant. “I am sorry that you were poisoned. That this happened to you. I know that some of my officers used violent language and threats against you in the past, but I assure you that none of my men were responsible for what happened to you. Just so that we are clear, none of us have tried to murder you.”

“There is no need to apologise, prefect,” Tobias replied in a hoarse voice. “I think if your officers had really wanted to murder me, I would be stone cold dead by now. The doctor says it was the woman, Sulpicia. Regalian’s wife. She poisoned me to steal the king’s treasure. You put me in charge of guarding that treasure. So, it is I who have failed you Sir and for that I am truly sorry.”

Riding his horse Corbulo hesitated, taken aback by Tobias’s surprisingly conciliatory tone which he had not been expecting.

“She was not entirely successful. She managed to make off with just one of the treasure chests,” Corbulo replied turning to look away. “The other one is still in our possession.”

“She came to me last night when I was just settling down to get some sleep,” Tobias continued closing his eyes again. His chest heaving from the exertion. “She said she wanted some money advice. And while I was trying to oblige her, she offered me and my men some broth that she’d made herself. I suffer from stiff joints Sir, and she said that it would help with the pain. The poison must have been in that drink. I was a fool to trust her.”

“You had no reason to suspect her,” Corbulo said evenly as he kept his eyes on the path ahead. “She caught all of us off-guard. But what is done is done. Did she say anything else?”

“No, nothing of importance,” Tobias replied wearily shaking his head, his eyes still closed as he slumped back against the doctor’s chest. “But that is not why I wanted to speak to you, prefect,” Tobias continued. “I wanted to thank you for saving my life. I am grateful to you Sir.”

“I did not save your life,” Corbulo said. “The doctor and the Gods are responsible for whether you live or die. That is their domain.”

“Yes, you did Sir,” Tobias replied refusing to be put off. “You saved my life. I know that I am not a popular man here with the soldiers. That you and I have had our disagreements. That things have been said and that threats have been made. But if you had wanted me to die you could simply have left me behind this morning. You could easily have rid yourself of another problem. I am still too weak to look after myself. I would not have survived another day on my own. If you had wanted to get rid of me, you could simply have left me behind and no one would have blamed you for that. By doing so you would have got rid of a threat. But you chose otherwise and for that I am deeply grateful. I am in your debt. You are a good man Sir, and I owe you, my life."

Riding his horse Corbulo gazed into the forest.

"I think you and I have got off on the wrong foot," Tobias said opening his eyes and wistfully gazing up at the blue sky. "When we first met back at Mediolanum, I thought you were just another barbarian officer looking to strike it rich. A man who only gave a shit about his own career. But now I see that I was wrong about you. And maybe I was too arrogant and sure of myself and for that I am sorry. I am very good at my job and sometimes that goes to my head. You should know prefect that when I was assigned to your unit by the imperial fiscus I had orders to keep an eye on you and your officers. The fiscus and the emperor are terrified that there will be another army rebellion. There is so much disaffection, ambition and suspicion these days. So aside from my official duties as an imperial accountant I was also ordered to spy on you, to judge your loyalty and to report back what I saw and heard."

"That you were here to spy on us is known," Corbulo said turning to give Tobias a hard sober look. "We have known this ever since you were embedded with us. So, what do you want from me?"

"I am going to drop my complaint against you, prefect," Tobias replied turning his eyes towards Corbulo and managing a weak smile. "From now on I will work only for you Sir. I can be useful. I know how the imperial bureaucracy works. I know how to get things done. An ambitious man will prosper with me at their side. From now on Sir, I would like us to become friends. To put past disagreements behind us. To start afresh on the right foot this time."

***

The marshes were vast, pretty much like everything else in these cursed barbarian lands, Corbulo thought as he moved on down the narrow path gazing out across the desolation. The waterlogged ground stretching away to the horizon interspersed here and there by lonely and forlorn looking trees trapped in watery misery. The stagnant pools of water and clumps of heather alive with armies of insects and teeming with noisy, nestling birds. The terrain made him feel vulnerable. The lack of cover meant he and his men would be visible from far away to any watching eyes. The lack of firm ground meant he had no room to manoeuvre if it came to a fight. Out here, Corbulo thought with growing despondency, he and his men were sitting ducks. Out here they were trapped. While over his head in the clear blue-sky flocks of screeching birds appeared to be mocking him. As if the wetlands were their domain and he an unwelcome intruder. The smell of rotting vegetation was discernible. The unhealthy environment a brooding, invisible threat.

It was morning and moving across the flat open terrain the Roman column was pushing westwards with the sun to their back. The men had dismounted and were leading their horses in a single file along the narrow sandy track that meandered through the swamp. The men taking care not to stray from the path. The soldiers casting uneasy glances at the treacherous ground to their left and right. The openness of the wetlands standing in sharp contrast to the claustrophobic and dense forest they had just left behind.

Leading his men Corbulo's expression darkened as he spotted the next gruesome effigy up ahead. The crude effigies appeared to be marking the route of the path through the marshes as if they were Roman milestones. For there was one every few hundred yards. The signs unmistakeable. But it was their very gruesomeness that had caught the soldier's attention and further dampened their spirits. For the simple wooden posts driven into the ground were each adorned with a human skull. The bones marking the way ahead. The meaning of this unknown. Who had erected these signs equally unknown. The guides being unable to offer any insights other than to say that the track was very old.

Squinting Corbulo saw that up ahead Atlas had come to a halt and his guides were hurriedly gathering around him. The men appearing suddenly unsure of themselves as if they had come across something unexpected. Then with a sharp intake of breath Corbulo saw what Atlas had already spotted. Across the marshes coming towards him down the path, heading east in the opposite direction to himself, a band of men had suddenly appeared. And the men were armed. They appeared to be warriors. And as the newcomers spotted the Roman column they too came to an abrupt halt. The two groups of travellers peering at each other.

Hastening up to the spot where Atlas was standing watching the newcomers Corbulo quickly raised his fist in the air bringing the Roman column to a halt behind him. A hundred paces up the track the newcomers had not moved. The warriors eyeing the Romans in guarded silence.

"Who are they?" Corbulo said as he came to a halt beside Atlas. His eyes trained on the newcomers.

“Hard to say from this distance,” Atlas replied in a tight voice without taking his eyes off the strangers. “They could be Quadi or maybe Vandals. They look like a warband. See they have a war banner. I count only thirty men.”

“There could be more hiding back along the trail,” one of the guides exclaimed speaking in German.

“We can’t go around them, they are blocking the path,” another guide blurted out. “Just a few determined men can hold up the whole column in this terrain. Nor can we easily outflank them.”

“What do you want to do, Sir?” Atlas asked gently.

For a long moment Corbulo did not reply. His mind working. His eyes fixed upon the men up ahead. Then without a word he pushed past Atlas and leading his horse on foot, alone he started out towards the strangers. His action forcing Atlas, the guides and the rest of the column to follow. And as Corbulo began to close the distance between the two groups, the newcomers too suddenly started to move. The heavily armed warriors walking towards him. Their hard, suspicious gazes fixed upon the Romans. But no one drew their weapons or prepared for a fight and as the two groups started to pass each other along the narrow track through the marshes, the Romans heading west, the barbarians heading east, no one spoke a word. The two groups passing each other in utter silence. The men simply ignoring each other. Taking in the bearded barbarians with their hard, wild and savage appearance, Corbulo maintained his cool. Then as the last warrior moved on past him, continuing down the track, he turned to look back down the path.

“Alright, so live and let live,” Atlas muttered tensely as he hurriedly drew level with Corbulo.

“Keep moving,” Corbulo replied quietly. “No one wants a fight.”

Turning his attention back to what lay ahead Corbulo frowned as he suddenly spotted the straggler coming towards him. The man was alone, trying to catch up to his comrades but he appeared to be wounded for he was hobbling along with the aid of a pair of crudely constructed crutches. Gazing at the approaching man Corbulo remained silent but just as they were about to pass each other Corbulo spoke up addressing the man in German.

“Friend, where have you come from?”

Coming to a halt along the narrow path the warrior hesitated, scrutinising Corbulo with a careful appraising look that revealed neither fear nor loathing. Then he cracked a broad smile.

“There is only one proper place for a warrior to go these days,” the man replied in heavily accented German. “To the civil war among the Marcomanni. There are many riches to be had if one chooses to fight for the right king. The Marcomanni lords pay well for any who will fight on their side.”

“And how goes the war among the Marcomanni?”

“It rages on, Roman,” the man replied with a shrug, cracking another broad smile. “War bands travel from afar to take part but the contest is yet to be decided. King Attalus may be the rightful king of the Marcomanni, but his rival Crocus has a legitimate grievance.”

“So, I hear,” Corbulo said.

“But my comrades and I did not go to fight for either of them,” the man continued puffing out his chest, eager to talk. “No. We went for another nobler reason. To slay the great warrior. The man they call Ignatz. The man who murdered Ganna, the priestess of Nerthus and who made himself an outlaw by doing so. For he too has joined the Marcomanni civil war. He is there with his band of mercenaries seeking fame and power like the rest."

"Ignatz," Corbulo said frowning. "I have not heard of this name before."

"Well, you should have, Roman," the man retorted. "They say that he was born a Roman but grew up as a Frank. That he fears nothing, not even the wrath of the immortal gods. His name is infamous. What he did – killing Ganna - was nothing less than sacrilegious. And now a great bounty has been placed on Ignatz's head. And much fame will be bestowed upon the man who manages to take down Ganna's murderer. But alas," the man said growing sombre and patting his thigh as if he were suddenly in pain, "in battle with Ignatz and his warband we failed and all I received in return for our effort was this wound and this poor leg which will never properly heal. We lost many good men. Now we return home," the German added. "But at least I still have my head. Many who tried to kill Ignatz were not so lucky. But that man is doomed. His name is cursed. No one gets away with offending the Gods!"

Watching the warrior moving away down the path across the marshes, Corbulo frowned.

"It's best when they are at each other's throats," Atlas muttered at Corbulo's side as the two of them resumed their journey, "then they have less time and energy to worry about us. Divide and rule. Let's hope that this Marcomanni civil war lasts for a very long time!"

***

"Forwards! Forwards! At them!" Corbulo bellowed as together with his bodyguards he followed directly behind his lead squadrons, urging his horse across the river towards the enemy held shore. His legs were completely submerged in the cold water. His hand was clutching his spear, his other the reins. His shield was strapped to his arm while his horse was snorting and straining. Its eyes and mouth were wide open. Its head bobbing up and down just above surface. While beside Corbulo the standard bearer of the ala, clad in his wolf's pelt, was grimacing and valiantly holding up the war banner of the equites foederati Germanica.

It was morning and the river was filled with hundreds of frantically swimming horses, their riders clinging on to their mounts, half-submerged. Their spears and shields raised, ready for battle. The Roman cavalry desperately trying to make it across to the western shore, where massed along the high bank, the Quadi horsemen were waiting for them. The enemy brandishing their weapons and shields and screaming their battle cries and defiance. The frontal river assault clearly showing the skill gap between the experienced Roman cavalrymen and the mass of infantrymen who had only recently converted to the cavalry role.

Cursing out loud Corbulo's eyes were fixed upon the enemy. The river around him alive with savage, yelling men and desperate, frantic horses. The river was the last obstacle before they could leave the marshes behind. But finding his path blocked by the enemy force he'd had little choice but to launch an immediate attack. The longer he delayed the more chance that Quadi reinforcements would arrive. And if he could not get across the river he and his men would die in the marshes. He had taken a risk Corbulo thought. But he'd had no choice. If the enemy had had archers, the assault would have already turned into a massacre but his judgement that the Quadi force consisted solely of spear armed cavalry appeared to have been right.

Observing the first of his soldiers as they made it into the shallower water along the western shore, he grunted but the enemy were not about to let them pass. There appeared to be only a hundred or so Quadi horsemen, but they occupied the top of the steep embankment and that gave them a major height advantage. The steep riverbank making it hard for his men to get up onto the dry land. Cursing again Corbulo urged his swimming horse onwards towards the shore as the Romans and their opponents jabbed ineffectually at each other with their long lances. Neither side making any progress. The outnumbered Quadi cavalry refusing to retreat. The Romans stuck in the water.

“Spread out! Spread out! We will outflank them! We need to get ashore!” Corbulo roared gesturing for the men closest to him to move towards the flanks of the enemy force.

But as the Roman cavalry began to extend their line so did the Quadi. The Germanic tribesmen quickly moving to prevent their foe from coming ashore. The warriors jabbing at the Romans with their spears. Using their height advantage to drive the Roman cavalry back. The furious skirmishing along the riverbank punctuated with screaming and yelling.

At last, feeling his horse’s hooves striking solid ground again Corbulo cried out in triumph as his beast abruptly reared up out of the water. Jabbing at a warrior ahead of him with his spear Corbulo tried to force his way up the steep embankment but failed. His horse sliding back into the water and nearly tumbling him into the river. Struggling to retain his balance and control Corbulo cursed again before hurriedly turning to look up and down the riverbank. But all along the shore the Romans were battling and failing to get onto firmer higher ground. The assault appeared to be in danger of stalling.

Suddenly Corbulo heard a familiar horn ringing out signalling *attack*. The sound coming from inland, *behind* the Quadi. The signal not unexpected. And as they heard and recognised the horn a great roar of encouragement rose up from among the hard-pressed Roman troopers.

Along the top of the embankment the Quadi too had heard the sound and for a moment they milled about in aimless confusion. The tribesmen's harsh guttural voices ringing out. Then with the speed of spreading fire, panic set in, order broke down and bands of Quadi riders began to flee. The horsemen making off in a mad, chaotic gallop. Seizing their chance the Roman horsemen surged up the riverbank and onto the dry firm land and as he joined his men Corbulo suddenly spotted prince Gummar and his four cavalry squadrons chasing the fleeing enemy across the open fields. The Franks racing after their quarry. Their surprise attack from the rear having destroyed the Quadi defence of the river crossing.

Grimly Corbulo looked on as more and more of his main force came surging out of the river and up over the embankment. The soldiers crying out in triumph. Water streaming from their mounts. Then raising his own horn to his lips Corbulo blew *recall* and a few moments later prince Gummar and his men gracefully broke off their pursuit and began to canter back towards their comrades. Approaching the spot where Corbulo was sitting on his horse, Gummar gave his commander a little conspiratorial grin which Corbulo returned.

"I believe I and my men once again saved the day Sir," Gummar said as he turned to survey the riverbank. "It's becoming a bit of a habit."

“Oldest trick in the book,” Corbulo replied looking pleased. “Fix the enemy attention on the main attack force before sending another force undetected around their flank and attack them from the rear. Works every fucking time!”

“There were only a hundred of them Sir,” the standard bearer called out. “We outnumbered them.”

"Yes, and this will be the last time that we outnumber the enemy," Corbulo replied. "It won't be easy from now on."

"We were lucky Sir," the standard bearer continued.

Ignoring his standard bearer Corbulo had turned to stare at a party of riders who were bringing a prisoner towards him. The enemy warrior was young and appeared to have fallen from his horse for he was limping and bleeding from a nasty cut to his forehead.

“Prisoner Sir,” one of the Romans called out in German as he led the man up to Corbulo. “What do you want me to do with him?”

Eyeing the man from his horse, Corbulo remained silent for a moment while the prisoner gazed back at him in sullen defiance. The troop of eager Romans crowding around.

“Where is king Hildimer? Where is your main army?” Corbulo called out. “Tell me what you know, and I promise you that I shall let you live. That you will go free.”

Gazing back at Corbulo the man appeared to be considering the offer. Then at last making up his mind he cleared his throat.

“The king is positioned further south covering the ford across the river,” the prisoner replied in his thick dialect. “He took his cavalry and moved on ahead. Our infantry is still marching to catch up. We were expecting you to take the southern route. That was what I was told. But the king sent me and my comrades north to cover this crossing point just in case you took the marsh road. We only arrived here this morning, just before you showed up and attacked us."

Quickly Corbulo exchanged a look with prince Gummar.

"How many men does the king have with him?" Gummar called out to the prisoner.

"The bulk of his cavalry, nearly a thousand men are with the king guarding the ford to the south," the warrior said with a shrug. "Ten thousand infantry are marching to join them. A hundred of us were sent to guard this crossing. We were not expecting to have to fight."

"Ten thousand!" a Roman voice groaned in Latin.

"So, we were right to take the marsh road," Gummar said turning to Corbulo with a guarded look. "If we had taken the other faster and more direct, southernly route like we were planning to we would have run straight into king Hildimer and his main cavalry force. They would have trapped us at the ford and annihilated us. The king was clearly expecting us to take that route. So, it seems Sulpicia betrayed us."

"Maybe," Corbulo replied cautiously. "She knew of our intentions, and she had a reason to sell us out, but it is also possible the king came to the same conclusion independently. Covering the southern route with my main force is what I would have done if the roles had been reversed. Lucky for us he seems to have badly misjudged us."

"So, these bastards who were here," Gummar said turning and pointing towards the riverbank with a contemptuous gesture, "were just a patrol sent to cover the secondary crossing just in case we showed up. That's why there were only a hundred of them. They were not expecting us. Good. I think it was very wise to change our plans Sir and when I get my hands on that woman there is going to hell to pay. She betrayed us to the enemy."

Sat upon his horse Corbulo's gaze was still resting upon the prisoner.

"Your king Hildimer has an uncle," he called out addressing the man. "Who he has tasked with guarding the western frontier in case the Marcomanni civil war spills over into Quadi territory. What news from him and his army? Will he not send men to aid the defence of your villages and farms?"

"I don't know about any of that," the man replied lowering his gaze. "I have told you everything that I know."

"We must assume that he will," Corbulo said glancing quickly at prince Gummar.

"That's another ten thousand men Sir," the standard bearer interrupted speaking in Latin and giving Corbulo a reproachful look. "Ten or eleven thousand to the east. Ten thousand to the west and us stuck in the middle. I don't like it Sir. The enemy appears to outnumber us by at least twenty to one. We should at least consider retreating across the Danube."

"No, not until we have achieved what we came here to do," Corbulo said in Latin, looking annoyed as he rounded on his standard bearer. "And we are not yet done. I have not come here to play at war. We have come here to win! To beat the shit out of an enemy who dared to raid Roman land. So, there will be no more talk about retreating!"

Turning to his officers Corbulo however could see the doubt and scepticism in their eyes. Even Gummar appeared to avoid making eye contact with him. The officers did not appear to share his confidence or enthusiasm.

Turning his attention back to the prisoner Corbulo frowned.

"Return to your king!" Corbulo called out addressing the young warrior, "and deliver this message from me. Tell king Hildimer that if he wants to see his precious treasure again, he will need to come and take it from us. We will be waiting for him along the banks of the Morava."

Then to his officers. "We ride for the fort. We ride fast. Back to Harald! Let's go! Go! Go!"

Chapter Twenty – Rome Defiant

"I have reinforced the palisade and added the spikes," Harald said gesturing at the high wall made from tree trunks that ran along the top of the steep earthen embankment which enclosed the rectangular shaped camp. It was morning and Harald and Corbulo were doing their rounds along the perimeter of the Roman fort. The two officers inspecting the defences while around them work parties were toiling to complete the work. The men moving about shouting instructions to each other. The Roman camp alive with the sound of hammering, sawing and swearing. Peering at the base of the ramparts Corbulo remained silent as he observed the line of sharpened wooden stakes, their ends blackened and fire-hardened and pointing outwards, set into the ground at a forty-five-degree angle. The spikes forming a protective collar around the fort.

It had been less than a day since he and his command had finally returned to the fort. Their journey uncontested by the Quadi. But he could not afford to waste any time Corbulo thought. Things appeared to be coming to a head. Shifting his attention, he turned to study the four simple wooden watchtowers that poked up from the corners of the fort. Their platforms manned by sentries armed with trumpets. The Draco banners of the 1st and 2nd cohort were fastened to their tops on wooden poles. The long serpent banners, made of colourful cloth, with their wide-open mouths, were moving crazily from side to side in the breeze as if they were alive. While from inside the camp the columns of smoke from the soldiers cooking fires drifted away. The smell of woodsmoke wafting through the camp. The nearby fields were filled with a mass of grazing Roman cavalry horses.

Turning to look to the west where the ground fell away towards the river valley and the ford across the Morava, Corbulo's eyes narrowed as he took in the lay of the land. Then quickly he turned his gaze to the south in the direction of the Danube just a few miles away, but his view of the great river was blocked by the forest. Then east across the open ground littered with tree stumps, all that remained of the small wood that his men had completely cleared to build their fort.

"Supplies?" Corbulo asked as the two officers continued their inspection.

"We have sufficient food to last us for a couple of weeks," Harald replied. "Water can easily be fetched from the Morava. Grass for the horses as you can see is in abundant supply. And if it comes to a siege," Harald added, a weary note entering his voice, "I suppose we can always eat the horses."

"Disease, illness?"

"Nothing unusual. A few men reported sick, and I have got the doctor checking all the Quadi civilians who turn up at our gates," Harald replied. "The doctor says he can handle it. There is no evidence of plague or a spreading infection among men or horses. We are good Sir."

Nodding, giving nothing away, Corbulo continued walking, his keen eyes taking in his surroundings and the construction work.

"But I had some trouble with that Christian priest, Clement, whom you left behind in my care," Harald added with a sudden frown. "That man I'm sorry to say has been nothing but a nuisance. First, he tried to seduce one of the civilians, a young girl but her father took offence, and it ended in a fist fight. Then afterwards Clement tried to escape. He managed to get to the river before my men caught him. I hauled his arse back into the fort but ever since then he has not shut up about his Christian God. I think he is doing it on purpose. Just to piss us off. He doesn't care. It got to the point where I had to gag him and stake him out. His incessant preaching was getting on the men's nerves Sir. Maybe you can do something about that," Harald concluded fixing Corbulo with a reproachful eye.

"I will speak with Clement."

"Also, while you were away," Harald said changing the subject and gesturing towards a patch of open field that appeared to have been left alone, "my men and I prepared some surprises for anyone who wishes to attack the fort. Plus - see those marker stones," Harald added pointing at the innocent looking stones that dotted the open country to the east. "They will tell us when the enemy comes into range. Some of my men know how to shoot. It's a shame that we don't have a company of trained archers to support us, but maybe a few missiles will fool the enemy into thinking that we are stronger than we actually are."

"War is deception! Good," Corbulo replied looking pleased and laying a hand on his friend's shoulder. "It looks like you have not wasted your time Harald. We are as ready as we are ever going to be."

"Sir," Harald replied looking away.

"So, now you can tell me what is bothering you?" Corbulo said as the two officers came to a halt at the corner of the fort beneath one of the watch towers. "I know something is bothering you. It is written all across your face."

Taking a deep breath Harald hesitated, his eyes fixed upon the Roman work parties. Then at last he turned to Corbulo, his expression grave.

"By making a stand here - in this fort - we are giving up our mobility," Harald said quietly. "Would it not be better to meet the enemy in the open on horseback, with room to manoeuvre. We are a cavalry unit after all."

"With room to manoeuvre, you mean the chance to retreat," Corbulo sighed. "No Harald, speak your mind, old friend. That is not what is truly bothering you. Come on, out with it!"

"Why must be make a stand and fight at all," Harald said sharply. "I don't understand, and I am not the only one. There is not an officer within the ala who does not share my doubts about the wisdom of all of this. There is real concern Corbulo. The others they came to me because they think that I somehow have influence with you. They asked me to discuss our situation with you and I do not blame them for asking. Think about it. What chance do we stand? What will we gain from meeting the enemy here in battle? We are not defending Roman land. The Quadi are likely to outnumber us twenty to one. You said it yourself. So, why fight? We have done all that we can do here. Maybe instead of offering battle a wiser course of action would be to retreat. Recross the Danube - back to our side of the river. The war here against the barbarians is over."

"I am aware of the concerns and you and I will address the officers and men later today," Corbulo said in a gentle, patient voice as he tightened his grip on Harald's shoulder. "We will do it together. I understand your fears Harald but the war with the Quadi is not yet over. Our job here is not yet done. At the heart of it, war is a battle of wills, and so we must break the enemy motivation, their willingness to keep on fighting. Only by doing so can we hope for a lasting peace along this stretch of the frontier. And to break the enemy's will and motivation we must demonstrate to him that he cannot defeat us. That we are too strong. But we have not yet broken the enemy. For that we must fight and inflict a decisive defeat. The worst thing we could do right now would be to retreat across the Danube. For king Hildimer will take that as a sign of weakness and this war would simply continue and there would be no true peace for any of our people along the frontier."

"But they are not our people! Most of them don't even speak German. Who cares about these civilians!" Harald shot back. "This is not the Rhine! We are far from home! These Romans are not like us, Corbulo. Why are we risking our lives for them? Why should we care!"

"No, you are wrong, Harald," Corbulo said shaking his head. "These bastards, these barbarians murdered my younger brother. Franks. Marcomanni. Quadi. I don't care what you call them. They are all the same. They all want the same thing. Barbarians! Raiders! You and I Harald we grew up along the Rhine. We know how dangerous the frontier can be. We have seen the aftermath of the barbarian raids. But the frontier is our home. The very first battle that I took part in as a young soldier was to repel a Frankish invasion. The barbarians will always be our worst and most dangerous enemy. And it does not matter where along the imperial border you live. In Pannonia or the lower Rhine. Defending the frontier will always be our fight!"

"But how can we win!" Harald hissed. "We have barely eight hundred men. Making a stand here is a risk Corbulo! If we are destroyed it will mean the whole frontier will be wide open to attack. If we are destroyed, we lose everything. You are rolling the dice and hoping for a six every time."

"It's a risk," Corbulo replied turning to look around at the fort, "but a calculated one. I am not blind or deaf. I am taking measures to even the odds and I would say we have a good chance of succeeding. Our position is stronger than it appears.

Don't judge our strength solely on numbers or what you see about you. Much remains hidden and things are in motion. But we are going to break the enemy beneath these walls and then we shall have a proper peace. That is the only way this war is going to end. That is the job that we have been given. That is why we are here and that is why we are going to fight. And we're going to win!"

"You are a stubborn bastard," Harald muttered looking away.

"So, I am told," Corbulo said retaining his firm grip on Harald's shoulder, "but if the Roman empire still means anything, then surely it must mean solidarity between people who face the same enemies. Together we are stronger. Only together can we defeat the common enemy. I refuse to forget that."

"I don't want to die just yet," Harald said sourly.

"Neither do I."

"This is all fucked up."

"Will you stand beside me when I address the ala?"

Taking a deep breath Harald looked unhappy. Then gathering himself he turned to Corbulo and his expression changed.

"I have never told you this before but when we were summoned to the East to serve emperor Valerian," Harald said looking grim. "Hostes made me swear that I would look after you. He told me to keep an eye on you. He said you were born to be a leader of men. That one day you would make a great general. The old warrior appears to have a soft spot for you Corbulo. He treated you like a son, even though you were not his real son. So alright then," Harald continued in a heavy voice, "we are lucky to have an officer like you in command, Corbulo. The men know it and I know it. So, I am going to do as Hostes asked me to do. I will stand beside you. If we must fight these barbarians, then so be it. We will kill them all! We will send them back into the fires of hell. Glory to the equites foederati Germanica!"

***

Squatting beside Clement Corbulo took a deep breath as he studied the old sorry looking priest who was sitting on the ground with his ankles chained together. The man's hands were bound behind his back securing him to a solid wooden post while he was gagged with a piece of cloth that had been stuffed into his mouth. Clement looked miserable with a fresh bruise around his one good eye, and it appeared that multiple persons had urinated on the Christian for his clothes were soiled and he stank. Reaching out Corbulo pulled out the gag and leaned back, observing the priest with an unhappy look.

"They tell me that you assaulted a young Quadi girl and tried to have sex with her," Corbulo said. "And that afterwards you tried to escape."

Licking his lips Clement did not immediately reply. The Christian merchant gingerly stretching and moving his body about as if he'd got cramp. Then slowly Clement turned his gaze towards Corbulo.

"She was not so young, and she was more than willing," Clement replied. "Believe what you like but I know women like few men do. And this one was well up for it. There is no shame in what I tried to do. I am a man. She is a woman. So, what was the problem?"

"And trying to escape?" Corbulo snapped.

"Well why not?" Clement replied with a shrug, looking away. "Wouldn't you? I have done nothing wrong. I am a Roman citizen, and I am being held against my will."

"You are also a Christian and a priest. If my men did not know that you were under my protection you would have been lynched long ago," Corbulo retorted. "I cannot have you causing disquiet in the camp, understood. That was why you were gagged. That is why you are tied to a post right now. And this will continue until you learn to shut up and not cause any more trouble."

"Yeah, well I can't help who I am," Clement replied before shooting Corbulo a good-natured smile.

"I thought we were friends," Corbulo said frowning. "I thought that was what you wanted when we last spoke. To be friends. So, it is disappointing to see you abuse my kindness. Must I remind you that I saved you from being lynched. I have treated you well since we freed you from captivity or have you already forgotten who it was who came to your rescue."

"Ah friends," Clement said lightly. "Yes, we are friends, and I apologise if I have offended you, prefect. That was never my intention. You are a good man. But the problem with friendship is that friends must learn to trust each other. Would you not agree?"

"You don't trust me?"

"Oh, I do," Clement replied. "But it's hard to be your friend when you are not telling me the truth, prefect. About whom you really are. And until you do our friendship will not be the real thing."

"What do you mean?" Corbulo said with a guarded look.

Leaning towards him in a conspiratorial manner Clement grinned and lowered his voice.

"I am not a stupid man. I know the hearts of men nearly as well as I know the hearts of women so tell me honestly prefect, are you a Christian? Are you one of us? Because I think you are. I think you are a secret Christian which is why you saved me. Which is why you are willing to help me. But don't worry I won't tell a soul. I don't want to get you into trouble. Your secret will be safe with me."

***

Nosing around a bend in the Morava River the Nemesis looked like a top of the food chain predator who feared nothing. The noon sun shining down benevolently upon the sleek Roman warship that was bristling with artillery, armaments and soldiers. It's square sail dominant, like a banner of war. The graceful curved wooden prow with its figurine of the god of vengeance riding high. The banks of rowers were plying the river in rhythmic harmony to the slow beat of a drum. While upon the deck the soldier's cries rang out across the still water.

Hurrying down the forested slope towards the riverbank and the Roman ship, Corbulo raised his hand as his bodyguards cried out to their comrades, hoping to catch their attention.

"A little further! Slow. Slow! Hold! Hold boys! We don't want to run her aground!" Crastus's powerful, urgent voice boomed across the river, yelling at the rowers as the big centurion stood beside the pilot at the bow of the Nemesis. The pilot appeared to be taking depth measurements with a length of rope and lead weights that vanished into the water while the galley slowly and carefully pushed upstream towards the ford across the river.

"Alright, drop the fucking anchor! Drop it! Now!" Crastus shouted at last turning to the banks of rowers. "This is as far as we are going boys! She stays right here until I tell you to move her!"

As the heavy anchor splashed down into the water Crastus turned to look up in the direction of the Roman fort that sat upon the high ground overlooking the valley. Then abruptly he became aware of the small party of Romans approaching the riverbank and as he recognised Corbulo, he broke into a huge grin, as if he were thoroughly enjoying himself.

"Launch the small boat!" Crastus bellowed grandly. "I am going ashore boys. The captain is leaving the ship!"

"Crastus!" Corbulo called out looking pleased as the centurion leaped over the side of the small boat that had ferried him ashore and began wading through the shallow water towards him.

"Sir," the big man replied coming to a halt before him and rapping out a smart salute.

"Well, this is new," Harald said eyeing Crastus with a little cruel look. "You look like you are enjoying being the captain of a ship. The infantry is wasted on you, Crastus. Maybe now you have an excuse to fuck off to join the marines and leave the serious business of war to the rest of us."

"Yeah, but then you would not have anyone to bitch about with your girlfriends," Crastus replied smiling sweetly at Harald.

"Any problems out on the river?" Corbulo asked addressing Corbulo as his two senior officers quickly swapped silent, familiar insults with their hands.

"No Sir," Crastus replied growing serious. "The Nemesis rules the water. None dare attack us. But whatever you did to the Quadi you have certainly got them pissed. The Danube is filled with returning warbands. You appear to have stirred up a hornets nest Sir."

"Did you get my message through to Probus?"

"Yes, I did Sir," Crastus said nodding. "The Moor, the liaison officer said he would take it to Probus himself. We landed him on the south shore soon after we left you a few days ago. It's done."

"Good," Corbulo replied. "Then I have another task for you. There are some wounded and sick men in the fort. I am going to need you to transport them across the Danube right away. Land them on our side of the river. They will have to make their own way back to Carnuntum. Then once you have done that return here at once and take up position to cover the ford over there," Corbulo said turning to point towards the shallows a little way upstream.

"You are expecting trouble from the west?" Crastus said frowning.

"Only ten thousand Quadi warriors' hell bent on revenge for all their settlements which we destroyed," Harald interrupted.

"Maybe," Corbulo responded coolly fixing his eyes upon Crastus. "The main threat however is coming from the east. I expect king Hildimer to approach from that direction and his arrival is imminent so there is no time to waste. So, when you return, anchor the Nemesis as close to the shallows as you can get her. Use your artillery to stop anyone from crossing the Morava. You are going to have to protect our backs Crastus. I am going to rely on you and your men to secure our rear and if all goes wrong," Corbulo added, "the Morava will be our only chance of escape."

Taking in what Corbulo had just said Crastus remained silent for a moment. His expression serious. Then his cheerful grin returned.

"Looks like I will be saving your arse again," Crastus exclaimed glancing at Harald. "Just like old times then."

"Nothing like old times," Harald retorted.

"So, you are set on this then Sir," Crastus said ignoring Harald and turning to Corbulo. "We are going to make a stand and fight."

"Yes, we are," Corbulo replied nodding.

"Good," Crastus growled. "About fucking time that we did. Let's teach these barbarians a lesson in how to fight!"

"I want you to go to the fort and start organising the loading of our wounded onto the Nemesis," Corbulo said addressing Crastus and ignoring the banter. Then to Harald. "You will stay here with me. We are going to need to dismantle one of the Nemesis's bolt throwers and haul it back into the camp. You had a good idea. It would be useful to have something to shoot with, even if only to make the enemy think that we are stronger than we really are."

"Want me to take the civilian, the accountant with me too?" Crastus said turning to Corbulo with a grin. "I could lose him in the Danube when we cross over. Accidents happen all the time on ships I am told. It would save us a heap of trouble when we get back. We may not get another chance."

"No," Corbulo replied. "Tobias will remain here. He won't be a problem anymore. Believe it or not but he is our friend. He works for me now and I trust him. He is not going to report anyone to the fiscus. He changed his mind."

"Tobias is our friend now!" Crastus said giving Corbulo a disbelieving look. "Hell Sir. How did you manage that?"

"Tobias had a change of heart," Corbulo said coolly. "Like I said he works for me now and we can use his financial expertise and knowledge of the imperial bureaucracy. He will be useful. He is not to be harmed by anyone, is that clear. He is one of us now. This talk of ending him must cease."

"Sir," Crastus said in a dubious voice as he quickly glanced at Harald for confirmation.

It was late in the afternoon and Corbulo was supervising the small party of Romans who were dragging the heavy bolt thrower up the steep slope back to the fort when a sudden warning cry alerted him. Rushing towards him, coming from the direction of the fort, a solitary Roman officer had appeared. The man was wildly waving his arm in alarm.

"What is it?" Corbulo shouted.

"Trouble Sir," the officer gasped. "You need to come right away."

Swearing out loud Corbulo hurriedly turned to Harald. "Get the bolt thrower into the fort!" Then he was off, running after the officer, covering the short distance towards the Roman fort. And as he rushed back into the camp, Corbulo became aware of a multitude of raised voices. The fort was alive with aggressive cries and shouts, as if something had got his men excited and worked up. Ahead beyond the horse pens filled with the ala's cavalry horses, occupying the remaining open space in the centre of the rectangular fort, a large crowd of soldiers had gathered and appeared to be watching something that was hidden from view. Crying out in a harsh voice Corbulo began to push his way through the crowd, the startled men falling silent and moving aside as they turned and recognised him. Then abruptly Corbulo came to a halt as he saw what his soldiers had been observing. Enclosed by a ring of spectators, who were keeping a respectable distance, Crastus and prince Gummar were fighting each other in single combat. The two men armed with knives. The two warriors snarling, circling and lunging at each other in deadly seriousness. Their faces contorted in hatred for each other. The violence very real.

But before Corbulo could speak or act prince Gummar had lunged again, moving swiftly and nimbly, his blade punching straight into Crastus's exposed shoulder. The stabbing blow causing the big man to roar in pain while among a section of the crowd of onlookers a collective groan of dismay rang out. Punching Gummar in the head with his left hand, Crastus drove his opponent backwards, but it was clear the centurion had been badly wounded. Grasping his wounded shoulder Crastus snarled as he staggered backwards.

"What the fuck!" Corbulo bellowed as he leaped into the middle of the fight. "Stop this right now!"

In his corner prince Gummar had been preparing to renew his attack and finish Crastus off but as Corbulo suddenly appeared the prince hesitated.

"Drop your weapons, both of you!" Corbulo roared as he pulled his spatha sword from his belt. "Or by the gods I swear that I will run you both through myself."

Glaring at him both Gummar and Crastus hesitated. Suddenly uncertain. Their raw aggression and desire to kill palpable. The smell of blood was in the air. But then suddenly the absurdity of what they had been engaged in appeared to reassert itself and their expressions changed.

"Drop your fucking weapons!"

Dropping their knives to the ground both prince Gummar and Crastus remained standing where they were. The crowd of spectators falling silent. The betting on who would win the fight ending abruptly.

"On your knees!" Corbulo bellowed as he turned from one combatant to the other, his face dark with rage.

Obediently both officers dropped down onto their knees. The crowd of spectators holding their breath as they waited to see what would happen next. For a moment Corbulo remained silent as Harald suddenly appeared, hurriedly pushing his way through the crowd, the old officer looking visibly alarmed.

"What the fuck do you think you were doing!" Corbulo yelled turning from Crastus to Gummar, still clutching his sword. "Did I or did I not forbid duelling and single combat in this ala?"

"He started it Sir," Crastus called out his words ending in a groan.

"I don't care who started this fight," Corbulo roared. "Both of you disobeyed me. You disobeyed a direct order and for that you will both be punished. Gods I should have both of you executed right here and now!"

Corbulo was about to speak again when he was interrupted by a commotion at the gates into the fort. Frowning he turned to see what was going on before abruptly a cavalry scout appeared, the man struggling to make his way through the crowd. The soldier crying out in a harsh, urgent voice.

"Sir. Sir!" the soldier yelled. "The outlying pickets report enemy cavalry approaching from the east. Hundreds of them Sir! It's king Hildimer! He is here!"

Staring at the solitary cavalry scout Corbulo did not move. A strange, strangled noise of frustration coming from his throat as his mind worked. Then hurriedly Corbulo sheathed his sword and turning to prince Gummar he glared at the kneeling officer. "Prince Gummar! Recall our pickets and get the rest of the men into their defensive positions along the ramparts! You are to hold the walls! The enemy must not be allowed to break into the camp. And you!" Corbulo said swiftly rounding on the wounded, bleeding Crastus. "Get our wounded onto the Nemesis and stay there with them. The Nemesis will remain where it is anchored right now. You are not to move her. We no longer have the time to transport the wounded across the Danube. Defend the ford across the Morava as best as you can. Like I instructed you. Now move. All of you move! Move!"

"What the fuck just happened?" Harald said hurriedly as he reached Corbulo while around him the camp sprang into frantic action, officers yelling orders and trumpets blaring as the Romans rushing to their defensive positions.

"Prince Gummar and Crastus got into a fight," Corbulo growled, "despite my explicit orders forbidding duels and single combat. When this is over both are going to be punished for disobedience!"

Standing up on the walkway behind the wooden palisade, his bodyguards, officers and men lining the defences, clutching their shields and spears, Corbulo peered across the cleared fields to the east where the hundreds of Quadi horsemen had come to a halt. The enemy, formed up in a long straight line, were studying the Roman fort in silence, making no attempt to attack. The Quadi cavalry, to his surprise, appeared to be organised in disciplined Roman style turmae, squadrons of around thirty men, led by a single leader positioned at the front. Many of the barbarians were clad in their traditional clothing, long trousers, shirt like gowns and capes over which some of the warriors were wearing captured Roman body armour. But here and there some of the men were clad completely in Roman style tunics. The fighter's heads adorned with a mixture of native caps and Roman helmets. While the horsemen were clutching long Sarmatian style lances and small round cavalry shields and some of their horses' manes were adorned with human skulls.

"That must be king Hildimer over there Sir," Harald said hurriedly pointing towards a band of enemy horsemen standing apart from the others, the riders clustered around a Germanic war banner. Then abruptly Harald stopped speaking, his expression darkening as there was a movement among the enemy ranks. The Roman soldiers looking on impassively as from the Quadi ranks a new banner was raised high into the air for all to see.

"Fuck!" Harald swore. "See there. They have a Draco. That is a captured Roman army banner!"

"I can't make out which cohort it belongs to Sir," a Roman voice called out. "But it is definitely one of ours."

"The barbarian scum are taunting us," Harald snapped.

Gazing at the distant enemy Corbulo remained silent. Then quickly he turned to look up at the men manning the nearby watchtower.

"What can you see?" Corbulo called out. "Are there infantry behind that line of horsemen?"

"No Sir," came back the reply. "I can't see any infantry. It's just cavalry. Maybe a thousand of them."

"This is just an advance guard," Corbulo said turning to Harald. "The king has taken his cavalry and moved on ahead. The enemy infantry must still be moving to catch up. They will be here soon."

"Should we attack them while the odds are still even Sir?" Harald said in a tight voice, his eyes fixed upon the Quadi.

"No," Corbulo replied shaking his head. "They will just lure us out of the camp and try and ambush us. No, we stay put. Let them come to us. That is the plan. If the king wants his treasure back, he is going to have to come and take it."

Corbulo was about to say something else when a Roman warning cry rang out and moments later, he saw that a small band of Quadi horsemen had broken away from the main force and were cautiously making their way towards the Roman ramparts. The riders holding up a flag of truce.

"They want to talk Sir!" a Roman voice yelled.

But as the enemy riders approached a strange silence settled upon the mass of Roman defenders lining the ramparts of their fort. Staring down at the Quadi horsemen Corbulo took a deep breath before quickly exchanging a glance with Harald. His expression grave. Harald looking troubled.

"That's far enough!" Harald bellowed at last in German from the ramparts, his cry bringing the small band of riders to a halt a dozen paces from the Roman defensive ditch and earthen embankment. "What do you want?"

For a moment none within the enemy party answered him. Then sitting upon her horse flanked by two Quadi warriors Sulpicia raised her bound hands in the air, her eyes searching the Roman faces peering back down at her before finally her gaze settled upon Corbulo.

"Prefect," the lady called out speaking in Latin, her voice pleading, her face pale. "I am here to make a deal with you. King Hildimer sends me to you with a simple proposal. If you were to return the remaining treasure chest and all its contents that you stole from him, in exchange, he is willing to hand me over to you alive. So that you may do with me what you like."

Sitting on her horse, her eyes fixed upon Corbulo, Sulpicia fell silent. But even from his vantage point up on the wall it was clear to Corbulo that the woman was in distress. Her bound hands showing that she was not at liberty. That she was in fact a prisoner of the king.

"What's this!" Harald bellowed in a contemptuous voice. "The king did not agree to the private deal that you were trying to make with him behind our backs. Your plans did not work out as you had anticipated, did they? Was betraying your own not good for the royal arsehole? I thought you said you knew the king well," Harald roared taunting Sulpicia, "that he had a soft spot for you! That you could negotiate with him. Well, how is that going? Not too good by the looks of it from where I am standing. You fucked up!"

"If you do not agree to his terms the king will execute me," Sulpicia cried out, ignoring Harald, her eyes firmly upon Corbulo. "Please prefect, we made a mistake by stealing the king's gold. It was a foolish thing to do. Please. I am begging you. I am begging you to spare my life!"

"You betrayed us!" Harald roared back. "You murdered two of my men. You tried to sell us out for your own personal gain. There can be no forgiveness for that. You made your bed, now lie in it!"

"Please Corbulo!" Sulpicia cried out, her face growing increasingly distraught. "I beg you. For whatever I have done, I ask you to forgive me. I was wrong. I made a stupid decision. Please. I beg you. I will do whatever you want me to do from now on. They will kill me if you do not accept the king's proposal. Please!"

But from his vantage point along the ramparts Corbulo remained silent.

"I am king Hildimer's son!" one of the young men sitting on his horse beside Sulpicia suddenly called out in surprisingly good Latin. "This is your last chance Roman. Accept my father's demands!"

But in response Corbulo again remained silent.

And as the silence started to lengthen and no one made a move at last the king's son turned to one of his colleagues who, urging his horse up to Sulpicia, suddenly lunged at her. The man expertly wrapping a thin cord around her neck. Pulling the cord tight around Sulpicia's throat, forcing her head and body backwards the man proceeded to tighten his grip and strangle her in full view of the whole camp.

Looking on no one spoke until at last it was done and the executioner roughly shoved Sulpicia's corpse from the horse and onto the ground.

"You are all dead men, Romans!" the king's son cried out glaring at the faces watching him from the ramparts. "We are not going to forgive you for what you did to our villages. You had your chance to surrender. Now only death awaits you! Death and eternal shame!"

And with that the young man turned his horse around and the band of riders rapidly started out back towards their colleagues leaving Sulpicia's corpse lying where it had fallen.

Chapter Twenty-One - Fight to the Death

Hurrying along the fort's congested walkway Corbulo kept his head down, his body half bent over to protect himself as volley after volley of barbarian arrows slammed into the Roman ramparts or went whining over his head into the camp. Lining the walkway, their bodies pressed tightly against the wooden wall, his men were in a defensive crouch as they endured the enemy bombardment in stoic silence. The soldiers clad for battle, clutching their small cavalry shields and long thrusting spears. The men looking grim. It was morning. An hour after dawn. The sky clear and blue with a powerful sun rising in the east.

Reaching the spot where the crew of the lone Roman bolt thrower, taken from the Nemesis, were huddled around their weapon Corbulo quickly risked a peek over the top of the palisade. Across the recently cleared fields to the east parties of barbarian archers were advancing towards the Roman fortifications. The enemy bounding forwards then stopping before moving again. One group covering the next with impressive discipline as if they had spent a long-time training to do so. While coming on behind the archers, moving at a steady brisk walk, was a great solid mass of Quadi infantry. The fields filled with thousands upon thousands of warriors. The silent men brandishing their weapons and shields. Confident in their ability, their cause and their numbers. And beyond them Corbulo could see that the enemy cavalry had extended their line and now appeared to enclose his position on three sides. The horsemen stationary and watching the unfolding battle. Their war banners fluttering in the warm summer breeze.

"Let them have it," Corbulo growled as he hurriedly lowered his head and turned to the crew of the bolt thrower. "Keep shooting until you run out of ammunition. Concentrate on killing their officers."

"Prepare for infantry assault!" an urgent Roman voice cried out from further down the walkway.

Turning his attention back to the enemy Corbulo once again raised his head to see what was going on. And as he did so he grunted with mixture of surprise and grudging respect. The enemy appeared to be better prepared, organised and trained than what he had been expecting from a barbarian army.

Out in the fields the parties of Quadi archers had finally come to a halt. Arrayed in a disciplined line, with wide gaps left in between their formations for their infantry colleagues to pass through, some of the archers were down on one knee while others were standing behind them. The men releasing their arrows at the Roman fort in disciplined practised volleys. The harsh cries of their leaders ringing out across the still morning. The continuous aerial bombardment pinning the Romans down into their positions and forcing them to keep their heads down. Making a sally out of the gates all but impossible.

"They don't seem to be short of ammunition Sir," a Roman officer called out as he crouched nearby.

"They have learned how to fight from us," Corbulo replied. "But no matter. They are not the equites foederati Germanica."

"Here they come!" a Roman voice yelled.

Biting his lip Corbulo looked on as the vast mass of Quadi sword and spearmen began to move on through the gaps left by the archers. Now less than fifty yards from the edge of the Roman defensive ditch. Some of the men were carrying assault ladders. Others war banners and accompanying them were packs of savage looking war dogs. Their collars studded with sharp wooden spikes. And as the enemy infantry closed in on the Roman fort with a sharp crack the Roman bolt thrower sent its first yard long projectile hurtling towards the enemy. The bolt slamming into the Quadi ranks and claiming its first victim.

Hollering in delight the crew of the bolt thrower punched the air, but their cries of triumph were swiftly and decisively drowned out by a great thunderous roar coming from thousands of throats. A great bellowing torrent of noise that sent flocks of birds in the nearby forest lifting into the air in panic and a sharp tremor of fear coursing down Corbulo's spine. Then suddenly the Quadi tribesmen broke into a charge. The mass of warriors storming towards the Roman ramparts. Surging forwards like a massive incoming tide. The ground shook. The noise drowning out any audible Roman response. The enemy voices were filled with real rage. The sheer venom palpable in the war cries of the Quadi.

Storming towards the ramparts, unafraid of any Roman missiles, all along the length of the fort, the foremost ranks of enemy infantry went crashing and leaping down into the deep V shaped ditch. Some of the men crying out in horror as they lost their footing and were swiftly trampled underfoot by their comrades. Others scrambling out of the ditch and up the earthen embankment towards the wooden wall behind which the Romans were sheltering. The Quadi lunging at the wall with their axes and bare hands as they boldly tried to cut and break a way through the barrier. Dogs barking and snarling. Some of the men were crying out in desperation as the crush and pressure of their colleagues pressing in on them from behind was impaling them on the collar of sharpened stakes that ran along the base of the wall. Their bodies being thrust onto the stakes like flies onto a needle.

While out in the fields a section of ground just beyond the ditch suddenly gave way instantly swallowing up a whole group of men as the Quadi went tumbling into Harald's carefully concealed killing pits, to be impaled on the sharpened sticks that awaited them at the bottom. But effective as the defences were proving to be they were mere isolated rocks unable to contain the sheer power and momentum of the incoming tide. The Roman defences too puny. The carefully thought-out and prepared works barely slowing the massive enemy assault.

"Hold lads! Hold your positions!" Corbulo suddenly heard prince Gummar's powerful voice ringing out from further down the walkway.

Hearing axes hammering into wood and the harsh, guttural enemy voices yelling and crying out to each other now just yards away on the other side of the wooden wall Corbulo pulled his spatha sword from its sheath as he readied himself. His expression grim, his lips moving silently as he recounted the song of his ancestors. While along the walkway on either side of him the tense Roman soldiers crouched in their positions as they awaited the first of the enemy. Suddenly Corbulo noticed that the enemy archers were no longer targeting the top of the Roman ramparts but had instead shifted their bombardment. The enemy now aiming their arrows high into the sky where they were plunging down nearly vertically into the middle of the camp and causing chaos among the corralled horses.

"Up! Up and at them!" he yelled instantly rising to his feet.

Moments later a Quadi assault ladder thudded up against the wall just a yard away to his right. Holding his shield strapped to his left arm Corbulo drew back his sword as all along the walkway the defenders rose to their feet. The men frantically jabbing at the enemy below them with their long spears. The

Quadi trying to climb up and over the wall. The Romans trying to push them back down. The whole walkway suddenly alive with savage yelling, screaming activity. But there was no time to dwell on what was happening further along the wall. Abruptly a warrior appeared at the top of the ladder, desperately trying to scramble over the wall and onto the walkway but before he could do so a Roman stabbed him in the face, the blow sending the man tumbling back down to the ground. His place was immediately taken by another man who quickly suffered the same fate, vanishing from view with a horrendous scream, a knife sticking into his eye.

Hurriedly sheathing his sword Corbulo leaned out over the rampart and ignoring the savage, heaving mass of humanity directly below him he caught hold of the top of the ladder and with a mighty shove sent it sliding sideways. The flimsy wooden construction abruptly collapsing and disintegrating under the weight of the men it was carrying. The remaining Quadi tumbling back to the ground with startled shouts. Drawing back into cover just in time as a Frankish throwing axe thudded into the wood just inches from where his head had been Corbulo gasped in shock.

Recovering he quickly turned to check the Roman line where his men were fighting a desperate and furious battle to stop the Quadi from breaking into the camp. But the ramparts appeared to be holding. The enemy had so far not managed to break through. Their ladders were too few and too exposed and the enemy attempts to hack a hole through the solid wall of tree trunks was having no success either. The enemy casualties were mounting. The wooden wall and earthen embankment were giving his men an advantage. But for how long?

Hurriedly Corbulo shifted his attention to the centre of the camp where several horses were lying dead in their corral, killed by arrows. But there was nothing he could do about that now. Down inside the camp, arranged in a single file along the base of the western wall, down on one knee, Harald's reserve company of men had not moved an inch. The soldiers waiting in disciplined silence for the moment when they would be needed.

Hearing a sharp warning cry close by Corbulo looked up and was just in time to see one of his men tumble to the ground from the top of the watch tower. The soldier had been hit by an arrow, his body landing on top of an unsuspecting, cowering Quadi civilian who had been seeking shelter from the arrow storm in the shade of the wall. Quickly Corbulo began to move down the walkway, past the line of fighting men, calling out encouragements to his soldiers. At last spotting prince Gummar savagely driving his spear into a warrior who was trying to clamber over the top of the wall Corbulo hurried up to his deputy.

"The enemy is properly pissed with us Sir," Gummar growled as he noticed Corbulo, his coat of body armour stained with someone else's blood. "They are fucking furious for all those settlements which we burned! They are fighting like demons! But it will not avail them! We are Franks! We were born to war!"

"What do you need to hold them back?" Corbulo cried, quickly turning to survey the carnage around him.

"Nothing, my men and I will hold the wall," Gummar replied, his face darkening. "I am not going to allow some Quadi son of a bitch to beat us. It would just not be right. Fuck them! The enemy are not going to get through. Not today. No need to call on Harald just yet."

"Good," Corbulo replied. "Do your job!"

"I am sorry Sir," Gummar exclaimed as Corbulo was about to push on down the walkway. "About what happened earlier. A lapse of judgment on my part. I should have known better than to get involved in that fight."

Saying nothing nor providing his deputy with any acknowledgment, Corbulo pushed on down the walkway.

***

Looking grim as prince Gummar conveyed the casualty numbers to him Corbulo carefully raised his head a little over the parapet to gaze out across the battlefield from his vantage point up on the walkway. The small group of senior officers were crouching around him in the shelter of the wooden wall. It was afternoon and after the morning assault had failed the Quadi had withdrawn leaving behind the bodies of their dead. The fields and Roman ditch filled with corpses, debris, broken ladders, discarded weapons, shields, clothing and equipment. The Roman wall peppered with arrows sticking into the wood. Surrounding the fort the dead were lying twisted into gruesome shapes, slain by weapons, trampled underfoot or hanging lifeless, stuck onto the wooden spikes that protected the fort. But the enemy had not gone far. Nor had their first assault being entirely unsuccessful for in numerous places the Quadi had managed to bridge the defensive ditch with wooden beams and planking. The bridges improving their access and making it easier to attack the walls. While small parties of archers were roving about shooting at anyone careless enough to expose himself along the ramparts. Their lone challenges and insults ringing out.

Regrouping just beyond the range of the bolt thrower the mass of enemy infantry appeared to be preparing to renew their assault at any moment. The lull in the fighting was only going to be temporary. For a moment Corbulo studied the enemy before lowering his head and shifting his gaze to the line of Roman soldiers sitting along the walkway eating their midday meal that was being brought to them by their comrades from down below in the camp.

"We continue to hold the wall," Corbulo said turning to his officers who were watching him closely. "The enemy must not be allowed to break into the fort. We stand and we fight."

"For how long Sir?" a centurion asked. "For how long must we hold?"

"Another day, perhaps two," Corbulo snapped. "And tell your men this. You all heard the barbarians. They are not here to accept our surrender. This has become a fight to the death. And I expect that every man will do his duty. First and foremost, to himself as a man, a soldier. Then to me as your commander and to Rome! Together we shall endure."

Turning to eye his officers one by one Corbulo's face was hard like rock, his resolve meeting the doubt in his officer's eyes. His presence stiffening the men's morale. None speaking out.

"Message from the Nemesis Sir," a decurion called out as he came hastening towards the small group of senior officers.

"Well, what is it?" Corbulo said quickly turning to the decurion.

"The Nemesis reports no sightings of the enemy along the west bank of the Morava Sir," the decurion said hurriedly. "Retreat in that direction is still possible. But centurion Crastus is too badly wounded to continue in command of the ship. He has lost a lot of blood, and the doctor thinks his wound has become infected. Crastus has been confined to his sick bed. He has therefore temporarily handed over command to his deputy."

Staring at the decurion Corbulo tried to hide his sudden concern. Then his gaze shifted in the direction of where, out of sight, the Nemesis lay at anchor guarding the ford across the river before Corbulo turned his eyes towards prince Gummar.

"If you wish to have me executed after the battle Sir," Gummar said looking down at his hands, "then tell me now for I would prefer to die like a warrior. I will jump down from the wall into the midst of the enemy and die with a sword in my hand. Will you grant me that favour at least?"

"No, you will do your job," Corbulo retorted. "I have not yet decided your fate and right now I need you. Fight well and lead your men like only you can prince Gummar and you will go some way to redeeming yourself. But if Crastus dies from the wound that you gave him then you will be treated as a murderer and nothing will save you. So, pray that he lives!"

Raising his head Gummar gave Corbulo a dark, brooding look, but he said nothing.

***

"Hold your positions men! We are all in this together! We are going to win!" Corbulo cried out as he hurriedly made his way down the walkway, keeping his head down as barbarian arrows came whirring over the top of the Roman wall. It was late in the afternoon and the Quadi had renewed their assault on the fort. Attacking not only the eastern facing ramparts but also this time from the north and the south. The Roman fort under relentless assault. The fields beyond alive with thousands of yelling and shouting men. Horns blaring and dogs barking. The barbarians were rushing across the makeshift bridges that spanned the defensive ditch. The Quadi baying for blood. Their fury palpable. Ladders were thumping up against the walls. The enemy were hammering away like demons at the wall of tree trunks that barred their way into the Roman camp. The defenders were jabbing at the attackers with their long spears and sending the ladders crashing back to the ground. The ferocious contest evenly matched, the success of the assault hanging in the balance.

Reaching the corner watchtower along the north facing ramparts Corbulo took a quick peek over the side of the wall, trying to assess the situation, before grabbing hold of the centurion in command of this section of the wall and quickly pulling him down into a crouch.

"What do you need?" Corbulo cried out over the din of battle. "What can I do to help you?"

Hastily the centurion turned to look down the line of men manning this section of the wall, his breathing coming fast, his chest heaving as he assessed the situation. Then he turned his eyes towards Harald's reserve company who were waiting down inside the camp. The reserve of a hundred and twenty men uncommitted to the battle. The soldiers down on one knee, gripping their weapons as they lined the base of the western wall.

"The reserve Sir, we could do with them up here right now," the officer exclaimed.

"No, they will only be committed as a last resort," Corbulo said abruptly rising to his feet. "Signal me only if you are in immediate danger of being overrun. For now, you will have to make do with the men that you have got. Hold the wall centurion. All of us are counting on each other to do their job. The enemy must under no circumstances be allowed to break into the camp! For if they do, we are all dead. Keep going. Do your job! We are going to win!"

Then gripping the officer's shoulder tightly Corbulo was off hurrying down the walkway yelling encouragements to his men. But he'd only gone a dozen paces before the soldier ahead of him suddenly slumped to the ground and a gap appeared in the Roman line. Taking advantage of the temporary weakness, a barbarian leaped over the top of the wall landing feet first onto the walkway. The lone man was clutching an axe but before he could do anything else Corbulo was onto him, ramming the point of his spatha sword repeatedly into the man's gut. The steel blade punching through flesh. Blood soaking the man's tunic. Then with a brutal shove Corbulo sent the dying warrior tumbling down into the camp. His body landing with a thud in the dirt. Turning to face the next threat Corbulo was just in time to see a second man scrambling over the top of the wall. This one armed with a spear. The man yelling obscenities at the Romans. But as the warrior was about to tumble headfirst onto the walkway a Roman nearby partially decapitated him with an axe. The blade getting stuck in the bone. The body of the barbarian hanging half over the top of the wall, his legs dangling into space. Blood gushing from the wound.

Staggering backwards against a comrade Corbulo swore out loud. His spatha covered in blood. But before he could rejoin the fight or issue orders, he suddenly heard a Roman trumpet ringing out from the southern ramparts. And as he recognised the signal a chill ran down his spine. The men along the southern ramparts were signalling for help. They were about to be overrun. Turning to stare across the camp towards the opposite wall Corbulo's chest was heaving. His feet rooted to the deck. His cheeks burning. But before he could act, he suddenly heard cries of alarm rising from the men along the eastern wall. Their increasingly frantic warning yells dramatically reinforced by another trumpet cry for immediate assistance. The eastern walls too looked like they were about to lose control. The enemy appeared to be about to break into the camp from two separate directions.

Swiftly Corbulo sized up the situation. His eyes switching from the fighting along the southern wall to that along the eastern wall. Then he was on the move. His decision made. Leaping down into the camp and landing with a roll he was up on his feet and racing towards the eastern wall.

"Harald!" Corbulo roared as he ran. "The eastern wall! Get over there! Now!"

But there was no time to see if Harald had heard him or was complying with his orders. Abruptly with a dreadful creaking, splintering sound part of the Roman ramparts along the eastern side of the fort came tumbling down. Pulled down by a dozen iron grappling hooks attached to ropes that had been flung over the top of the wall and which the defenders had been unable to dislodge. The collapse of part of the Roman wall eliciting a great triumphant cheer from thousands of barbarian throats that seemed to grow in strength and volume as they sensed victory.

Directly ahead of Corbulo a gaping hole in the defences had appeared. The collapse of part of the wall cutting the walkway above and isolating prince Gummar's men from the rest of their colleagues. Staring at the breach with growing dismay Corbulo gasped as within seconds dozens of Quadi warriors came charging unopposed into the camp brandishing their weapons. The barbarians yelling in savage triumph as they sensed that the end was near.

Coming to a halt, alone, clutching his spatha, his shield strapped to his left arm Corbulo bravely prepared to face the enemy onslaught as the Quadi came charging straight towards him. But suddenly Corbulo was no longer alone. Rushing past him, counter charging the enemy, Harald and his men had appeared. The reserve company storming towards the breach. Their spears lowered as in a phalanx. Their counterattack sending them crashing into the front and flanks of the enemy. The momentum of the Roman charge impaling the enemy on their spear points and abruptly halting their attack. And as Corbulo looked on Harald's men began to drive the howling mob back towards the breech in the walls. The Roman spears causing havoc among the densely packed enemy who had no room to manoeuvre. Bodies tumbling to the ground to be trampled upon by their comrades. Bones breaking. Men losing their footing. The cries of triumph swiftly turning to screams of alarm and panic.

"Remember Samosata!" Harald roared as he locked eyes with Corbulo. "I am saving your arse again, prefect!"

Staring at the desperate struggle to contain the breach Corbulo swore. Then swiftly he turned his eyes towards the southern wall. But his men were still in their positions along the walkway. The enemy were not yet in control of that section of the ramparts. Maybe the crisis there had come and gone. But it was a different story along the eastern wall.

"Drive them back! Drive them back!" Harald's voice boomed over the din of the fighting.

Moving forward to join his soldiers Corbulo grimaced as he saw that the struggle to contain the breech had become a relentless shoving and pushing contest. A trial of strength. The Roman spear points pressing against the shields of what remained of the Quadi breaching party. The two sides struggling to push each other back. The breech in the wall packed solid with snarling Quadi warriors trying to get into the camp. The Romans trying to push them out and no side making much headway. Hurriedly Corbulo assessed the fighting, but he had no more reserves to commit to the battle. Every available man was already in the fight.

Suddenly Corbulo heard prince Gummar bellowing orders and as he looked up, he saw frantic activity taking place along the walkway on either side of the breech. His men appeared to be preparing something. Then without warning the first earthen jar filled with black pitch was hurled down onto the heads of the Quadi directly below who were packed into the breech. The jars shattering on impact, the pitch getting everywhere. The barbarians crying out in alarm at the unexpected assault from above. But packed tightly into the breach the enemy were barely able to move. The gap in the wall plugged solid with men.

And as more and more earthenware jars filled with pitch began to rain down on the heads of the enemy and shatter on impact, prince Gummar's deep powerful voice rang out once more.

"Set the bastards on fire! Set them on fire!"

Within seconds his men had complied hurling half a dozen burning torches down onto the helpless multitude directly below. The torches swiftly setting the pitch drenched enemy warriors on fire and moments later the breach had been transformed into a fiery hell of burning human beings. The greedy flames spreading rapidly, catching hold of anything flammable. The smell of burning flesh growing. The enemy's panic stricken, terrified screams rising to a crescendo. And as the fire spread and men began to burn alive the Quadi assault collapsed. The mass of warriors fleeing in great disorder. The breach rapidly emptying. Some of the barbarians leaping down into the ditch, their clothes on fire as they desperately tried to save themselves. Others running off in panic or rolling over the ground as their colleagues frantically tried to put out their burning clothes. The chaos and panic rapidly spreading across the whole assault force.

Looking on as Harald's men rapidly secured the breach in the wall and began to fortify it with anything they could find Corbulo hissed in delight. There was no need to tell Harald what to do. His old friend knew exactly what was required. The second enemy assault of the day appeared to have been repelled for up on the walls the intensity of the fighting had begun to diminish. His men had started to call out, checking on each other. The relief in the men's voices clear. Quickly looking up to check the position of the sun Corbulo saw that the afternoon had given way to evening. The light was already starting to fade.

Shifting his gaze as his men hurriedly worked to fortify the gap in the wall, he caught sight of prince Gummar standing on the walkway proudly surveying the fiery carnage and destruction he'd just wrought upon the enemy. And as he gazed up at the Frankish prince Corbulo paused. Spotting him at last Gummar grinned before quickly and silently raising and shaking his fist in a sign of triumph.

***

"They are licking their wounds for now," Harald said quietly as he and Corbulo stood alone up on the walkway gazing out across the darkened fields towards the enemy campfires that stretched off into the night. The numerous little pin pricks of flickering light surrounding the fort on all sides in an ominous, suffocating embrace. "But I expect they will renew the assault tomorrow at dawn and we are weaker now. That makeshift barrier which we erected to plug that breach is not going to hold for long against a determined assault," Harald added turning to glance at his commander, his expression concealed by the darkness of the night.

"I know," Corbulo said quietly. "They will attack again tomorrow and try and overwhelm us. That is what I would do. The battle tomorrow will be decisive."

"We could still slip away in the night," Harald said sighing. "The Nemesis still controls the ford across the Morava. We could break out and head west. We would stand a fair chance of getting away."

"If we did that, all the men who have died here will have died in vain and we would not be able to take our wounded with us," Corbulo replied in a quiet, sober voice. "No, Harald there will be no breakout tonight. No retreat. We will make our stand here. We will fight and we will win."

Standing beside Corbulo Harald made no reply as he gazed out towards the enemy campfires just a few hundred yards away.

"I am going to trust that you have a plan to get us out of this," Harald said at last. "The men - they all think that you have a plan. They believe in you. They trust you. They really do. But fuck me, I sure hope that you know what you are doing Corbulo. And having now said that, if we are to die tomorrow, then I shall do so at your side. That is how it should be. That is how old Hostes would want us to go. He would be proud of us. Brothers in arms, right!"

"Brothers in arms," Corbulo replied as the two officers gently bumped fists.

***

The makeshift barrier that plugged the gap in the Roman wall was on fire. The Quadi fire arrows slamming into the crude wooden defences. One after the other in a slow but never-ending barrage. The resin-soaked cloth tied to the arrows constantly adding to the fire. While Harald and his men rushed about inside the fort trying to put out and smother the flames with army blankets, but it appeared to be a hopeless task Corbulo thought as he observed his men's actions from atop of the walkway. The flames were refusing to die. The smoke was getting thicker and thicker. Inhaling the smoke his men were coughing and spluttering. It was morning and as expected the Quadi had renewed their assault for a third time. But instead of a full frontal attack the mass of enemy infantry was hanging back, waiting for their moment. Biding their time. In their place, the barbarians had sent their archers forwards again, and it was they who were now taking the Roman ramparts under aim. The parties of enemy archers lined up all along the perimeter of the fort, shooting at any Roman who was foolish enough to expose himself and present a target. The debris and corpse strewn battlefield strangely quiet and calm.

Biting his lip in frustration Corbulo looked on as Harald's men started to lose the battle against the flames. The barrier they had erected to plug the gap was going up in flames - once again exposing the breach in the Roman defences. He had no formed and trained archers to shoot back at the enemy and drive them away from the walls, nor could he risk a cavalry sally with the mass of enemy infantry so close by. Turning to look down the walkway where the Romans were clutching their weapons, crouching behind the shelter of their wooden wall, Corbulo took a deep breath. There was nothing he or his men could do but remain where they were and wait for the barbarian infantry to launch their attack.

"Harald, let it be!" Corbulo called out at last in a resigned sounding voice. "Let it burn. There is nothing you can do to stop it."

Looking up at him from where he was standing in the camp supervising his men's efforts Harald appeared displeased but seeing that Corbulo was right at last he reluctantly called off his men. Ordering them back. The soldiers from the reserve company retreating from the flames and the billowing smoke, some coughing and gasping for breath.

"Let it burn," Corbulo called out. "Then take up positions around the breach. We will catch the bastards from three sides if they try to enter again." Then to prince Gummar who was crouching on the walkway on the opposite side of the gap in the ramparts. "If they try to come through here again Harald will hold them up and we will set them alight again like last time."

"I will burn them all, Sir," Gummar called out gleefully from across the gap, pointing at the mass of small earthen ware pots filled with pitch that sat readied along the walkway at his feet.

Shifting position Corbulo carefully raised his head a little over the top of the parapet and peered at the groups of enemy archers camped just along the edge of the Roman ditch. What were the enemy waiting for? Why had they not launched their main assault? Puzzled he studied the barbarians. The lightly armed Quadi archers appeared confident that they were not going to get shot at or attacked for many were standing out in the open in exposed positions. Some of the barbarians were hurling insults at the besieged Romans while others were busy scavenging among the corpses that lay strewn across the ground and throughout the V shaped ditch. Idly Corbulo watched them going about their business before shifting his gaze in the direction of the lone Roman bolt thrower whose crew had long since run out of ammunition. The giant cross bow silent and no longer used. If only he'd had some missile troops he thought.

"Enemy assault parties approaching!" a Roman voice suddenly cried out from high up in one of the watchtowers. The sentries lying flat on the deck to present the smallest possible target to the archers. Hurriedly Corbulo shifted his gaze to the main infantry force and sure enough he soon spotted the small groups of men moving purposefully towards the Roman fort. The Quadi were moving fast, half running and they appeared to be carrying something. But from his vantage point he had only a partial view of what was going on.

"What do you see?" Corbulo bellowed turning to the watchers high up in their tower.

For a moment no reply came.

"They are carrying grappling hooks and ropes!" an alarmed Roman voice screamed. "They are coming from everywhere. North wall, south, east, west!"

"Confirm?" Corbulo bellowed across the fort to the men manning the opposite wall.

"Enemy assault parties advancing Sir!" the shouted response came followed by another hurried confirmation from the south wall.

Swearing softly Corbulo turned to peer at the enemy to the east as the small groups of men came rushing towards the fort. The Quadi swiftly passing through their supporting formations of archers. The bowmen covering their comrades advance and shooting at anything that revealed itself up on the wall. And as he observed the enemy Corbulo's expression tightened as he saw that some of the men were carrying grappling hooks attached to iron chains. While coming on behind their colleagues' other parties of Quadi were leading sturdy looking oxen towards the Roman fort. The animals bellowing in frustration.

"The enemy are going to try and pull down another section of the wall!" Corbulo called out turning to Harald who was waiting down below in the camp. "They have hooks with iron chains so that you cannot cut the rope, and they are going to use oxen to pull down our defences. Prepare to face multiple breaches all at once. They will probably wait until they have created enough gaps to stretch us and then they will launch their main assault."

"What do you want me to do?" Harald shouted back.

"Stay where you are! Hold your position around this breach for now. Let's see how successful they are going to be at pulling down our defences," Corbulo called out. Then he was off scurrying along the walkway, his head lowered as he hurried over to the northern end of the fort.

Crouching along the walkway Corbulo looked on as the first enemy grappling hooks came flying over the top of the wall. Their iron claws scraping ruthlessly along the wooden deck or smacking into his soldiers as from outside the fort the enemy quickly worked to pull the ropes tight against the ramparts. The base of the Roman defences crawling with Quadi. The men shouting excitedly to each other. While up on the wall the Romans scrambled to cut the grappling ropes or fling them back down before the hooks could do any damage to the wall. The soldiers swearing and shouting to each other as they in turn were taken under aim by the enemy archers. The air thick with whirring arrows.

It was nearly noon, and the Roman defences were beginning to look distinctly ragged and forlorn. The battered wooden wall was partially pulled down in places, the palisade cracked and splintered, the timbers half bent and sticking out at crazy angles. While in other parts small gaps in the defences had appeared forcing Harald to disperse the men from his reserve company to cover the growing number of breaches. The struggle between the grappling parties and the defenders still ongoing, when Corbulo suddenly heard the urgent warning trumpet blast. Instantly his head whipped round. The trumpet blast had come from the west, in the direction of the Morava. It had come from the Nemesis and the signal was clear. *Am under attack*.

"What do you see?" Corbulo yelled turning to the men in the nearby watchtower. "To the west! What is happening?"

For a moment the watchers manning the watchtower remained silent as they turned to peer in the direction of the Morava.

"Enemy cavalry Sir!" a Roman voice yelled out at last. "Hundreds of them! They are approaching from the west. They are attempting to cross the ford across the river. The Nemesis is trying to stop them with her artillery! They are fighting! They are trying to force the ford."

Staring up at the men in their watchtower Corbulo swore. Then quickly he turned his eyes towards the west, but he could not see what was going on in the river valley beyond the fort.

"Enemy skirmishers! To the west also!" the Roman watcher in his tower yelled again, his voice filled with alarm. "Archers and slingers Sir. Loads of them! They are engaging the Nemesis. The enemy are shooting at the Nemesis! Our men are responding! It's becoming a missile duel. Gods..."

"Enemy infantry?" Corbulo shouted.

"No Sir can't see any. It's just cavalry and skirmishers, missile troops. But there are loads of them! I see enemy banners!"

Swearing again Corbulo looked frustrated.

"What is going on?" Harald shouted as he came running up, looking concerned.

"The Nemesis is under attack," Corbulo replied hurriedly turning to look down at Harald from the walkway. "Looks like king Hildimer's uncle has finally arrived and he has brought his cavalry and skirmishers with him. They are attempting to cross the river at the ford. But the enemy appear to have only brought cavalry and skirmishers. The king's uncle must have left his main infantry force behind to guard the Marcomanni border. If he took only his cavalry and light troops then he must have wanted to move fast."

Staring up at Corbulo Harald's expression darkened but he was too professional a soldier to express what had now become abundantly clear. The arrival of the king's uncle from the west threatened to close the ala's last remaining line of escape. He and every man inside the fort were about to be trapped with no way out.

Suddenly the Roman trumpet rang out again, the noise coming from the direction of the Morava and as he recognised the signal Corbulo lowered his eyes.

"Sir! Sir!" the watchers up in their tower yelled in alarm. "The Nemesis! She has cut her anchor and is retreating. She is drifting away downstream. She is abandoning her position at the ford. The enemy archers are still shooting at her. Horsemen are moving across the ford. They are getting across the river. They are heading towards us! We have lost control of the ford!"

Looking down at the planking of the walkway Corbulo made no reply. If Crastus had still been in command of the Nemesis, the ship and its crew would never have surrendered their position so easily and quickly. But Crastus was already out of the fight before it had even begun. Looking sombre Corbulo at last raised his head and turned his eyes to the west feeling the sudden crushing burden of command weighing him down. Conscious that hundreds of men were looking to him for hope and leadership. But his entire command was now trapped and likely to be massacred within the next hour and that was all on him. His decision.

"Harald;" Corbulo called out at last, gathering himself, as from outside the fort sudden cheers of delight rose up from the ranks of the Quadi as they saw their mounted allies moving towards them; "they will launch their main assault within the hour and try and overwhelm us. I am going to send you what men we can spare from the walls to reinforce your company. Your men are to hold the breaches as long as they can. Then if we are about to be overwhelmed, we will retreat up onto the walls and make our last stand along the walkways. If you are about to be overwhelmed set the horses free and stampede them into the enemy. Then come and find me! Understood."

"Surrender?" Harald called out looking up at his commander with a questioning look but in reply Corbulo silently shook his head.

"To the death it is then," Harald replied harshly as he hurriedly turned away and started bellowing instructions to his command.

It was sometime later, the sun riding high across the clear blue sky, when the enemy grappling parties, their job complete, started to beat a hasty retreat taking their oxen with them. Watching them, with his standard bearer down on one knee at his side, the ala's war banner held aloft for all to see, Corbulo's expression abruptly hardened as he saw what was coming next.

"Here they come! Prepare for infantry assault!" a shrill Roman voice cried out.

Biting his lip Corbulo crouched along the walkway among his men as he watched the mass of Quadi infantry who had begun to move towards the fort at a brisk walk. The thousands of tribesmen eager to finish off the stubborn defenders. To have their revenge and massacre the Romans. The Quadi confident that this time they would be successful. Large groups were veering towards the battered Roman wall and the numerous breaches in the defences.

For a moment Corbulo watched the approaching enemy. Then he shifted his gaze to the two proud Draco banners that were still fluttering from their masts atop the watchtowers. The serpent banners snaking in the gentle breeze. His eyes moving on he turned his attention to prince Gummar's men who were crouching along the walkways as they awaited the enemy attack. The men silent. The soldiers gripping their weapons and shields, their heads down. While inside the camp covering the breaches in the wall Harald and his men too were ready. The soldier's spears pointed at the gaps through which the enemy would come. His command was ready Corbulo thought. Every available man was in the line. He had done everything that he could do. Nothing had been neglected. Observing his men, Corbulo silently began to recount the song of his ancestors, recalling their names and famous deeds in the song that his mother had taught him when he'd still been a boy. Wondering if they would welcome him with pride or disgust. The familiar names of his ancestors still lending him strength and resolve.

"Here they come!"

With a great bellowing cry of rage, rising from thousands of throats, the mass of Quadi infantry broke into a sudden charge.

The enemy surging towards the fort. The fields covered with running men. The human tide storming towards the battered fort and the bands of defenders still holding out.

Surging into the breaches the foremost tribesmen ran straight into Harald's men blocking the way and instantly a furious shoving contest erupted. The Quadi pushing forwards through the Roman spear points, trying to drive the defenders back. Steel blades jabbing into unprotected flesh. Men sinking to the ground, screaming in pain, panic and rage. Axes, spears, swords and shields clattering into each other in the narrow-confined spaces between the walls. The Roman officers frantically yelling at their men as they desperately tried to hold back the onslaught. But the Quadi were too many and the breaches too numerous and as he looked on from his position up on the walkway Corbulo could see that his men were beginning to lose the fight. The enemy assault was relentlessly beginning to drive the defenders back. The Quadi were about to break through.

Swearing softly Corbulo shifted his gaze across the fort to where Harald was rushing about doing his best to contain and repel the assault. If he did not act soon one of the bands of defenders would soon be overwhelmed, letting the enemy into the camp and if that happened the rest of his men down in the fort would be in immediate danger of being surrounded and cut to pieces.

"Give the order to retreat up onto the walls!" Corbulo said hurriedly turning to the trumpeter crouching nearby, holding his long straight instrument. Then Corbulo pulled his spatha sword from its sheath as he prepared to fight.

Moments later the trumpet rang out, issuing the orders. Hearing the signal Harald come to an abrupt halt as he quickly turned to gaze back in Corbulo's direction. Then to Corbulo's horror his friend was struck by a throwing axe, the blade embedding itself into Harald's chest and instantly he crumpled to the ground. Crying out in shock Corbulo stared at the spot where Harald lay motionless on the ground, the Quadi axe sticking out of his chest.

"Give the order again!" Corbulo roared turning to the trumpeter as the Roman line began to falter. "The men are to get up on the walkways or else they are going to be overrun!"

And as the urgent trumpet once again rang out the Romans down in the fort began to act. Some men retreating towards the ladders that led up onto the walkway in good order whilst others broke into a frantic, chaotic sprint to the relative safety of the walkways. And as the defenders began to abandon their positions the Quadi surged forwards, yelling triumphantly as they broke into the fort from all sides. Watching the growing chaos unfolding inside the fort Corbulo expression darkened as some of his men came frantically clambering up the ladders to join their colleagues crouching along the ramparts. The Roman camp filled with rushing, yelling men. The panic and chaos growing.

Down inside the camp a small group of screaming Quadi women who had been sheltering by the wall, raised their hands in the air as they tried to surrender to their compatriots, but the Quadi were not in the mood to take prisoners. Their rage unrestrained. Their bloodlust unsatiated. The women were ruthlessly butchered, their bodies left where they fell. While beside the crude wooden gate behind which the ala's horses were tightly corralled a lone Roman officer bravely cut the ropes and flung open the gates trying to stampede the horses with his hands and voice before he was felled by a Quadi spear driven straight into his back.

"Fight men!" Corbulo cried out. "We fight! The Germanica fights!"

But the battle was becoming increasingly hopeless. The camp now crawling with enemy warriors and with more pouring in through the breaches in the wall. The remaining Romans, those who had not managed to get up onto the walkways, were now being cut to pieces. Isolated and trapped, the soldiers were putting up a brave final but futile resistance. Their defiant yells and battle cries dwindling as the men were cut down one by one. Soon the enemy would turn their attention to the wooden supports holding up the walkway and bring them crashing down or they could simply send their archers in to finish off the surviving defenders. Gazing at the carnage and bloody chaos Corbulo felt a sudden and great calm come over him. As if he had been relieved of a heavy burden. This then was the end. He was going to die here with his command.

Suddenly a new sound entered the battle making Corbulo blink in startled confusion. The noise had come from the west and it had sounded like a horn. But not a barbarian one! Turning his eyes to the west he frowned. But he could see nothing beyond the confines of the Roman fort. Then once again he heard the sound. And this time it sounded like multiple horns. They were rapidly drawing closer. Abruptly some colour shot into Corbulo's cheeks. Down below in the camp the Quadi too had heard the blaring horns and confusion suddenly seemed to have seized the enemy. The warriors looking around to see what was going on. Their rage and bloodlust evaporating and turning to unease.

"Riders to the west!" the last remaining sentry high up in the nearby watchtower suddenly yelled, the man pointing, the excitement growing in his voice. "Horsemen! I see hundreds of them. They are attacking the ford. They are driving the enemy back across the river. They are across the river. They are ours! Roman banners! I see imperial banners!"

And as the soldier cried out a stir ran through the survivors huddled up on the walkways. Rising to his feet, risking getting shot, Corbulo hurriedly turned his eyes to the west and the river valley. Moments later from among the forest that led down the slope towards the Morava a mass of fleeing Quadi skirmishers appeared. The warriors running for their lives. Their voices raised in panic. Their mad flight infecting the parties of Quadi archers still stationed around the fort and who now also began to waver. And moments later the reason for their flight became clear. Bursting from the forest in pursuit, charging after the lightly armed skirmishers, hundreds upon hundreds of cavalrymen suddenly appeared. The Moors on their small, fast, shaggy African horses slicing through the fleeing Quadi ranks, their spears and arrows sowing death and tumbling men to the ground. The riders flowing around the sides of the fort as they drove their enemy before them like wolves after a herd of sheep. The panic among the Quadi growing and spreading. The surprise attack from the west clearly having caught them off-guard. The Moors showing no mercy.

Staring at the scene in disbelief Corbulo gasped as he watched the Moors galloping after their fleeing enemy. The short little men controlling and wielding their horses and weapons like they had been born to do so. And as the Quadi skirmishers fled the mass of barbarian infantry inside the fort began to retreat also. Large groups of tribesmen rushing back out of the fort through the breaches in the wall. The barbarians yelling to each other in confusion. Their order disrupted. The Quadi retreat threatening to turn into a full-blown rout and defeat.

"Look at those little fucking Africans ride!" a soldier yelled in German, marvelling at the sight. "We have been saved lads!"

For a moment longer Corbulo stared at the Roman cavalry pursuing their quarry across the fields. The riders were driving the Quadi away from the fort. The Roman force was growing in strength as more and more cavalrymen appeared, bursting out of the forest from the direction of the ford across the Morava. The men crying out to their horses and comrades. The ground shaking to the beat of thousands of horses' hooves. Catching sight of a tight band of riders clustered around the war banner of the equites Mauri, Corbulo was suddenly unable to suppress a relieved smile. Then hurriedly he turned to the men crouching along the walkway.

"Reclaim the fort! At them lads!" Corbulo cried out as he leaped down into the Roman camp landing on the ground with a roll.

His men did not need to be told twice. With loud encouraged cries the survivors came leaping and clambering back down into their camp from the walkways that lined what remained of the walls. The Romans quickly setting about killing the few remaining Quadi warriors, butchering the enemy wounded and those who were not fast enough in getting away. Seeing that the barbarians were not putting up any significant organised resistance and his men were regaining control Corbulo ran across to the spot where he'd seen Harald collapse to the ground. Hurriedly pulling away the corpse of another man who had fallen across Harald he crouched beside his friend, feeling for a pulse. The throwing axe was still sticking out of Harald's chest and his tunic and body armour were stained with blood. His body motionless. His eyes closed. Moments later, with the Roman camp filled with shouting, rushing men, Corbulo was joined by two soldiers, the anxious looking men quickly crouching beside Harald's body as if they were his friends.

"Find the doctor and if he still lives bring him here at once," Corbulo cried swiftly turning to the two men. "Tell him that this man here gets medical priority. He's alive. Harald is still alive!"

Saying nothing the two men ran off and as they did Corbulo reached out to take Harald's hand and grip it in his own. And for a long moment he remained where he was silently crouching beside his friend and holding his hand.

"The fort has been secured Sir," prince Gummar called out as he came striding up, the warrior's face stained with blood from a cut to his forehead but otherwise looking unhurt. "The last of the enemy has been driven out. We are back in control. Your orders Sir?"

Letting go of Harald's hand and noticing the doctor and the two men he'd sent to search for him hastening over to him, Corbulo rose to his feet and turned to his deputy and as he did so Gummar rapped out a stiff salute. The two grim faced officers eyeing each other.

"Well done," Corbulo said at last in a stiff voice. "You fought well prince Gummar. I am going to need a strength report." Then he stopped. Trotting into the camp through one of the large breaches in the battered wall a party of horsemen had suddenly appeared. The riders slowing their mounts to a walk as they headed over towards the spot where Corbulo was standing. The horsemen were clad in smart, gleaming coats of mail body armour and one of them was holding up the proud war banner of the equites Mauri. The small, black haired, darkish looking Moors gazing about at the carnage. Turning to face Probus as the Roman commander walked his horse up to him and came to a halt, Corbulo took a deep breath. While Probus gazed back at Corbulo from his horse with a cool, perplexed look.

"You came to our rescue then Sir," Corbulo called out.

"Yes, I did," Probus replied jutting out his chin. "The enemy has been driven back for now and we even managed to capture the king's uncle. That old arse was complacent. He was not expecting to be attacked. Now he is my prisoner. But king Hildimer is still out there, and his men will soon regroup, and they still outnumber us. This fight is not yet over I am afraid."

"The ford across the Morava?" Corbulo asked hurriedly. "The bridge at Carnuntum. It still stands?"

"Yes. Both controlled by the legionaries of the Fourteenth," Probus replied in a calm competent voice. "I managed to rally them to our cause and bring them and some other remnants of our garrisons with me across the Danube. They may have been rebels once, but they are still professional soldiers. Now I have got two thousand loyal infantrymen guarding the ford and our line of retreat. Don't worry. The situation over there is under control, and we saved you."

Gazing up at Probus Corbulo paused. Then he lowered his eyes. "Well done, Sir," he said humbly. "On your great victory."

"You are fucking insane, you know that Corbulo," Probus replied, feigning anger. "When I got your message and understood what you planned to do, I thought you had gone mad. If we had arrived any later than we did, you would have been dead. You are fucking lucky that my men and I bothered to ride to your rescue at all. And I will add that we have also wasted a lot of precious time in doing so. This was not part of our original plan! We were supposed to be on our way south by now to join general Aureolus and confront the Macriani usurpers!"

"You said you were my friend," Corbulo said with a shrug. "Is this not what friendship looks like? I knew you would come to our aid."

"Oh, and how is that?" Probus replied.

"Because if you had allowed us to be destroyed it would have looked bad on you," Corbulo replied. "A defeat like this would not be good for the career of an ambitious man. Instead, now I have given you a chance to boast about a great victory at the imperial court. My men and I have made you look good Sir. Plus, your sister would never have forgiven you if you had not come to our rescue. You still owe me for saving her in Syria and bringing her back to you."

Gazing down at Corbulo Probus remained silent before he slowly shook his head and turned to look around at the bloody carnage and death that lay strewn all around the camp.

"Like I said," Probus called out, "you are fucking mad Corbulo. You took one hell of a gamble. But this, this magnificent stand of yours; you are right. This is exactly what the empire needs right now. A great victory on barbarian soil no less. A victory for our people to savour in a time of endless trouble. A boost to morale. A message to the world that we are not yet done. Rome defiant!" Pausing Probus turned his attention back to Corbulo, his expression suddenly changed. "You and your men have my congratulations on making a most magnificent stand," Probus called out. "A famous stand. We shall call it the battle of the Morava. The people and Senate of Rome are grateful to you and your men. I will make sure that the whole empire learns of what happened here."

"We need to make peace with the Quadi Sir," Corbulo called out fixing Probus with an earnest look. "And now is the time to do so. When we are at our strongest and the enemy has suffered a defeat."

"I agree," Probus replied. "It is necessary. We have already wasted enough time up here. Remember general Aureolus needs us in the south in the war against the Macriani usurpers. We cannot linger here for much longer."

"Sir," Corbulo said nodding quickly in agreement.

Falling silent Corbulo wearily turned to survey the remains of his fort. No one speaking. The ground littered with corpses, debris, discarded weapons, broken shields and abandoned equipment, dead horses and splintered wood. Suddenly without warning the men of the equites foederati Germanica who were standing closest to Corbulo lifted their weapons into the air in triumph. Their voices raised. The silence abruptly shattered. Their cries of swiftly taken up by all the survivors across the Roman camp as elation became swollen with relief. The men's voices ringing out. Spears and shields pumping into the air.

"Victory! Victory! Corbulo! Corbulo! Corbulo!"

Chapter Twenty-Two - Peace

In the empty, tree stump covered field, under the noon sun, the table and chairs looked utterly out of place. A ridiculous sight Corbulo thought and for a moment he wondered where they had found the furniture at such short notice. Riding his horse, trotting towards the table, with the Roman fort and lines of stationary Moorish cavalry to his back, he glanced at his companions. Probus leading the Roman party of four, his expression set like a conquering general, calm and confident as if this was a job he did every day. Tobias looking excited as if he was relishing the forthcoming negotiations as a chance to show off his wonderful intellect. Only prince Gummar looked glum and uncertain, his demeanour changed, as if he knew something which bothered and troubled him.

Shifting his gaze to the party of four barbarian horsemen who were also heading towards the table but from the opposite direction, where in the distance the mass of silent Quadi warriors, both infantry and cavalry, stood arranged in a long, solid looking line, Corbulo took a deep breath. Conscious of the importance of what was about to occur. The great prize that beckoned if they played this right. The silent voices of the two hundred and forty-eight soldiers he'd permanently lost in getting to this point.

Arriving at the solitary negotiating table the Quadi leaders said nothing and made no acknowledgement of the Romans as upon reaching their destination the two negotiating parties stiffly dismounted and turned to eye each other, grasping the reins to their horses. The silence full of crackling tension and sullen resentment. The field quiet like a mouse. The eight negotiators wedged in between the two armies who were facing each other across the field.

Standing to Probus's right, acting as his second, Corbulo gazed across the table at king Hildimer. The Quadi king was a tall man in his thirties with a full black beard and to Corbulo's surprise he was clad in a Roman style toga. The only indication that this was a barbarian king, the mass of tattoos that disappeared up the man's arms and the golden torc that adorned his neck. Glaring back at the Romans king Hildimer looked like he wanted to throttle them with his bare hands. His three companions were clad in the traditional clothing of the barbarian tribes. Their bearded faces hard and tough like rocks that had weathered the wind and rain for an eternity and among them Corbulo recognised the king's son. The same man who had executed Sulpicia in front of the fort's gates just a few days earlier.

"Shall we sit and talk king Hildimer," Probus called out at last in Latin grandly gesturing to the chairs around the table.

"Let's talk," the king replied in a tight, unhappy voice, speaking in good Latin.

Carefully sitting down at the table in the middle of the tree stump studded field, the four Romans on one side, the four Quadi leaders on the other, Corbulo waited for Probus and the king to start the peace negotiations.

"So," Probus said getting straight to the point. "We are here to propose an official peace treaty between Rome and the Quadi. This war between us, the raiding. It has gone on long enough. Too much blood has already been spilt and too much treasure expended. It must come to an end today."

"You have the authority to negotiate such a settlement from emperor Gallienus and from your Senate?" King Hilimer snapped not allowing Probus to continue. "I do not wish to waste my time. My army is ready to renew the war at any moment and as you can see, we outnumber you."

"Yes, I have that authority," Probus replied nodding, looking grave. "I have been given full command of all Roman forces along this stretch of the Danube frontier and right now I am the acting governor of the province of Upper Pannonia. Emperor Gallienus will of course need to ratify what we agree here today, but he has delegated authority to me to negotiate on his behalf and I am confident that the emperor will agree if the terms of our agreement are fair."

"Fair!" king Hildimer growled unhappily. "You attacked our villages and burned them to the ground. Your men were very brave fighting against defenceless women and children."

"Maybe you should not have crossed the imperial frontier and left your settlements undefended," Probus retorted. "You launched an unprovoked war of aggression against us. You attack us, we attack you. War with Rome will never be without a cost to your people. We have demonstrated that we can reach you anywhere and defeat you even beyond the imperial borders. In your own land. We can do this again. You would do well to remember that."

"Your empire has become weak and corrupt," the king said. "The number of your enemies grows by the day. Tell me how many emperors rule the Roman world right now. You are not what you used to be, and we do not fear the name of Rome any longer. You are dying. Rome is the past."

"And yet we still managed to cross the Danube and defeat you in your own land," Probus replied keeping his cool, a little cold smile creeping onto his lips. "You may outnumber us king Hildimer but it is you who has shown weakness, which will not go unnoticed by your rivals. You could not even take one small Roman fort north of the Danube. You could not take Carnuntum. You could not protect your own treasure. You could not even defend your own people and now we have taken your uncle as a prisoner."

"Get to the point," the king said growing irritated. "What terms do you propose for this peace treaty?"

Pausing Probus shot Corbulo a quick look.

"I propose the following peace terms," Probus called out raising his voice and turning back to face the king. "There shall be a ten-year peace treaty between Rome and the Quadi which will also include your vassals the Vandals. Effective immediately. The war between us will end. The Quadi will be allowed to keep all the loot that you took from us, but you are to return all our people who were taken as slaves. All of them. They are Roman citizens, and we want them back. We will return your personal treasure to you king Hildimer, all of it and we will release your uncle too but in return we demand that you hand over to us the two Roman officers responsible for murdering Regalian the former governor of Pannonia. We know that you have been giving them political asylum but that ends now."

Gazing at Probus from across the table king Hildimer said nothing as he digested what had just been said. His companions looking uncomfortable as they too mulled over the offered terms.

"You ask much," the king replied at last, "and offer little in return. During your raids on our homes your men murdered the family of one of my extended kin. A man named Guntheric. He was the leader of his village. You decapitated him and his son after they had already surrendered. I demand blood money for that crime."

Hesitating Probus quickly glanced at Corbulo.

"The blood money for that incident has already been paid," Corbulo said stiffly, addressing the king. "When you executed Sulpicia in front of me and my men. There was no need to have her killed. She may have been misguided and deceitful, but she was no threat to you. That too was a crime. There will be no blood money paid for the death of your kinsmen."

"You speak boldly, be careful," king Hildimer said his eyes narrowing angrily as he glared at Corbulo.

"You can have all your treasure back," Corbulo replied coolly, "but you will not be getting the iron chest they were stored in. That chest is Roman, from a bank in Londinium and it belongs to me now. I am going to keep it as a reminder of all the men I lost here fighting in your land to achieve this peace."

Glaring at Corbulo king Hildimer's face darkened and for a long moment a resentful, brooding silence descended upon the table.

"Remember that the amber road runs through my lands," the king exclaimed turning his attention to Probus. "Without my consent none of your merchants will be able to travel to the amber producing lands to the north. We will simply not allow it. We can kill the trade."

"Ah yes," Tobias said quickly interrupting and giving the king a careful deferential look as if he had been waiting for the topic to be raised. "We understand that this is so. Therefore, as part of the peace treaty, we demand free, safe and unfettered access for all Roman amber merchants to cross your land. The amber trade between the northern sea and Carnuntum is to be restored at once. Trade will make us all richer and," Tobias continued looking suitably grave, "in return for this concession we are prepared to lower the tariffs that we charge your people. We are willing to lower the import taxes that you currently pay to do business with us, an exclusive arrangement that the Quadi alone will benefit from. As part of this treaty, we will give your people preferential tax treatment. No other barbarian tribe will be getting a deal as good as the one that you are now being offered. I suggest you take it."

Glaring at the accountant king Hildimer grunted. Then the king turned to his three companions and a brief conversation ensued.

"It's not good enough," the king said at last, turning back to Tobias. "We demand no tariffs on our trade with you at all. And we demand that Rome pays us an annual subsidy like that which the Thuringi receive from emperor Postumus who rules in the West."

"No subsidies for the first five years of the treaty," Probus replied firmly. "After five years we will review the subsidy policy. You have devastated the frontier, and it will need time to recover."

"Fine but then reduce our trade tariffs to nothing," the king retorted.

Feigning amusement Tobias quickly shook his head. "That is impossible Sir," the civilian replied. "We can lower the tax but not lift the tariffs entirely. If your people want to continue doing business with us, they will need to pay the taxes. But we do want trade to increase between our two peoples. Like I said, increasing trade will make us all richer and both our people will need time and money to rebuild after all the recent destruction. The financial cost of this war in terms of lost taxes and economic destruction is enormous for us and for your people too. Destruction from which only our enemies will benefit." For a moment Tobias paused, the bureaucrat appearing to be enjoying himself. "I am sure," he continued, "that you Sir would not want us to start diverting trade and the wealth it brings, through other provinces along the imperial frontier which we could do. There are after all alternative trade routes that could carry our merchants to the amber producing lands to the north that bypass your territory entirely."

Glaring at Tobias the king looked displeased but from his seat Corbulo could see that Tobias's quiet threat had struck home.

"Fine," king Hildimer said at last turning to Probus. "I agree to the offered terms. There shall be peace for ten years between my people and Rome. Let no man say otherwise."

"Good," Probus replied looking pleased. "On behalf of emperor Gallienus and witnessed by the immortal gods I too agree. For ten years there shall be peace between Rome and the Quadi. The war ends today."

"There is one final matter that needs to be agreed upon," Corbulo said gazing across the table at the Quadi king. "How this peace treaty is to be policed and governed. We suggest an exchange of hostages to ensure that each party will adhere to the terms of this agreement."

"Hostages, yes," king Hildimer said nodding. "I agree."

"From our side," Corbulo continued, "we will hand over prince Gummar, close personal friend and ally to emperor Gallienus and second son of Jonar, brother of the Frankish king Adalheim. This man here," Corbulo said gesturing towards Gummar. "He is of royal Frankish blood and also a Roman citizen. He shall be handed over to you as a hostage and we expect him to be treated according to his rank and status. Do you accept?"

And as Corbulo finished speaking Gummar lowered his eyes, and it was clear that he already knew what was going to happen to him and that he had willingly if grudgingly accepted his fate. Turning to study Gummar king Hildimer muttered something under his breath.

"Allow me to confer with my companions in private," the king said turning to Probus as he swiftly rose to his feet and gestured for his companions to join him a little distance away from the table. And as the barbarians conferred among themselves Corbulo turned to prince Gummar, his expression like stone. The prince raising his head and meeting his gaze.

"Accept your fate prince Gummar," Corbulo said speaking in a patient voice. "Count yourself lucky that this is your punishment for disobeying my orders and putting a valuable officer out of action immediately before the fight of our lives. Count yourself lucky too that Crastus lives. And know this, you will not be a hostage of the Quadi forever. One day you will return to us. One day you may yet become king of the Franks in your brother's place."

"I served you well and do not deserve this," Gummar replied forcing a bitter smile as he gathered himself, pride suddenly shining through like the sun breaking through on a cloudy day. "I fought well and have nothing to be ashamed of. The gods see me and will smile upon me again."

"You are a soldier, and you will obey," Probus said sternly, turning to Gummar. "Now do your duty to Rome."

Ignoring Probus, Gummar's gaze remained fixed upon Corbulo and it was clear to all that something had irretrievably broken down between the two men. Gummar had it seemed acquired a new grudge, this time against Corbulo. Lowering his eyes prince Gummar spoke.

"I shall do my duty not to Rome but to my friend the emperor Gallienus," Gummar said with a hint of menace in his voice before raising his head and turning to Corbulo. "And you are right. I shall not be a hostage forever and one day I shall be king of my people, and no one will be able to order me about. I will be seeing you again, Corbulo, maybe sooner than you think."

Returning to the table king Hildimer cleared his throat as he turned to address Probus, his hand resting upon the shoulder of his son. The younger man looking disappointed but resigned to his fate.

"We will accept your hostage," the king said with a curt nod, "and in return we shall exchange him for my son here. The exchange happens as soon as emperor Gallienus ratifies the terms of the peace treaty. And there may be more hostage exchanges in the future. Are we agreed?"

"Agreed," Probus said reaching out with his hand, which after a pause, the king finally grasped with his own hand. The two men shaking hands.

Taking a step back with the table in between them, their horses grazing and snorting in the background, both parties fell silent, the tension slowly dissipating, the negotiators reflecting on what had just been achieved. Then at last king Hildimer turned to Corbulo with a frown.

"You were in command of the fort along the Morava?" the king called out. "You are the one who held out against us?"

"Yes, that was me," Corbulo replied coolly.

For a moment the king did not respond. Then to Corbulo's surprise he chuckled. "Maybe one day when you get tired of Rome, you should come and fight for me," the king called out to

Corbulo before breaking into laughter as he turned and started back towards his horse. His laughter carrying across the deserted field as he and his companions mounted their horses and rode away.

Chapter Twenty-Three - Hope for the Future

Watching the spitting, crackling, funeral fire Corbulo looked grave, his hands clasped behind his back. It was morning and a short distance away from him the tranquil waters of the Danube gleamed in the sunlight. The river dominated by the magnificent Roman pontoon bridge that stretched across the wide water towards the city of Carnuntum, clearly visible along the opposite bank. The northern end of the bridge was guarded by a detachment of legionaries and marines from the Fourteenth and the Pannonian fleet while parties of Moorish cavalry were moving back across the bridge, retreating towards the Roman city, the clatter of their horses' hooves ringing out upon the wooden deck. Moving on by some of the Moors were idly glancing in the direction of the solitary fire and the small party of Roman officers and civilians who were gathered around it.

Gazing into the flames into which he had just consigned Sulpicia's body Corbulo at last turned to the two Roman officers who were on their knees before him. The men had their hands tied behind their backs and were bareheaded, clad in just their white army tunics. The men looking up at him with pleading looks. While four of Corbulo's soldiers stood guard directly behind them.

"You cannot do this," one of the officers cried out with mounting desperation, "we are Roman officers, we are Roman citizens. We are entitled to a trial in a proper court of law. You must obey the law, prefect!"

"So, I should," Corbulo said coldly, "but you forget one thing. That over there," he said pointing towards the pontoon bridge and the south bank of the Danube, "is where the jurisdiction of Roman law ends. As we are on the north side of the river, we are in the territory of the Quadi, which means that we are beyond the reach of the law. I as military prefect am in command here and that makes you my responsibility and I will decide what your fate is to be."

"Mercy Sir," the second prisoner called out. "I beg you. I can pay you. I can give you what you desire. Please let me live. I beg you."

"What have we done to deserve this," the first prisoner cried. "I told you already. We were captured by the Quadi and taken as hostages. We did nothing wrong. We are on the same side. Spare us!"

"You stand accused of helping murder Regalian, the governor of Upper Pannonia," Corbulo retorted. "You stand accused of arranging the assassination of a Roman governor after which you fled to the Quadi. And you have been found guilty of these charges. You know the penalty."

"What!" the first prisoner blurted out. "This is nonsense. Where is your proof? We did nothing of the sort."

"But Regalian was a usurper!" the second prisoner cried. "He attempted a revolt against emperor Gallienus. He was your enemy! Why do you care what happened to him?"

"He may have been a usurper and an enemy of emperor Gallienus," Corbulo replied with growing disgust, "but he was still the lawful governor of this province. He was still your commander and you as his closest advisors murdered him. You betrayed your friend. You dishonoured your rank and the trust that was placed in you. I don't care whose side Regalian was on. We cannot have Roman officers going about murdering their commanders at will without punishment."

"What proof do you have that we did this!"

Turning to stare into the flames Corbulo remained silent for a moment.

"She knew it was you," he said at last gesturing at the fire that was still devouring Sulpicia's corpse. "She was the proof. This is justice. For her."

Then Corbulo turned and gestured to the four soldiers standing behind the two prisoners. Grasping hold of the protesting officers two of the soldiers raised their swords and quickly and expertly drove the blades down into the prisoner's necks killing them instantly. Watching the bodies flop onto their sides Corbulo took a deep breath as his men wiped their blood smeared blades on the officers clothing before sheathing their swords.

"This brings a final end to this sordid revolt, this ends the Regalian rebellion once and for all," Corbulo called out turning to the group of officers and men of the Fourteenth who were watching him in silence. "From now on there will be no more retaliation, no more shame. We move on together. We are Romans, all of us. Soldiers! Our enemy resides beyond our frontiers, not within them. And today we stand united behind our one true emperor, Gallienus! Throw their bodies into the river," he commanded gesturing to the pair of executed officers, "traitors should not have an eternal resting place."

Observing him the gaggle of Roman officers and soldiers remained silent. Then one by one they started to drift away. The sombre, tense mood lifting like the warm sun breaking through the clouds. Watching them go Corbulo at last turned to Tobias who was studying Corbulo with an expectant, inquiring look.

"I have a task for you," Corbulo said quietly reaching out to lay a hand on the civilian's shoulder. "You know the treasure chest that we took from the Quadi king, the iron strong box with the name of that London bank on it. Well, I want you to create a new fund and keep its assets inside that chest. I want you to take responsibility for all the monies and their investments. The purpose of this new fund will be to create a pot of money for the families of all those we lost fighting here and those we are going to lose in the future. The fund will be just for our ala, a private endeavour. I will arrange for an initial deposit which I am going to rely on you to invest wisely. Can you manage that for me Tobias?"

"Like a group pension," the accountant said smiling, "yes of course I can handle that. I can start as soon as I have the initial funds."

"You are not going to fuck this up?"

"No Sir," Tobias replied, feigning offence. "When it comes to money, I am the professional here. You can trust me. I promise. The fund will be in good hands."

"Good man," Corbulo said nodding before leaving Tobias to it and moving across to where Mattis was still down on one knee, his head bowed in solemn respect before the crackling funeral fire. Looking up at Corbulo as he came to stand beside him the centurion looked ashen.

"Thank you, Sir, for granting her this final respect," Mattis said hurriedly straightening up as Corbulo turned to gaze into the flames. "That was noble of you. You know that we were lovers, she and I," Mattis continued gesturing at the fire. "We were close. She meant something to me, but I did not know what she was planning to do. Otherwise, I would have warned you. I know what she did Corbulo. I know about her betrayal, but at heart

Sulpicia was a good woman who loved her husband and who was just overwhelmed by the injustice of these times. All she wanted was revenge upon the men, her one time friends, who betrayed and murdered her husband and now it is you who have granted her that wish, Corbulo."

For a moment Corbulo stood staring into the flames. Then he turned to Mattis.

"I hear congratulations are in order," he said. "I hear that Probus has promoted you to acting governor of the province of Upper Pannonia. And that you will be handling the implementation of our peace treaty with the Quadi. Well-done on your promotion governor. I am sure that the frontier will now recover with you in charge. I told you once that things would start to get better and now, they are. With you in charge here at Carnuntum there is hope for the future."

"Thank you," Mattis said dipping his head, "yes I too am pleased although I am not so sure my new job is going to be a blessing. The Fourteenth are back in the fold and under my direct command, but much has been lost. There is a lot of destruction and much work to do. It is going to take years before we are fully back on our feet, but I am going to give it a go and it starts today. You are right Corbulo, things are beginning to look brighter."

"Then I must bid you farewell," Corbulo said smiling and offering his hand. "For Probus is impatient to ride and we have urgent business in Illyria. We are leaving today. Take care of my wounded men. I am leaving them in your care until they are recovered enough to join me."

"I will Sir," Mattis said snapping out a salute that Corbulo quickly returned. Then calling out to his men Corbulo turned away and joined the stream of retreating Moorish cavalry who were moving southwards across the bridge.

***

The hospital inside the city of Carnuntum was packed with wounded, ill men. The soldiers were lying scattered about on camp beds, straw mattresses or on the hard cold stone floor. The hospital crammed and overwhelmed. A band of dedicated doctors and slaves were moving about among them doing what they could. The floor stained here and there in blood. The building filled with soft moans and groans and the occasional loud scream. The place smelling of vinegar. Moving slowly past the wounded from his ala, accompanied solely by Atlas, Tobias and the standard bearer holding the war banner of the equites foederati Germanica Corbulo busied himself gripping his wounded men's proffered hands. Pausing now and then to speak a few words to the men. Some of the soldiers reaching out to touch the war banner as if it were a holy relic.

At last pausing beside the camp bed on which Harald lay stretched out, his bare chest wrapped in a white bandage that covered his chest wound, Corbulo reached out and gently shook him awake. Harald's eyes opening. A resigned look appearing on his face as he saw who it was.

"I have come to say goodbye," Corbulo said looking down at his friend. "We are moving out within the hour. We are heading south to Illyria, to the next crisis. More usurpers!"

"Good for you," Harald said weakly. "I am pleased. Kick arse Sir."

"Acting Governor Mattis has reassured me that you and the rest of our wounded will be well taken care of," Corbulo said. "So, rest and recover, and then when you are able to, I am going to need you to rejoin the ala with those men who are fit enough to be able to fight. Understood?"

"Yes Sir," Harald nodded in agreement before pausing. His expression wracked with a sudden spasm of pain. Recovering he grimaced. "I hear that you did it," Harald said at last. "That a ten-year peace treaty has been concluded between us and the Quadi. Is it true?"

"Yes, the treaty has been concluded," Corbulo said nodding. "We did it. There will be peace along this stretch of the frontier."

"So, our men did not die in vain in some foreign land," Harald nodded looking relieved. "From the ala, how many survived?"

"Five hundred and two officers and men are fit for duty," Corbulo replied. "Another two hundred and three are too badly wounded or sick to be able to join us right away. They are all here in this building with you. Once you are recovered Harald, I am going to need you to prepare them to rejoin us as soon as they can."

"Sir," the standard bearer said leaning towards Harald and showing him the war banner of the equites foederati Germanica. "See. We have added a new battle honour to the standard. See there. The battle of the Morava. I had it engraved just now. I thought you would like to see it."

Gazing weakly at the new battle honour Harald smiled. Then he lifted his eyes to look up at Corbulo.

"And Crastus, he lives?" Harald asked. "I have not seen him."

"Yes, he lives, he is doing better," Corbulo replied with a nod. "His wound got infected, but he is recovering now. The doctor says he will live. He is being kept in a separate building for now and will remain behind here in Carnuntum with you until he is fully recovered." Pausing Corbulo took a deep breath. "I had to punish Crastus for disobeying my orders and getting into that knife fight with prince Gummar. That is why you have not seen him."

"What punishment did Crastus receive?"

"I demoted him to junior centurion and fined him a year's pay."

"And Gummar?

"Is to be handed over to the Quadi as a hostage," Corbulo replied. "He didn't take it so well. He is pissed off with me now. You know how easily he holds a grudge."

Looking up at the ceiling of the hospital Harald seemed to be weighing the punishments in his mind. Then he shrugged.

"That is about fair for both," he said weakly. "They cannot complain. How did Crastus take the news?"

"I think," Corbulo said taking another deep breath, "that as long as he can command men and can fight, that Crastus really doesn't give a shit. He told me that I was still the same arse he'd met years ago."

And as Corbulo smiled Harald too broke into a grin.

"There is one final thing," Corbulo said as he prepared to leave. "Now that Gummar is being handed over to the Quadi as a hostage I need a new deputy, a new second in command of the ala and so I am promoting you Harald. From this moment on you are the new deputy commander of the Germanica."

***

Arranged in a long column that filled the street leading towards the southern gate of Carnuntum, ready to ride, the men of the equites foederati Germanica were sitting upon their horses waiting for the signal to move out. The soldiers gripping their spears. Their shields slung over their backs. Their army blankets rolled up and their marching packs strapped to their horses while here and there the horse drawn supply wagons were filled with supplies, tents and the ala's large iron cooking pots. The soldier's coats of mail armour and helmets gleaming in the afternoon sunlight. While a crowd of eager townsfolk were moving along the sides of the stationary column of horsemen. The women handing out flowers and hunks of bread and calling out blessings. The children rushing about shrieking in excitement. Dogs barking.

Leading Clement on foot with just Atlas for company Corbulo ruthlessly drove the Christian priest down the deserted alley. His hand resting menacingly on the hilt of his sword. The three men moving away from the waiting column. Their boots thudding across the paving stones. At last, at an intersection with another alley Corbulo reached out and brought Clement to a halt before quickly turning to look around but the three of them were alone.

"What are you going to do?" Clement exclaimed casting a wary look towards Corbulo's hand which was resting upon the pommel of his sword. "Is this it? Have you decided to get rid of me before I even go to trial?"

"You are not going to go to trial," Corbulo replied sternly. "We are friends are we not?"

"We are," Clement said guardedly still looking dubious, glancing at Corbulo and then Atlas with his one good eye. "So, what the fuck are we doing here in this alley? I was told that once we reached Carnuntum I would be handed over to stand trial for the crime of being a Christian."

"No. Not anymore," Corbulo replied lifting his hand from his sword and folding his arms across his chest as Atlas looked on impassively. "I am letting you go. I am setting you free. Officially it will be reported that you escaped. Unofficially I want you Clement to come and work for me."

"Work for you!" Clement exclaimed looking startled.

"That's right," Corbulo said. "I have a task that I need you to do for me. An important task. And you owe me. Twice now I have saved your life."

"I don't understand, what task?"

Pausing Corbulo considered Clement.

"You said before that you are an amber merchant who works for the house of Ulpia Severina in the city of Rome. Well, I didn't mention this to you before, but I have heard of this family," Corbulo said growing serious. "They say that the Ulpia hail from a most distinguished and ancient blood line that goes right back to the time of emperor Trajan. And you told me yourself that the lady Severina is a friend of Gallienus. So, I want you Clement to return to your mistress, to the lady Severina and convince her to become the patron of the equites foederati Germanica. It is time our ala gained a wealthy and powerful patron who is willing to stand up for our interests in the imperial court."

"What! This is crazy!" Clement blurted out looking shocked. "My mistress maintains good relations with Gallienus for a reason. She wishes to live. She wishes to stay out of imperial politics. She has no desire to add to her troubles. Gallienus's agents are already suspicious. They are watching all the great houses, testing their loyalty to the emperor. Gallienus is paranoid of another revolt. And you know who my mistress is related to, right?"

"The lady Severina is a relative of the Legate Laelian who now serves the usurper Postumus in the West," Atlas interrupted. "Yes, we know. We are aware. Which is why we want her to become our patron. The Ulpia family bear a famous name. They sit astride the great political divide that has recently split the empire, which makes them interesting. They are survivors! Like us."

"Anyone who has spent time along the Rhine knows who Laelian is," Corbulo said taking over. "Laelian may be serving a usurper, but he is a good man. He has done much good for the Rhine frontier, our home, my men's homes. He is an important and powerful man who has led diplomatic missions to the barbarian tribes, to help contain the threat from the Franks. And he is close to Postumus. One does not get to choose who one's relatives are. Nor can anyone ever truly stay out of politics however much they may wish to."

"Right. But you will understand that my mistress's family, like so many, are divided in their political loyalties, which is a most dangerous place to be," Clement exclaimed raising his eyebrows. "She supports Gallienus but Laelian supports Postumus. My mistress does not wish to make matters worse. Hence her lack of interest in dabbling in imperial politics."

Exchanging a glance Corbulo and Atlas remained silent leaving Clement confused.

"Oh, I see now," Clement suddenly exclaimed, blushing. "Right. You wish to play both sides. You profess loyalty to emperor Gallienus but if he were to fall or be assassinated you intend to shift your support and loyalty to Postumus. And you think having a connection to the Ulpia family will help."

"The ala needs insurance," Atlas said with a little smile. "Emperor Gallienus is a good man but we cannot take it for granted that he will always be emperor. We must be ready for any changes if they occur. We do not wish for a repeat of what happened to us after Valerian was captured last year and we ended up drafted into the army of the Macriani usurpers."

"We are not asking your mistress to do anything but look after the interests of the equites foederati Germanica. We are just asking her to become our patron, nothing more," Corbulo said taking over from Atlas in a patient voice, his eyes fixed upon Clement. "We are not asking her to change her loyalty to Gallienus. But emperors don't last very long these days. These are troubled and dangerous times and when things happen, they happen fast. We should be prepared for change."

"So, insurance?" Clement said looking sceptical.

In reply Corbulo nodded, looking serious. "So, will you do this for me?"

"I don't know," Clement said shaking his head.

"You once berated me about friendship," Corbulo said taking a step towards Clement. "Now I am letting you go. I am setting you free. This is the act of a friend. But if we are not to be friends, then do this for me because you owe me. Atlas here will accompany you to see your mistress in Rome. I want her to become our patron. The patron of the Germanica."

Staring back at Corbulo Clement appeared to be mulling over what had just been said. Then at last he sighed, looking resigned.

"Alright Corbulo," the priest said. "I will do this for you, but I cannot guarantee that my mistress will be interested in your proposal."

"Then make her interested," Corbulo said sharply, "both of you," he added turning to look at Clement and then Atlas. "Use your charm and wit. Do whatever is necessary. And tell the lady Severina this, that when the time is right, I would like to meet her in person."

Quickly glancing at Atlas who simply shrugged, Clement hesitated before reaching out to grip Corbulo's shoulder, his expression softening. "Alright my friend," the priest said in a changed voice. "I hear you. I will see what I can do. I will do my best. Thank you Corbulo for what you have done for me. It is most appreciated, and I will not forget. May God protect you and guide you on your path."

"Go," Corbulo said hurriedly gesturing towards the alley.

Chapter Twenty-Four - The Emperor's Favour

Illyria, summer 261 AD, General's Aureolus camp

Trotting into the vast Roman army camp at the head of his column of men, Corbulo turned to gaze at the rows of white tents that stretched off into the distance. The place packed with soldiers and corralled horses. It was afternoon and the men were going about their business. The camp alive with noise and activity, the smell of horse manure and woodsmoke. Blacksmiths were hammering away in their workshops. Civilian merchants were setting up their stalls while along the avenue that led to the centre of the camp, hundreds of soldiers were sitting about around campfires, resting, some of them bearing wounds. The men turning to gaze at the long column of Salian Franks and Moors who were entering their camp.

"You are too late bitches! We have already destroyed the enemy!" an officer cried out to Corbulo as he rose to his feet and turned to gaze at the newcomers. His cry bringing forth a smattering of contemptuous laughter and other cries from the men lining the street.

"You are too late! Where were you boys! What are you doing here! Fuck off back to the Rhine! Lazy Frankish bastards!"

Ignoring the cries as some of his men exchanged insults with general Aureolus's men Corbulo shifted his attention to the cluster of larger army tents that occupied the centre of the Roman camp. The Roman HQ was guarded by a detachment of praetorian guards. The cavalry army's battle standards arranged proudly in a double line just outside the HQ, like an avenue of trees. Draco banners snaking from wooden poles above the tents. While what looked like a host of captured enemy banners were lying thrown into a pile upon a makeshift altar dedicated to Sol Invictus that had been erected just outside the entrance to the foremost Roman army tent. A band of children playing a ball game around the captured standards. Their delighted shrieks and cries ringing out.

Reaching the area around the Roman headquarters Corbulo raised his fist in the air bringing his column to an abrupt halt. While the children turned to stare at him in silence, their ball game all but forgotten. Lining the track ahead the Moors had already started to dismount, the little black-haired Africans moving about and tending to their horses. Their officers shouting orders to their men in their own language as the soldiers started towards their billets. The supply wagons and mules carrying their supplies, tents and iron cooking pots drawn up alongside the horsemen. The avenue crowded with men and horses.

Dismounting Corbulo handed the reins of his horse to a bodyguard before turning to one of his officers.

"Find the camp prefect and ask him where he wants our men to pitch our tents," Corbulo said. "Then see that the men and the horses get something to eat. I am going to speak with general Aureolus."

"Sir," the officer said hurriedly, saluting.

Leaving his men, accompanied only by his standard bearer clutching the battle standard of the equites foederati Germanica, Corbulo headed towards the cluster of tents. Spotting Probus, Corbulo veered towards him. The young dashing general giving him a cautious look before turning his gaze to the Roman HQ and the praetorian guards standing guard outside.

"Oh, this is going to be rough," Probus said in a sudden weary voice as Corbulo came up. "Aureolus is going to have our balls. It seems that we were too late to take part in the battle against the Macriani usurpers. Aureolus is not going to be pleased. Brace yourself."

"Let's just get it done," Corbulo said as the two officers and their small entourage turned and headed towards the HQ of the Roman cavalry army.

General Aureolus commander of the imperial cavalry was sitting in a chair inside his spacious and luxuriously decorated tent, shaving himself with the help of a handheld mirror, when Corbulo and Probus entered. The two officers approaching their superior before coming to a halt and rapping out a stiff salute. Pausing his work Aureolus glared at them in unhappy silence before laying down the mirror and rising to his feet. The forty-year-old posing a formidable figure. A tall man with a shock of thick black hair styled in the shape of a cock and the colour of a crow. A bully. His hideous face disfigured by old wounds and evidence of a childhood disease.

"What's this!" Aureolus bellowed glaring at Probus and then at Corbulo as he wasted no time and got stuck in. "You missed the battle! You missed the fucking war! Where the fuck were you? Did I or did I not specifically instruct you to rejoin me before our fight with those Macriani arseholes!"

"I am sorry Sir," Probus replied stiffly, "it took us longer than we expected to subdue the Quadi. But in the end, we were successful. The enemy were driven back across the Danube and defeated. Peace now reigns along the frontier in Upper Pannonia. A lasting peace."

Glaring at Probus, Aureolus remained silent as he came up to the young general and thrust his face at Probus. For a long moment no one spoke, the tent crackling with aggression and the hint of violence as the two men faced off with each other. Their noses nearly touching. Then abruptly without warning Aureolus turned and scowled at Corbulo.

"And what the fuck is your excuse, Frank!" he roared.

"I was busy fighting with the Quadi Sir," Corbulo replied coolly staring straight ahead. "We carried out your orders."

"Not all my orders!" Aureolus boomed. "You missed the battle with the Macriani, which was vastly more important than driving some filthy barbarian horde back across the Danube."

"Well at least you won the battle Sir," Corbulo said.

Staring at Corbulo as if he were mad, Aureolus's eyes bored into him. The general looking furious.

"You thought that I may lose the battle!"

"No Sir."

Swearing out loud Aureolus glared at Corbulo. His body growing tense with pent up aggression as if he needed an outlet for the violence that was natural to him. His hands clenched into fists as if he wanted nothing more than to beat the crap out of his subordinates. At last, controlling his temper, Aureolus took a step back shifting his attention to Probus.

"You damn right that I won the battle," Aureolus snapped. "A great victory. I crushed those Macriani like bugs. I Aureolus did that. Without your help may I add. The enemy outnumbered us. They had the support of the Danube legions, but they were not counting on facing my cavalry army. We enveloped them and surrounded them so fast they had no time to react. Then I forced them to surrender. The Macriani were killed by their own soldiers. We are still searching for their bodies, but I am told that they died upon the battlefield. Their army belongs to me now. They have changed sides as have all the detachments sent by the Danube legions. My army has almost doubled overnight. I am victorious."

"Both Macrianus major and minor are dead?" Probus said hurriedly.

"Yes," Aureolus said looking satisfied. "That is what I have been told. Both usurpers, father and son are dead. I crushed their little rebellion. It is over."

"With respect Sir," Corbulo said in a tight voice, "the revolt in the East is not over until the remaining usurpers have been dealt with. Both Quietus and Balista still rule the eastern provinces. They must not be allowed to rebuild their forces. They still pose a threat to the emperor."

"You don't think I know that, Frank!" Aureolus boomed, his anger returning. "Who are you to try and lecture me on what I should do next! You," Aureolus said jabbing a finger at Corbulo. "Yes. I remember you now. You are that officer who came to us from the East. You served under the Macriani and Balista before. Well, you know what those bastards look like. So, get your arse out onto the battlefield right now and start helping my men to look for their corpses. And once you find the bodies of the Macriani cut off their heads and bring them to me. I can only report our success to the emperor once I have actual proof that the bastards are dead. So, find their bodies! Now get out of my sight, both of you!"

***

It was evening, as accompanied by Tobias, Corbulo strolled back into the Roman camp from the battlefield less than a mile away, coolly carrying a sack slung over his shoulder that contained the severed heads of the two Macriani usurpers. A bloodied axe hanging suspended from his belt. Tobias grim faced and tight-lipped as he carried a second smaller bag filled with loot he'd taken from the battlefield. Some unnoticed blood staining his cheek. The two men not speaking. Content to remain silent. Heading towards the cluster of tents at the centre of the camp where Aureolus had set up his HQ Corbulo idly glanced at the soldiers who were going about their business. Taking in the scent of baking bread and woodsmoke as the men sat around their campfires. The mood relaxed and jovial.

The camp was filled with a growing army of civilian traders and craftsmen who had come to sell a huge variety of products and services to the cash rich soldiers. With more merchants waiting at the gates to be allowed into the sprawling encampment. The opportunity to make some money was simply too good to be missed. The traders appeared to have come from all over Corbulo thought judging from their accents and the languages that he could hear being spoken all around him. The news of general Aureolus's great victory must have spread fast for now everyone wanted a piece of the spoils.

Pushing on down the camp's main avenue, which was lined on both sides with civilian stalls and handcarts selling everything from freshly slaughtered meat to tattoo services, Corbulo tightened his grip on the cloth sack containing his former commander's head and that of his son. Remembering the last time he had seen them alive. Back in Syria. When they had been so confident. The Macriani so full of themselves. So ambitious. So powerful. The two usurpers appeared to have committed suicide. He'd eventually found their bodies under a pile of corpses in a spot where the fighting had been particularly fierce, lying next to each other on the battlefield, their hands linked together in death. But now they were missing their heads. Their bold dreams of ruling the greatest empire the world had ever known, reduced to ignominious defeat and death. A sorry ending.

Contemplating his evening meal Corbulo tapped Tobias's shoulder and was just about to cross the main avenue and approach a fishmonger's stall when he suddenly heard voices nearby speaking in German. Pausing he turned to gaze at a band of men, newcomers to the camp, who appeared to be asking for directions. The soldiers looked tired and were clad in mail body armour, their clothes, cloaks and boots covered in dust as if they had just completed a long ride.

"We are looking for the Frankish horse! The equites foederati Germanica. Do you know where they are billeted?" one of the men asked addressing a party of soldiers who were sitting around their campfire.

"What's this!" Corbulo called out in German as he and Tobias approached the band of newcomers. "You say you are looking for the Germanica?"

Quickly turning around the leader of the group of men gazed back at Corbulo. "Yes, we are," the man said. "Do you know where they are billeted?"

"And you are?" Corbulo said sternly.

"Reinforcements," the man replied quickly. "All of us here are German speakers. We are soldiers. I am from Noricum myself. My companions and I have come from all over the empire. We heard that they had created an all-German cavalry unit. Some of us served in other units before requesting a transfer to the Germanica. Some of us are volunteers. Others I don't know. But all of us want to join the Frankish horse. We have heard they are a first-class combat unit. We have been on the road for a week, some of us even longer than that."

"Well, you have come to the right place," Corbulo said. "I am the prefect of the equites foederati Germanica."

Staring at Corbulo the soldier said nothing before abruptly some embarrassed colour shot into his cheeks. Hurriedly he saluted.

Suddenly Corbulo was no longer paying attention to the soldier. Instead, his eyes widening in surprise and a little noise of disbelief escaped from his mouth, as standing among the band of newcomers he caught sight of Badurad and Linus. The two youths were staring back at him with mounting trepidation. The dread clearly visible across their youthful faces.

"You!" Corbulo burst out pointing a finger at Badurad.

And as Corbulo pushed towards Badurad and Linus, the two youths shrank back from him. Inching back. The teenager's faces growing pale like milk. Badurad manfully trying to stand his ground but failing while Linus sought cover behind his friend as if they had just come across an angry, hungry bear in the forest.

"You! Down on your knees right now, both of you," Corbulo roared as he came up to the youths, his hand dropping to rest on the handle of his axe. "You are deserters!" he cried out as Badurad and Linus obediently fell to their knees and their travelling companions looked on in astonishment.

"Uncle, please I can explain," Badurad called out hurriedly as Corbulo towered over his cousin.

"You have one chance and one chance only," Corbulo growled, "to explain what you are doing here. You are deserters. Speak!"

"We just wanted to go home Sir!" Linus cried out.

"You shut the fuck up," Corbulo roared silencing Linus with a single look.

"It is true," Badurad exclaimed, bowing his head in defeat. "I do not deny it uncle. We deserted because we wanted to go home - to defend our homes from the Franks. We thought that was the right thing to do. But when we finally got back to the Colonia on the Rhine, my father was furious with us for what we had done. Hostes said we had brought nothing but disgrace to the family. He decided to send us straight back to you. My father ordered me to return to you and the ala and not bother coming back home if I disobeyed him. He said that we should accept whatever punishment you deemed was right. Hostes has written you a letter uncle which I am to give to you. Please Corbulo, I have it on me here."

Staring at his cousin Corbulo frowned and for a moment he was lost for words.

"Ah yes I remember you," Tobias said studying Badurad with a sudden pleased look. "You were assigned to me as my assistant and liaison when I first joined the ala back in Mediolanum. You are the one who stole my purse. Thief. I am going to be wanting it back."

Gazing from Corbulo to Tobias and back again to Corbulo, Badurad looked increasingly glum.

"So, let me get this straight," Corbulo called out. "You deserted, went home and then Hostes sent you straight back to me."

"That's right uncle."

Pausing Corbulo's eyes moved from Badurad to Linus and back again. The two youths looking up at him with glum, anxious expressions. Then without warning Corbulo threw back his head and roared with laughter.

***

Standing in the entrance to his tent, sipping water from a cup, Corbulo idly gazed out into the rain that was pouring down into the vast Roman camp. The afternoon sky was grey and covered in clouds. The heavy rain pattering loudly across the canvas roof of his tent. Outside he could see the soldiers and civilians were sheltering inside their tents or huddling under their makeshift stalls. The people waiting for the storm to pass. The corralled horses standing motionless in the rain. A few campfires were still flickering defiantly against the deluge while a few yards in front of Corbulo's tent, out in the open, Badurad and Linus were sitting on the ground, their backs resting against wooden posts that had been driven into the ground. Their hands tied behind their backs. Their ankles bound together by iron slavers chains. The youths were getting soaked. Their heads bowed. An empty discarded plate and cup sitting on the ground beside each of them.

For a while Corbulo watched his cousin and Linus in contemplative silence. For seven days now he'd kept the pair of them tied up to the wooden posts in front of his tent. Day and night, they had slept, eaten and pissed where they sat. Punished in full view of the whole camp. This then was the punishment which he had decided upon. This and a financial fine of a year's pay. And with that done he had decided to accept them both back into the ala. To give them another chance. For he could not deny it. He was glad that Badurad and

Linus had returned. He could have been much stricter and harsher. Desertion was punishable by execution, but the fact that both Badurad and Linus had returned to the ala voluntarily and Hostes's private letter asking him to show mercy to the boys had persuaded him to use a softer hand. Besides there was no way he would be able to execute his own cousin Corbulo thought, however infuriating Badurad could sometimes be.

At last, with a sigh Corbulo placed his cup back on the table and reached for the vine staff. Emerging from his tent and into the rain Corbulo came up to the two bound youths and kicked Badurad in the leg. The youth opening his eyes and squinting up at him with an exhausted look. His clothes soaked. The teenager smelling like a latrine. His chin and cheeks unshaven.

"Up! On your feet!" Corbulo ordered.

Reluctantly, saying nothing, Badurad struggled to his feet, his hands remaining bound to the wooden pole. Moving behind the youth Corbulo produced a knife and quickly cut the rope, freeing Badurad's hands. The boy groaning in relief as he quickly reached out to rub his skin where the rope had cut deep.

"Stand still!" Corbulo barked. "Twenty lashes!"

Then swiftly and brutally he struck Badurad across his back with his vine staff. The blow making the youth cry out sharply in shock and pain. "One...two...," Corbulo called out as he began to work his vine across Badurad's back. The blows coming in quick succession. The dull whacks of the staff across human flesh ringing out as from their shelters the soldiers of the Germanica looked on in sombre silence, the rain pattered the ground and Badurad yelled in agony.

"You are both free to go. Your punishment is over," Corbulo called out at last as Linus sank to the ground after having received a beating of ten lashes from Corbulo's vine staff. "I do hope that you have learned your lesson and that you will not be causing me anymore trouble."

"We won't be any trouble Sir," Badurad said quickly, his face still wracked with pain. "Understood Sir," Linus said groaning. The two youths not daring to look up at Corbulo.

"Good," Corbulo replied sternly. "Then find yourself a place to sleep and I shall see you both back on the morning parade as usual. Dismissed."

Retreating into his tent Corbulo sighed as he watched the two youths slinking off into the rain. Then abruptly he caught sight of Probus hurrying towards his tent. The young general was on his own and he appeared to have something on his mind. His face set in a frown.

"Corbulo," Probus called out as he came hastening into the tent, rainwater dripping from him. "There has been an unexpected development. The emperor is here and so is my sister. They just arrived. Completely unannounced. No one was expecting them."

"What! Gallienus is here in the camp? Claudia too?"

"Yes," Probus nodded. "Gallienus is here. He travelled in secret with just ten men to accompany him. They have come straight from Mediolanum, riding with great haste as soon as they heard about our victory. They brought Claudia with them. She insisted on coming. The emperor has called for a council of war at sunset. The meeting is going to take place in Aureolus's HQ. Gallienus has requested that both you and me be present."

"A council of war," Corbulo muttered looking down at the ground with a sudden thoughtful look. "That will be about next steps then."

Nodding Probus watched Corbulo.

"Aureolus is not pleased," Probus said forcing a little smile, "he thinks the emperor has come to steal the glory that should rightfully be his. But let's see what the evening will bring. And Claudia," Probus added with a cryptic smile, "she has asked to see you afterwards. Looks like you are going to have a busy important night, my friend. So, let's not fuck it up."

***

Inspecting the two severed heads of the Macriani that had been stuck on poles and placed in the middle of the large tent, Gallienus looked pleased. The emperor taking his time as he slowly circled around the heads, studying them. Gallienus was still clad in his dusty travelling cloak, bareheaded, with a sword hanging from his belt. The emperor's appearance proving him to be a man of daring, of action. The tent filled with the reddish flickering light coming from two lit braziers that stood on opposite ends of the confined space. While the party of senior officers, three ranks deep, were standing rigidly to attention inside the Roman HQ. Their arms were pressed tightly against their sides, their faces staring straight ahead. The men clad in their white army tunics. The tent silent like a mouse.

"At ease gentlemen," Gallienus called out at last turning to his officers with a little amused smile. "Relax."

Then the emperor turned and approaching Aureolus, who was standing at the front of his officers, he clasped the general's shoulders with both hands in a loose embrace.

"Congratulations general Aureolus," Gallienus called out smiling, "on this great victory that you have achieved. Your emperor recognises you. And in recognition of this glorious victory, I have instructed the state mint to start producing gold coins bearing the motto *fides equitum*. The loyalty of the cavalry! So that the whole empire will know what you have achieved. And to all of you," Gallienus added turning to the assembled officers, "well done on crushing the usurpers and bringing me their heads. Long live Rome. Long live the house of Valerian!"

Standing in the back row directly behind Probus Corbulo quickly joined in the three sharp and short cheers that the officers raised in response to the emperor's praise. The men stamping their boots onto the ground.

"Gentlemen," Gallienus called out grandly, appealing for calm, "this is just the start of many victories. We are going to take back what is rightfully ours. We are going to reunite the empire under one rule. We are going to restore the glory that is Rome and her empire! Death to our enemies!"

Once more the assembled officer's cheers rang out.

"The Macriani usurpers are dead," Aureolus said addressing Gallienus as the noise inside the tent finally subsided. "But the Danube legions must still be punished for their disloyalty to you and Balista and Quietus still remain in control of much of the East and the barbarian threat to Dacia is growing ever more pressing."

"Yes," Gallienus replied coolly turning to size up Aureolus, "so they are, and you are right, much work remains to be done. Which is why I am here. So next steps. You general Aureolus will take your cavalry army and move to pacify the legions along the Danube. And once you have successfully carried out your task you are to return to Mediolanum and help me prepare for war with the usurper Postumus. The next step in our campaign to reunite the empire is to recover the western provinces. To destroy Postumus and his ridiculous Gallic empire. The destruction of Postumus and the recovery of the West now becomes our top priority."

As Gallienus finished speaking an awkward silence descended upon the tent. Some of the Roman officers glancing at each other uneasily.

"Sir," Aureolus said carefully clearing his throat as he prepared to address Gallienus. "You wish me to take my cavalry army to the West. But that will leave Dacia and the Danube frontier wide open to attack from the Roxolani, Iazyges and the other barbarian tribes. The pressure on Dacia is already immense. If we now get entangled in fighting in the west the barbarians will take advantage of our absence. Dacia is my home province Sir."

"I know. I know," Gallienus said with a hint of weariness in his voice. "But we simply do not have the resources to be strong everywhere all the time. Sacrifices must be made. The focus for now must be on the West. I intend to concentrate all our strength on crushing Postumus. We must win a decisive battle in the west before we can deal with the other threats along the Danube."

But as Gallienus finished speaking Corbulo could see that Aureolus was not pleased. The general's silence suddenly turning sullen.

"And what about the East, Sir," Probus called out. "What do you intend to do about Balista and Quietus?"

"The East," Gallienus said taking a deep breath as he turned to Probus, "will have to look after itself for now. Like I said we do not have the resources to send an army to crush the remaining usurpers."

"So, we are to do nothing?" Probus asked raising his eyebrows.

"No," Gallienus replied. "I did not say that. Balista and Quietus must be dealt with and crushed. King Shapur and the Sasanians must be punished for what they did to my father but that will be the task of king Odenathus of Palmyra. I..." for a moment the emperor paused as he turned to look at the faces gazing back at him. "I have been corresponding with the king since my father was captured," Gallienus continued as if he were revealing a great secret. "In the East we must look to a diplomatic solution to our problems. Hence king Odenathus and I have come to an understanding. An arrangement. Necessity dictates that I have had to recognise him as the de facto ruler of our eastern provinces while he has agreed to respect the fact that I am still the rightful and legal emperor in the East. We have common enemies and so for now we are allies of sorts."

"I see," Probus said nodding. "A clever arrangement my lord."

"A necessary and practical arrangement," Gallienus said fixing Probus with a little amused smile. "Which will last only as long as we remain weak and divided, hence the importance of crushing Postumus as soon as possible."

For a moment silence returned to the tent.

"However, if we are to rely on king Odaenathus to regain control and stabilize the East for us," the emperor continued and to Corbulo's surprise Gallienus's eyes had suddenly come to rest upon him. "I want at least some men fighting alongside the king who I can trust. Men from my own armies. So that when the king proves victorious, he cannot claim to have done it all on his own. For victory makes men ambitious for more. So, you, yes you prefect of the Germanica!" Gallienus called out pointing straight at Corbulo. "I seem to remember you came to us from the East. You have met with king Odaenathus in Palmyra before, and you even know his second wife Zenobia which makes you the perfect choice. So, I have decided to send you and your men to the king's assistance and help him crush our common enemies. You will prepare to leave for the East in the next couple of days."

"My lord," Corbulo said rapping out a stiff salute. "The Germanica will do as commanded."

"Good," Gallienus said studying Corbulo with a careful appreciative look. "You understand the importance of your mission, prefect. This will not solely be about a military operation to destroy the usurpers and take revenge for the disaster at Edessa last summer. It will also require diplomacy. The budding alliance between myself and king Odaenathus, between us and the Palmyrenes, is still young and fragile. Our enemies will seek to undermine and destroy our alliance in any way they can. You must ensure that this does not happen. I need Odaenathus to remain on my side. I need *you* prefect, as my representative, to be *the* bond that binds and holds this alliance together."

"I understand my lord," Corbulo said hurriedly. "My Germans and I will not let you down."

"Good," Gallienus said his gaze lingering upon Corbulo for a moment longer. Then the emperor shifted his attention to Probus.

"And I hear that congratulations are in order to you my dear and strong Probus," Gallienus said breaking into a pleased smile. "For driving the Quadi back across the Danube and forcing peace upon king Hildimer. That was well done. You should know that I have ratified the peace treaty. Hostages are being exchanged. Our people will once more be able to live in peace thanks to you."

"My lord," Probus said dipping his head in acknowledgment.

Pausing Gallienus eyed Probus in silence, a cunning look suddenly appearing on the emperor's face.

"You two," the emperor said gesturing at Probus and Corbulo. "I wish to have a word with both of you separately and in private after this council has been concluded."

***

The evening had advanced well into the night and Corbulo was alone in his tent when he heard movement just outside the entrance. A moment later a figure appeared, stepping into his tent and as the person carefully lowered their hood, in the dim flickering torch-light, he saw that it was Claudia. The two of them alone, both remaining silent. Claudia looked alluring, her long blond hair tightly braided. The young woman's cloak held together at the throat by a fibula shaped to look like a pair of swords. Her perfume settling around her like a magic invisible cloak. Her eyes taking in the sparsely decorated space with its solitary camp bed, iron chest and the wooden frame which was holding up Corbulo's coat of mail body armour, helmet, army boots, belt and weapons. Then her eyes came to rest upon Corbulo, observing him coolly and with no smile.

"Claudia, it is good to see you again," Corbulo said as he came up to her and the two quickly and formally embraced before he took a step back.

"Corbulo," Claudia said quietly in response as she studied him for a moment before looking away. "I am glad that you survived the fighting in the north. My brother tells me that it was touch and go. That you nearly did not make it. I am glad also," Claudia continued preventing Corbulo from speaking, "that your endeavours were met with success. You have my congratulations on your victory, prefect."

"Thank you," Corbulo replied as he slowly folded his arms across his chest unsure of where things were heading. "I must say that I am surprised to see you here," he continued. "Neither Probus nor I were expecting you but here you are. Probus told me that you wished to see me."

"Yes. That is right. I had to come and see you," Claudia said quietly turning her cool gaze to Corbulo and still not smiling. Her demeanour strangely distant. "My brother tells me that the emperor kept you behind after the council tonight. That he allowed you both a private audience. That is a rare opportunity and privilege afforded to few men."

"So it is," Corbulo nodded.

"While you were away on the Danube," Claudia continued carefully undoing her cloak and draping it across the camp bed. "Gallienus too has been busy. But not with preparations for war or conquest. No. He has been neglecting his duties to the empire by spending all his time searching for Pipara, his young Marcomanni princess and hostage who became the emperor's lover but now has run away from him. The emperor is most upset by her disappearance. He seeks the barbarian princess everywhere, to the consternation of his officials." For a moment Claudia paused as she turned to gaze at Corbulo, the young attractive woman now just clothed in her long-sleeved woollen tunic. "Do you know that Gallienus granted my brother Probus a favour tonight during their little private one on one audience. The emperor asked my brother what he wanted from him in lieu of his success along the Danube frontier and the peace with the Quadi."

"That is good. So, what did Probus ask from the emperor?"

"He asked to be given command of the imperial cavalry army. Probus says that whoever commands the new cavalry army controls the empire. He asked the emperor to sack Aureolus and give him the command instead."

"That's bold," Corbulo replied raising his eyebrows. "Let's hope Aureolus does not find out. What was the emperor's response?"

"Gallienus said he would think about it."

"Well, that is something," Corbulo said smiling. "Good for Probus. At least he gave it to the emperor straight and simple."

"And you?" Claudia said advancing towards Corbulo, her perfume enveloping him. "You were also given a private audience with the emperor. What I wonder did the two of you discuss? Did the emperor grant you a request like he did for my brother? Did Gallienus ask you what you wanted from him in return for your loyal service up on the frontier?"

Reaching up to rub his chin Corbulo remained silent. "The emperor and I talked," he replied at last. "It was a good conversation. Gallienus is a sophisticated, educated and clever man, and I can see why he has survived for so long. He is likeable. He is good at making friends. He told me that he was grateful for what I had done for him along the Danube frontier. He wished to congratulate me and yes he asked me what I wanted from him in return."

"I see and what answer did you give," Claudia said lifting her chin in a little challenging gesture as she came up close, her large eyes looking up at him, her lips slightly parted. Their faces dangerously close together. Claudia examining him carefully as the strange tension between the two of them started to rise.

"You need to tell me what is going on with you Claudia? What has happened between us. We used to be friends."

"You need to stop lying to me," Claudia snapped, steel entering her voice, her eyes hardening. "I know who you are, what you have become Corbulo."

"And what am I?"

"You are a Christian," Claudia said her eyes growing damp as if she had uttered a curse upon a friend. "You have converted to the Christian god. Don't deny it for I know it is the truth. In Mediolanum I followed you to the house of that priest, a known Christian. I know that he initiated you into the rituals of the Christian faith. I know that you have been keeping it a secret all this time, even from my brother, your friend. You are a traitor Corbulo. You have betrayed the old gods. You have betrayed Rome, and you have betrayed me!"

Turning to gaze down at the floor Corbulo took a deep breath. "I do not deny it," he said at last. "Yes, I am a Christian. The Christian god is more powerful than all the others. It is my free choice. So now you know Claudia. There I said it."

"Being a Christian can destroy your career," she hissed. "Being a Christian can get you executed. Is that what you want? Have you no shame!"

"What do you want from me Claudia?" Corbulo said suddenly sounding tired. "Are you going to report me?"

"What I want," Claudia snapped, anger flaring across her face, "is to have the old Corbulo back. The man I came to trust and yes love. Christians are traitors to Rome. I hate them. They follow a false god. So, what I want you to do Corbulo is to save yourself and renounce your Christian faith. To stop being a Christian and return to the old ways. Do this and you and I can be together. Do this and I will not tell Probus the truth."

"No," Corbulo said shaking his head. "I will not do that. I will not renounce the Christian god. I cannot. This is who I am now. You will have to do what you have to do."

Glaring back at Corbulo Claudia's beautiful face darkened. "This is not over," she hissed. "I can destroy you Corbulo. I can ruin your career and even bring legal charges against you! Cross me at your peril!"

"You asked me what answer I gave to the emperor tonight, when he asked me what he could do for me," Corbulo said. "Well, I asked him to issue an imperial decree that would tolerate Christians and make it lawful for them to gather and worship the Christian god throughout the empire."

Staring at Corbulo as if he had gone insane, Claudia's chest rose and fell in rapid succession, her large eyes growing even larger. Then snatching up her cloak from the bed she turned and stormed out of the tent.

Watching her disappear into the night Corbulo at last lowered his eyes before carefully reaching up to touch the small fish amulet that hung around his neck concealed under his tunic.

"Hi uncle," a voice said suddenly from the entrance of the tent, "is this a bad time? I saw that woman storming out just now. I can come back later if that works better for you." A moment later a sheepish looking Badurad appeared, gingerly stepping into the tent and the light, fidgeting awkwardly with his hands as if he had something on his mind.

Blinking, Corbulo gazed at his cousin without saying anything.

"It is alright, what do you want?" Corbulo said at last in a patient voice, gathering himself, gesturing for Badurad to approach.

"Well Sir," Badurad said hesitating, looking at Corbulo nervously as if he were expecting another beating. "Maybe I should have told you about this earlier, but well with all that was going on and all, I forgot."

"You forgot to tell me what?"

"Well, you see," Badurad began fidgeting again with his hands, "when I got back home to the Colonia Sir. There was news. For you. A letter had arrived from your aunt Helena, from the isle of Vectis, from Britannia. She writes that she and the family are all well and that the farm is doing great," Badurad went on, a hopeful smile suddenly lighting up his youthful face. "Your aunt says that you were not to worry about your family. That they are safe and that Balista's men were unable to do any harm because your brother Veda stopped them." Oh," Badurad called out with increasing confidence, his face growing excited, "and there is more uncle. Great news! Your younger brother, Munatius, the one who went missing all those years ago. The one everyone thought had been murdered by Frankish raiders. Well, he is alive! Veda came across him when he was in free Germany. Munatius lives!"

Epilogue

Rome Defiant is historical fiction. The third book in the **Guardian of Empire** series of many books that will follow the adventures of three brothers, Corbulo, Veda and Munatius, during the crisis of the third century. The brothers are descendants of the characters in my **Veteran of Rome** and **Soldier of the Republic** series, so all three-book series are linked.

Emperor Gallienus, Probus, Aureolus, the Macriani, Regalian and his wife Sulpicia were real people who are known to have existed. Probus did have a sister called Claudia, but nothing is known about her. Emperor Gallienus did mint coins bearing the inscription *fides equitum* and he apparently did have an affair with the barbarian princess Pipara, daughter to king Attalus of the Marcomanni, another historical character. More on them in book 4. It is also likely that Gallienus was estranged from his father emperor Valerian. The ancient sources are generally negative about Gallienus, claiming he was idle and a womaniser, but these sources originate from the Roman senatorial class who hated Gallienus because he stripped them of many long-held privileges. The fact that Gallienus survived a lot longer than all the other emperors during the crisis of the third century, suggests he had significant support among the ordinary people and the army but make of that what you will. The Quadi were a Germanic people who inhabited roughly modern-day Slovakia. The Roman town of Carnuntum lies just east of modern Vienna in Austria. The battle site where Aureolus defeated the Macriani usurpers is not known, some put it in Thracia (Bulgaria), others in Illyria or even Pannonia (modern Hungary). There is no actual detailed description of how Aureolus managed to defeat the usurpers, so I had my characters miss the battle. The artwork for the book cover was done by my wife.

Until the next book my friends!

Romans, Celts and Germans

Corbulo's Family

Tadia, mother of Corbulo (deceased)

Vennus, biological father (fate unknown)

Gamo, stepfather (murdered)

Hostes, uncle, Gamo's brother

Helena, aunt, Tadia sister

Veda, middle brother

Munatius, youngest brother

Cata, sister

Holda, Hostes wife

Jutta, daughter of Hostes and Holda

Badurad, son of Hostes and Holda

Caledonus, family slave and now freedman

The equites foederati Germanica

Crastus, a centurion

Harald, a centurion from the Rhine, promoted to deputy of the ala

Prince Gummar, outcast Frankish prince, deputy commander of the ala

Atlas, A Roman speculatore, intelligence officer

Tobias, imperial accountant working for the Roman fiscus, attached to the ala

Linus, Badurad's childhood friend

Characters appearing in book 3 for the first time

Sulpicia Dryantilla, wife of governor Regalian (deceased)

Regalian, governor of the province of Upper Pannonia, usurper (deceased)

Emperor Gallienus

Probus, Claudia's brother and prefect of the equites Mauri

Aureolus, general of Dacian descent, commander of the new imperial cavalry army

Clement of Antioch, amber merchant and Christian priest

King Hildimer, Quadi king

Mattis, centurion and commander of the marines from the classis Pannonica

Characters from book 2

Sulpicia, Tadia's female friend

Adron, estate manager at Veda's farm

Odo, Munatius's former master, a Frankish warrior

Bertrada, Odo's wife

Senovara, young junior banker in London

Buccaddus, partner at B&M Brothers banking house

Dubnus, rival banker at First Imperial bank

Laelian, Roman diplomat

Abbe, captain and owner of the Frisian Glory

Jorina, Abbe's daughter

Ganna, high priestess of Nerthus (deceased)

King Hadugato, Saxon King

Postumus, Roman usurper and emperor in the West

Members of Munatius's mercenary warband

Heller, member of Munatius's war-band

Blaz, member of Munatius's war-band

Frederic, member of Munatius's war-band

Penrod, member of Munatius's war-band

Characters from book 1

Macrianus, Emperor Valerian's chief treasurer (deceased)

Balista, Valerian's praetorian prefect

Uranius Antoninus, lord of Emesa (deceased)

Claudia, Antoninus' wife and sister of the future Emperor Probus

King Odaenathus, king of the city state of Palmyra

Queen Zenobia, second wife to king Odaenathus

Asher, Sasanian born Jewish lord (deceased)

Fadel, Bedouin slave and Asher's man servant

Arif, leader of the Arab mercenaries (Deceased)

Hypatia, Christian woman

Probus, future Roman Emperor

Wulfaz, Ripuarian Frankish leader, Balista's bodyguard

Kartir, Zoroastrian priest

Macrianus Junior, Macrianus son and co emperor (deceased)

Quietus, Macrianus's son and co emperor